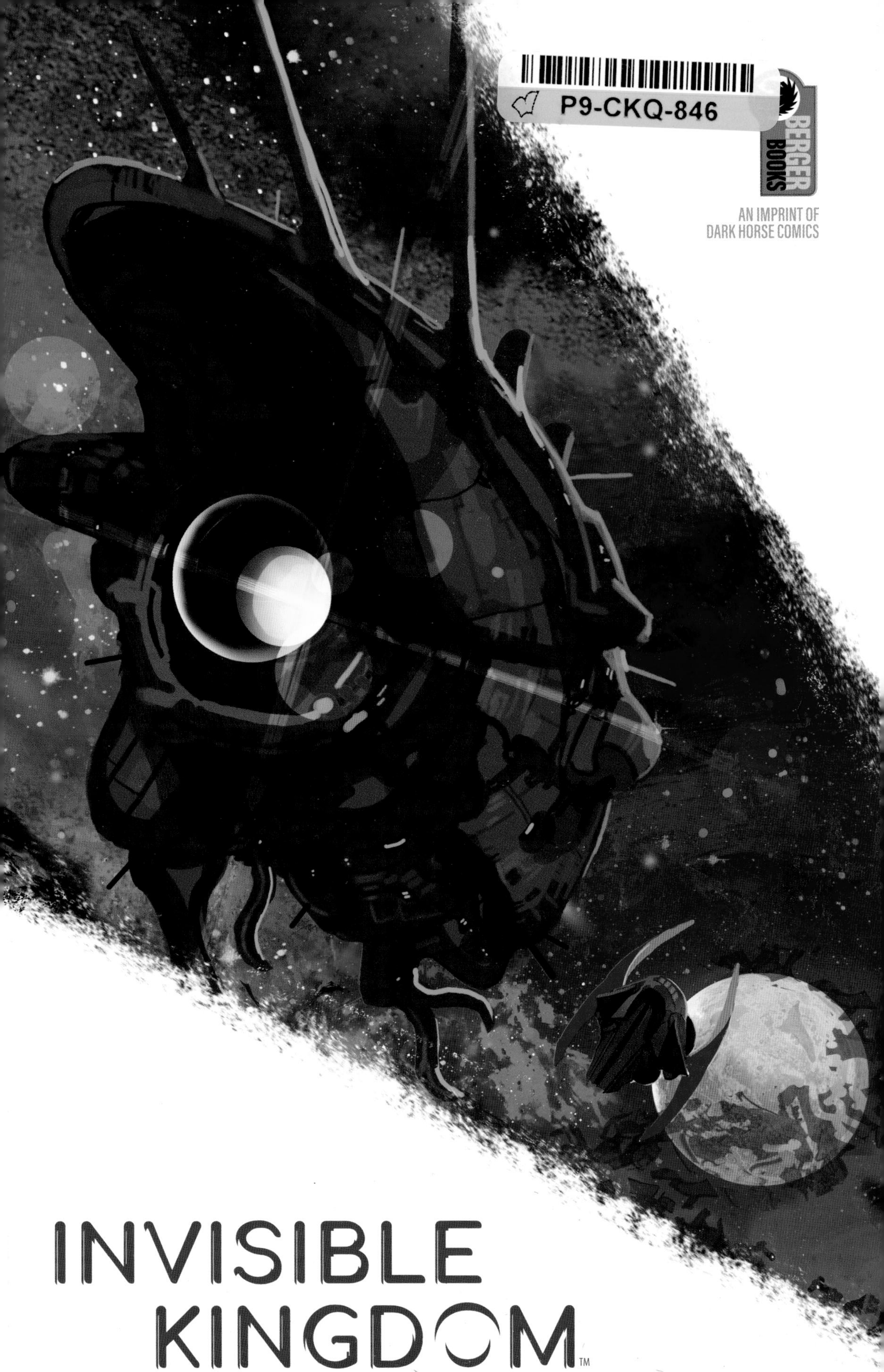

BERGER BOOKS
AN IMPRINT OF
DARK HORSE COMICS

INVISIBLE KINGDOM™

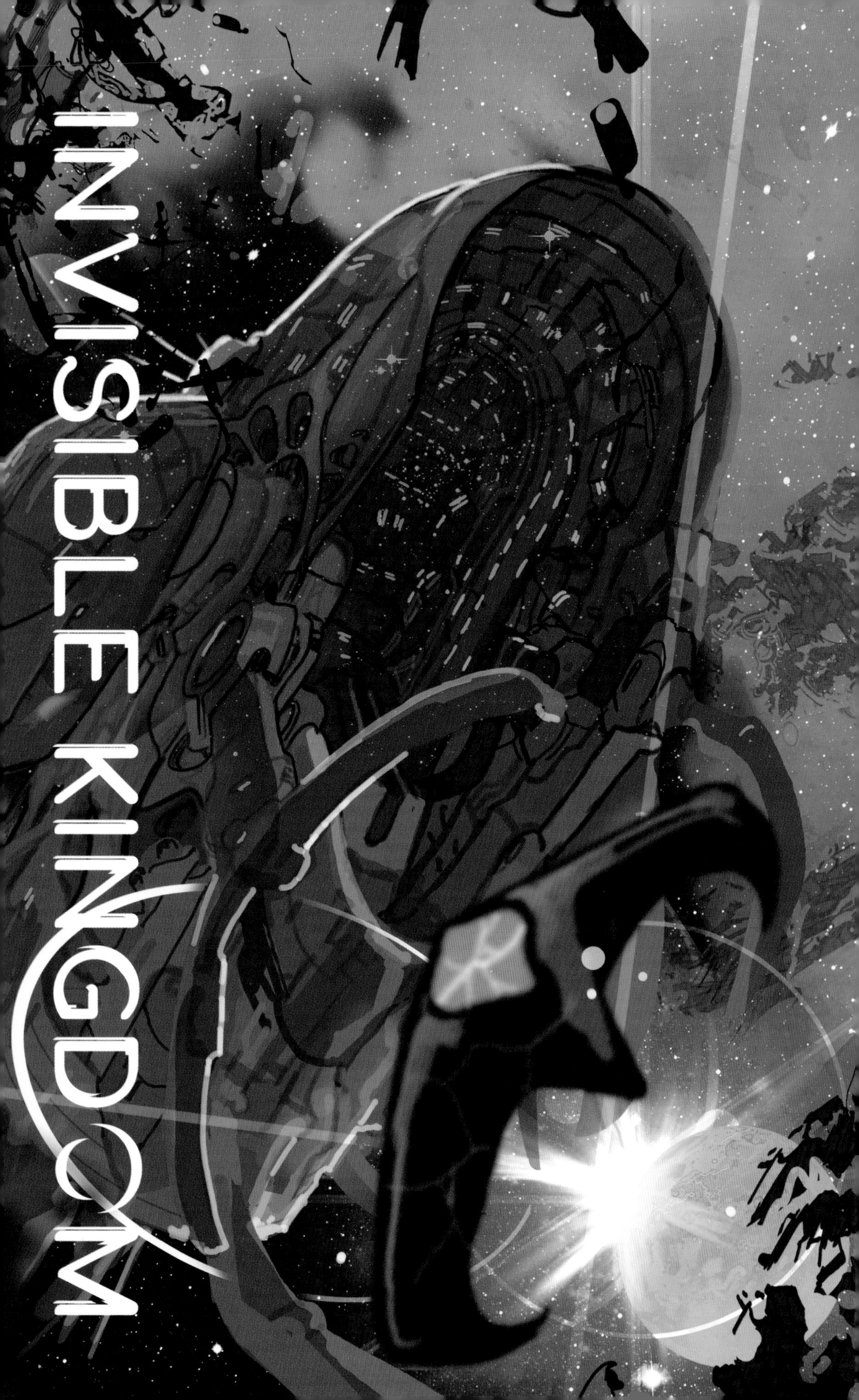
INVISIBLE KINGDOM

WRITER
G. Willow Wilson

ARTIST
Christian Ward

LETTERER
Sal Cipriano

VOLUME 2

EDGE OF EVERYTHING

EDITOR
Karen Berger

ASSISTANT EDITOR
Rachel Boyadjis

BOOK DESIGNER
Richard Bruning

DIGITAL ART TECHNICIAN
Adam Pruett

PRESIDENT & PUBLISHER
Mike Richardson

to Imogen
• • •
G Willow Wilson

for Catherine
• • •
Christian Ward

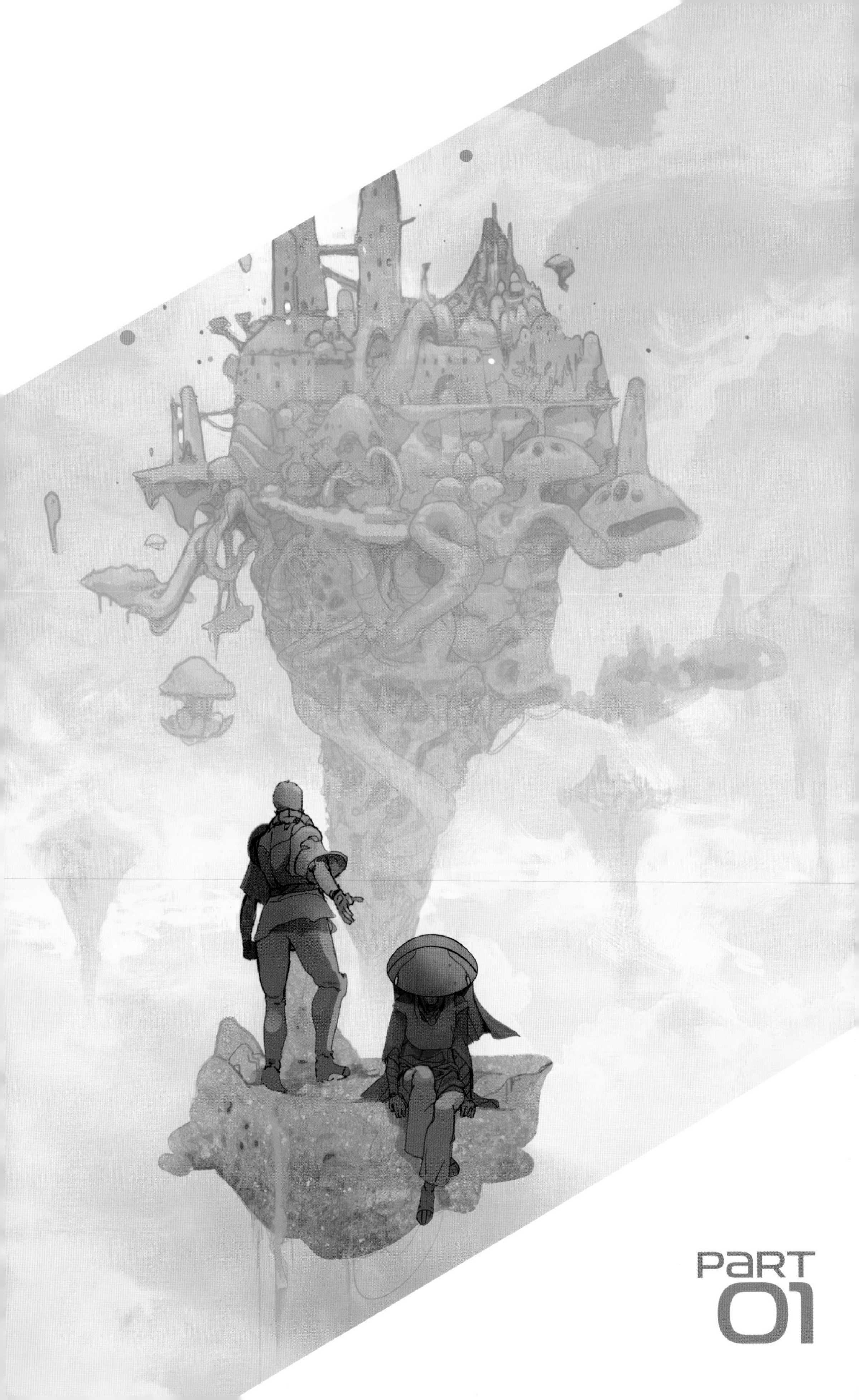

PART 01

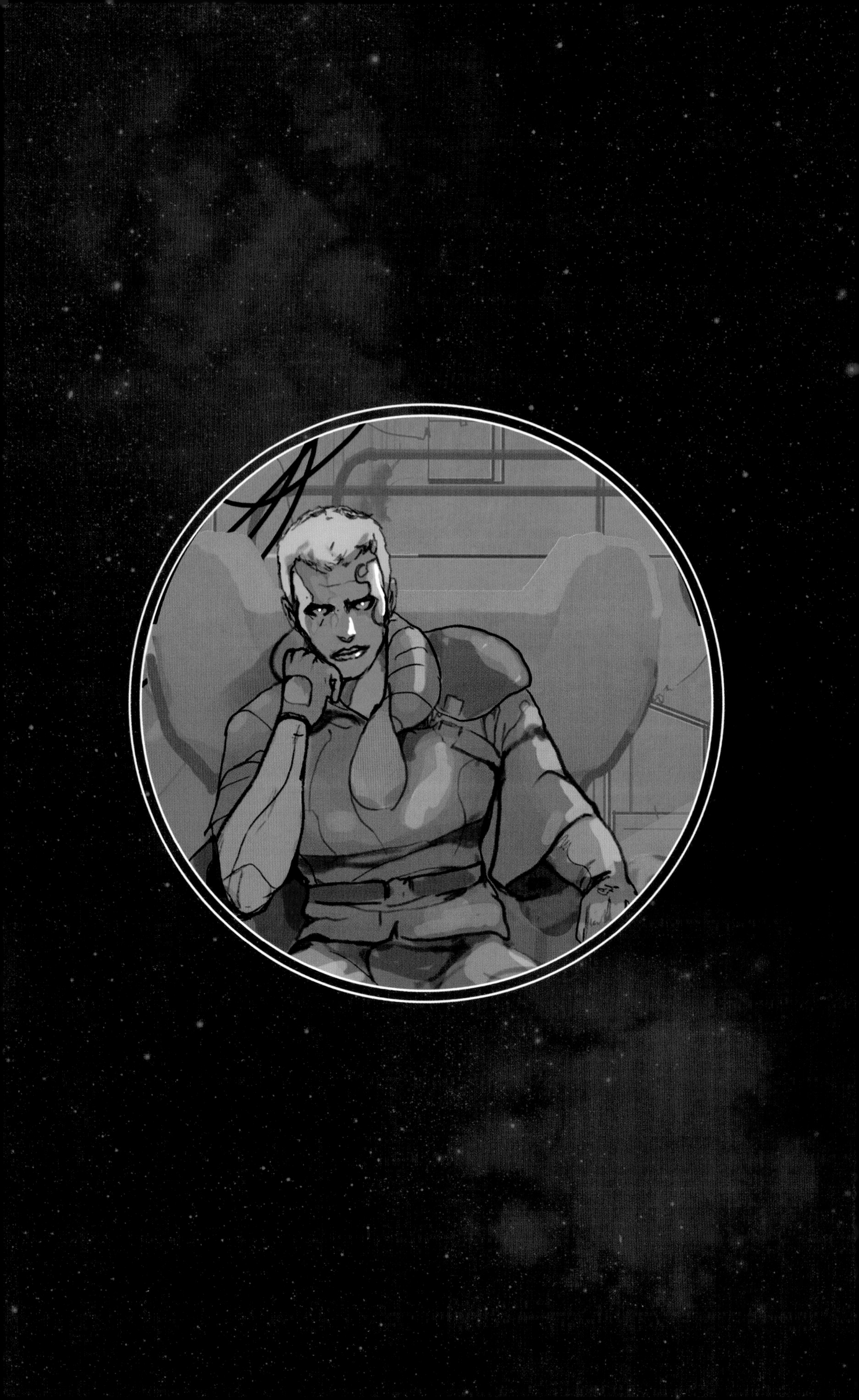

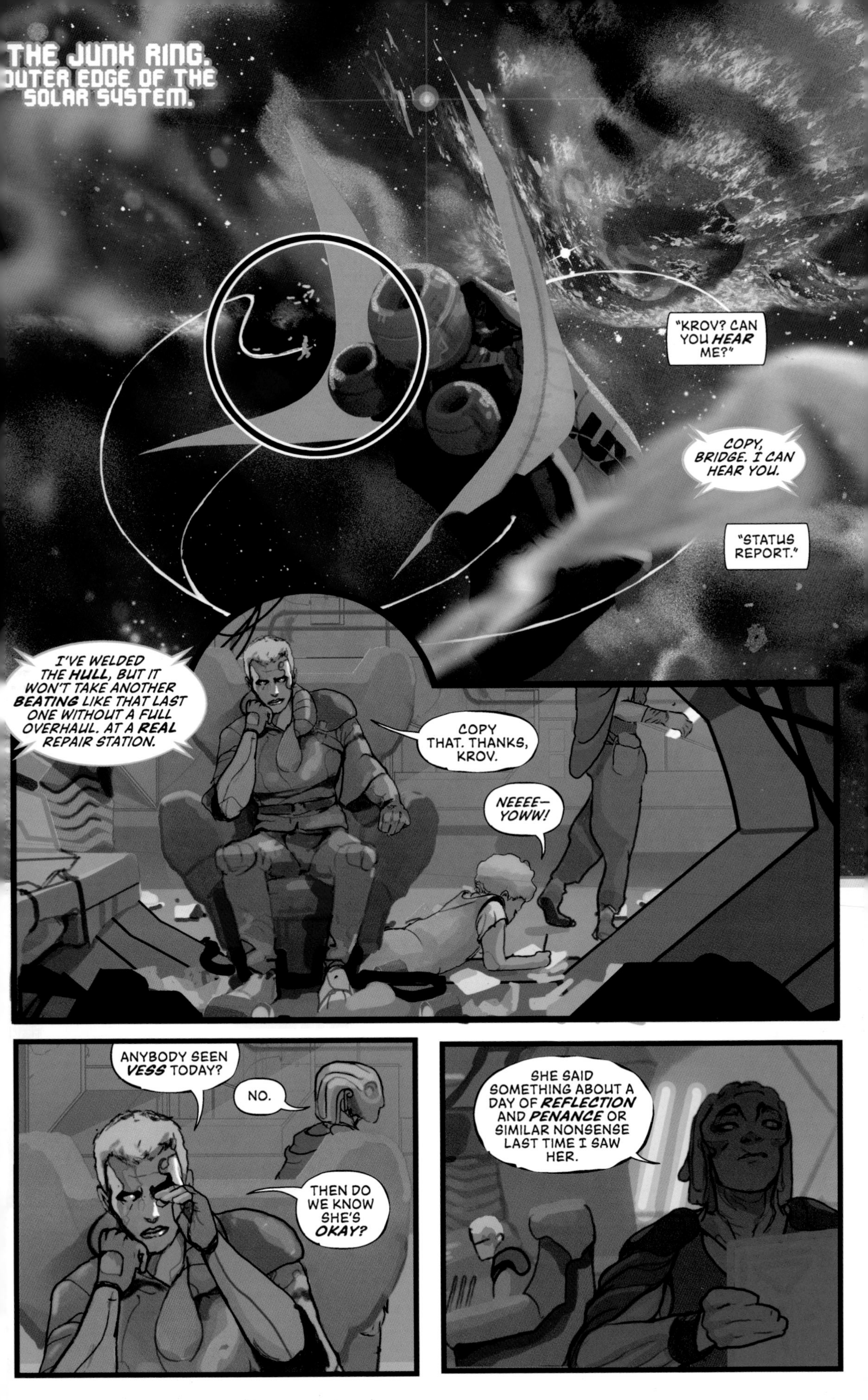
THE JUNK RING. OUTER EDGE OF THE SOLAR SYSTEM.
"KROV? CAN YOU HEAR ME?"
COPY, BRIDGE. I CAN HEAR YOU.
"STATUS REPORT."
I'VE WELDED THE HULL, BUT IT WON'T TAKE ANOTHER BEATING LIKE THAT LAST ONE WITHOUT A FULL OVERHAUL. AT A REAL REPAIR STATION.
COPY THAT. THANKS, KROV.
NEEEE—YOWW!
ANYBODY SEEN VESS TODAY?
NO.
THEN DO WE KNOW SHE'S OKAY?
SHE SAID SOMETHING ABOUT A DAY OF REFLECTION AND PENANCE OR SIMILAR NONSENSE LAST TIME I SAW HER.

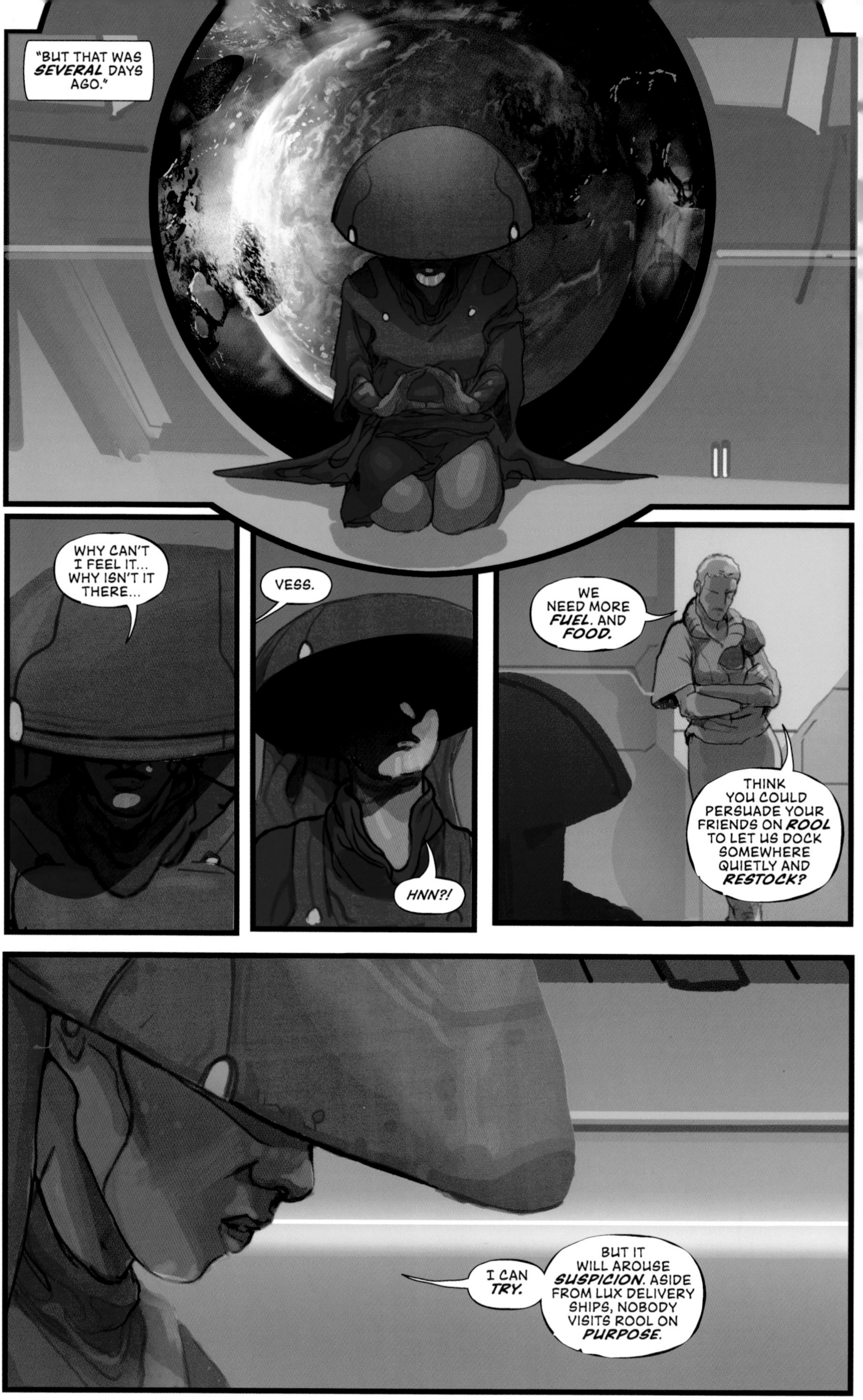
"BUT THAT WAS SEVERAL DAYS AGO."
WHY CAN'T I FEEL IT... WHY ISN'T IT THERE...
VESS.
HNN?!
WE NEED MORE FUEL. AND FOOD.
THINK YOU COULD PERSUADE YOUR FRIENDS ON ROOL TO LET US DOCK SOMEWHERE QUIETLY AND RESTOCK?
I CAN TRY.
BUT IT WILL AROUSE SUSPICION. ASIDE FROM LUX DELIVERY SHIPS, NOBODY VISITS ROOL ON PURPOSE.

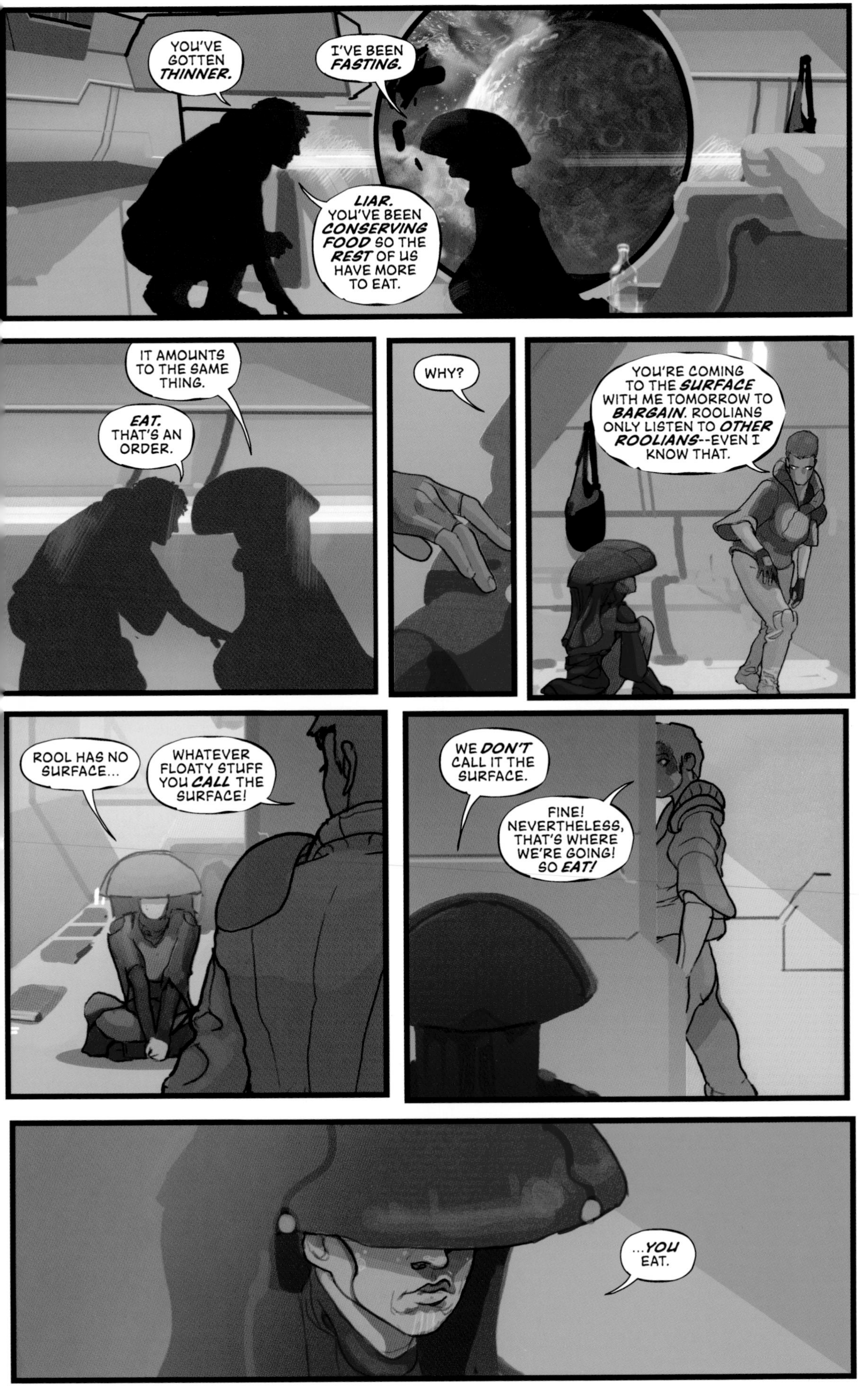
YOU'VE GOTTEN THINNER.
I'VE BEEN FASTING.
LIAR. YOU'VE BEEN CONSERVING FOOD SO THE REST OF US HAVE MORE TO EAT.
IT AMOUNTS TO THE SAME THING.
EAT. THAT'S AN ORDER.
WHY?
YOU'RE COMING TO THE SURFACE WITH ME TOMORROW TO BARGAIN. ROOLIANS ONLY LISTEN TO OTHER ROOLIANS--EVEN I KNOW THAT.
ROOL HAS NO SURFACE...
WHATEVER FLOATY STUFF YOU CALL THE SURFACE!
WE DON'T CALL IT THE SURFACE.
FINE! NEVERTHELESS, THAT'S WHERE WE'RE GOING! SO EAT!
...YOU EAT.

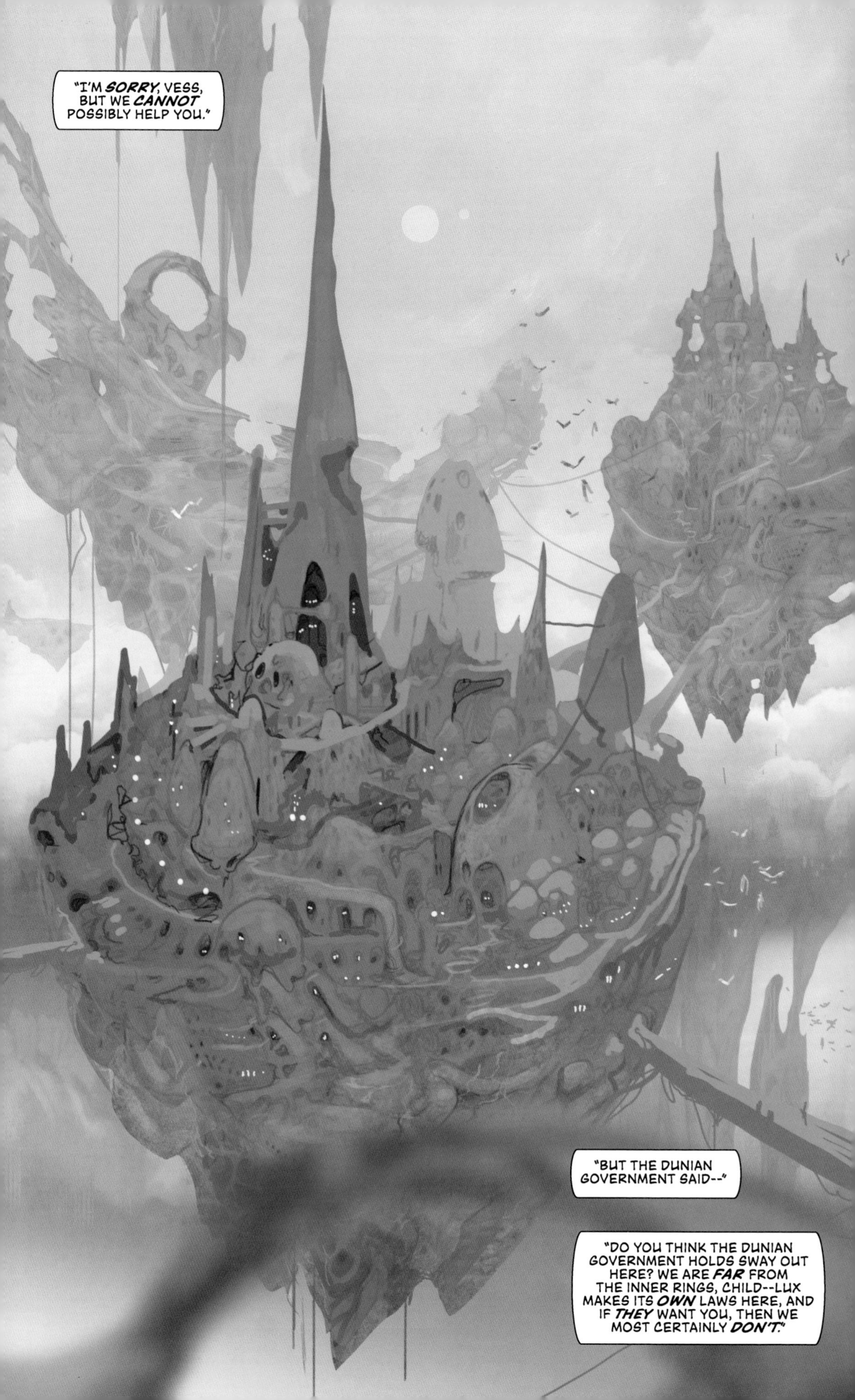
"I'M SORRY, VESS, BUT WE CANNOT POSSIBLY HELP YOU."
"BUT THE DUNIAN GOVERNMENT SAID--"
"DO YOU THINK THE DUNIAN GOVERNMENT HOLDS SWAY OUT HERE? WE ARE FAR FROM THE INNER RINGS, CHILD--LUX MAKES ITS OWN LAWS HERE, AND IF THEY WANT YOU, THEN WE MOST CERTAINLY DON'T."

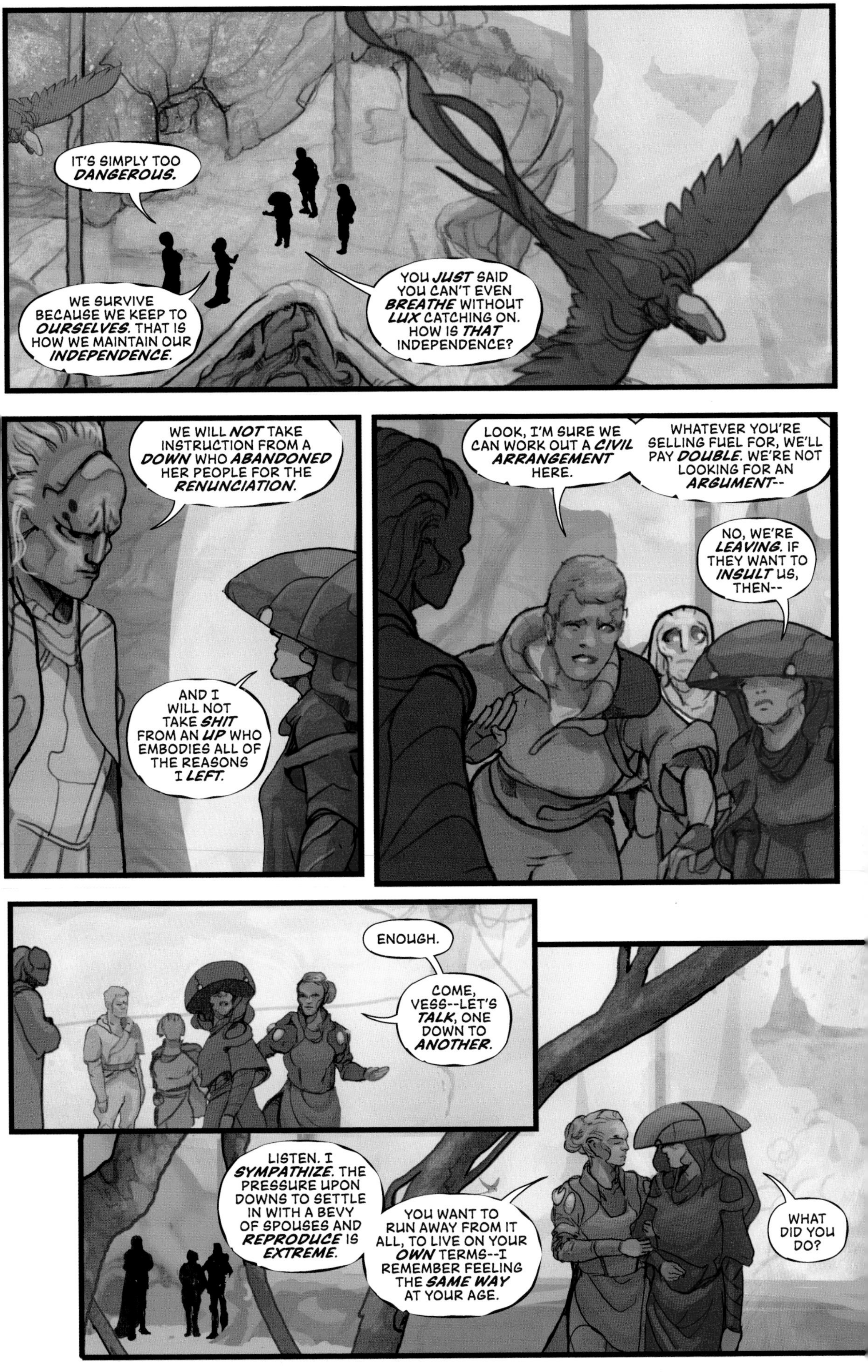
IT'S SIMPLY TOO DANGEROUS.
WE SURVIVE BECAUSE WE KEEP TO OURSELVES. THAT IS HOW WE MAINTAIN OUR INDEPENDENCE.
YOU JUST SAID YOU CAN'T EVEN BREATHE WITHOUT LUX CATCHING ON. HOW IS THAT INDEPENDENCE?
WE WILL NOT TAKE INSTRUCTION FROM A DOWN WHO ABANDONED HER PEOPLE FOR THE RENUNCIATION.
AND I WILL NOT TAKE SHIT FROM AN UP WHO EMBODIES ALL OF THE REASONS I LEFT.
LOOK, I'M SURE WE CAN WORK OUT A CIVIL ARRANGEMENT HERE.
WHATEVER YOU'RE SELLING FUEL FOR, WE'LL PAY DOUBLE. WE'RE NOT LOOKING FOR AN ARGUMENT--
NO, WE'RE LEAVING. IF THEY WANT TO INSULT US, THEN--
ENOUGH.
COME, VESS--LET'S TALK, ONE DOWN TO ANOTHER.
LISTEN. I SYMPATHIZE. THE PRESSURE UPON DOWNS TO SETTLE IN WITH A BEVY OF SPOUSES AND REPRODUCE IS EXTREME.
YOU WANT TO RUN AWAY FROM IT ALL, TO LIVE ON YOUR OWN TERMS--I REMEMBER FEELING THE SAME WAY AT YOUR AGE.
WHAT DID YOU DO?

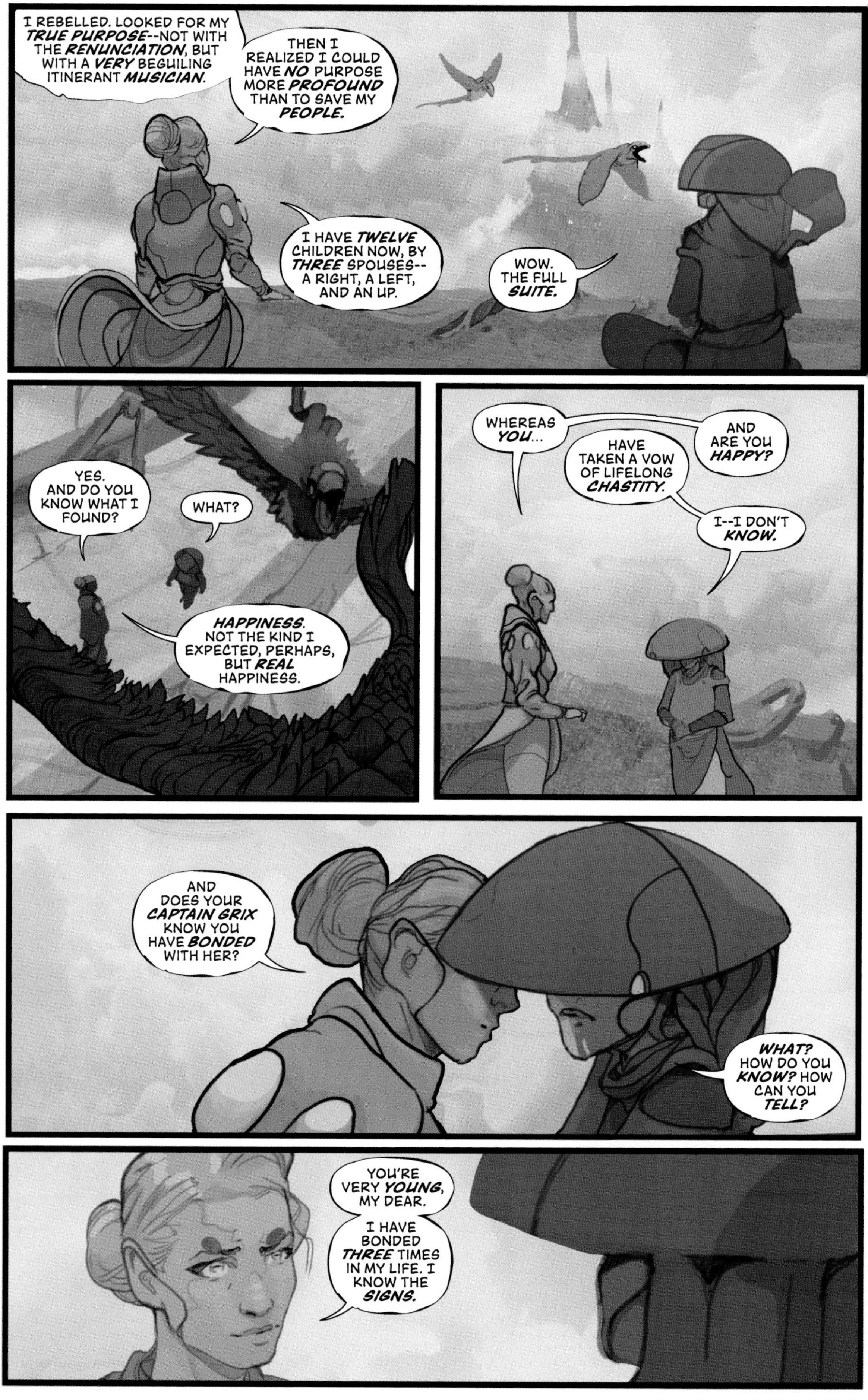
I REBELLED. LOOKED FOR MY TRUE PURPOSE--NOT WITH THE RENUNCIATION, BUT WITH A VERY BEGUILING ITINERANT MUSICIAN.
THEN I REALIZED I COULD HAVE NO PURPOSE MORE PROFOUND THAN TO SAVE MY PEOPLE.
I HAVE TWELVE CHILDREN NOW, BY THREE SPOUSES-- A RIGHT, A LEFT, AND AN UP.
WOW. THE FULL SUITE.
YES. AND DO YOU KNOW WHAT I FOUND?
WHAT?
HAPPINESS. NOT THE KIND I EXPECTED, PERHAPS, BUT REAL HAPPINESS.
WHEREAS YOU...
HAVE TAKEN A VOW OF LIFELONG CHASTITY.
AND ARE YOU HAPPY?
I--I DON'T KNOW.
AND DOES YOUR CAPTAIN GRIX KNOW YOU HAVE BONDED WITH HER?
WHAT? HOW DO YOU KNOW? HOW CAN YOU TELL?
YOU'RE VERY YOUNG, MY DEAR.
I HAVE BONDED THREE TIMES IN MY LIFE. I KNOW THE SIGNS.

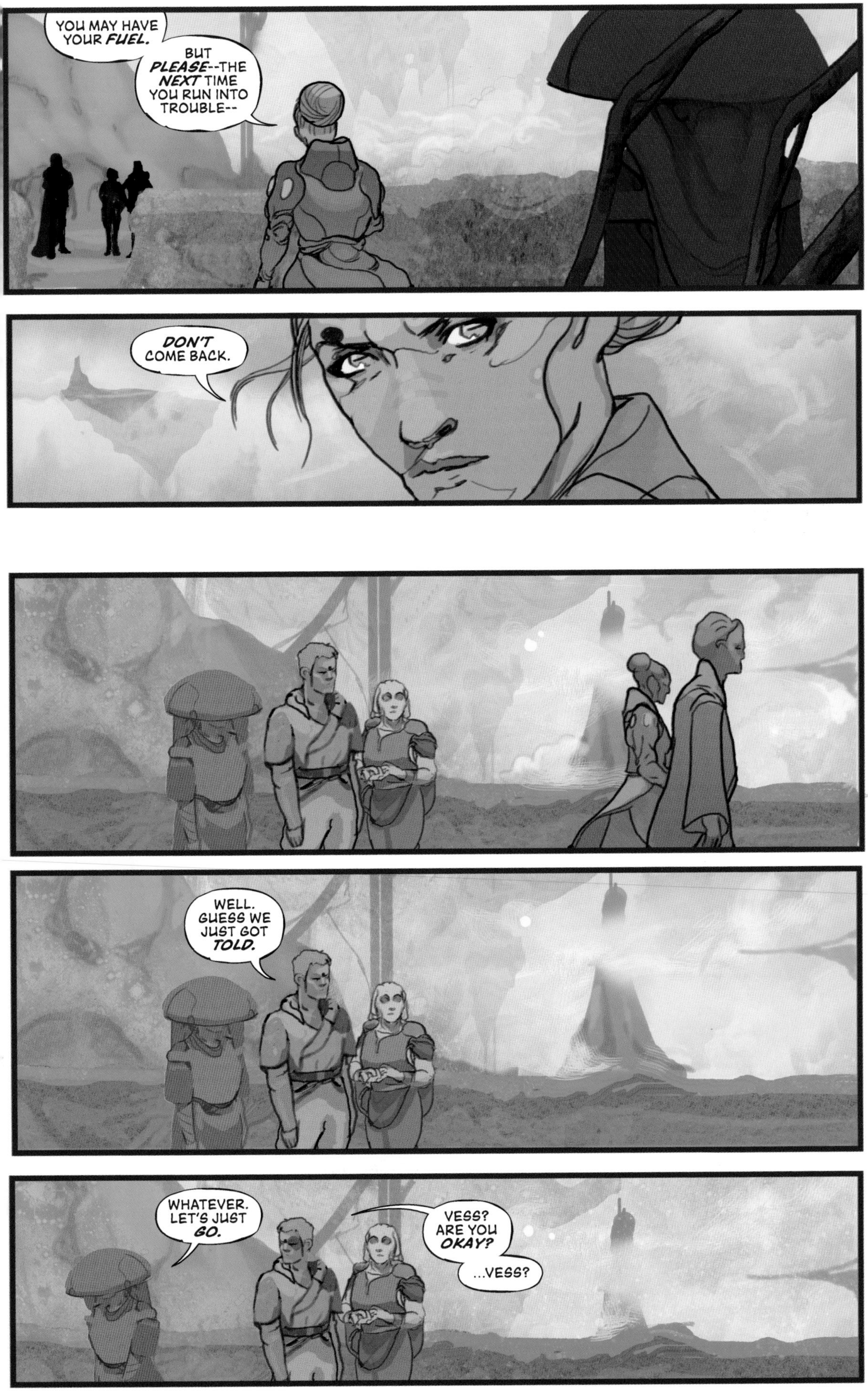
YOU MAY HAVE YOUR FUEL.
BUT PLEASE--THE NEXT TIME YOU RUN INTO TROUBLE--
DON'T COME BACK.
WELL. GUESS WE JUST GOT TOLD.
WHATEVER. LET'S JUST GO.
VESS? ARE YOU OKAY?
...VESS?

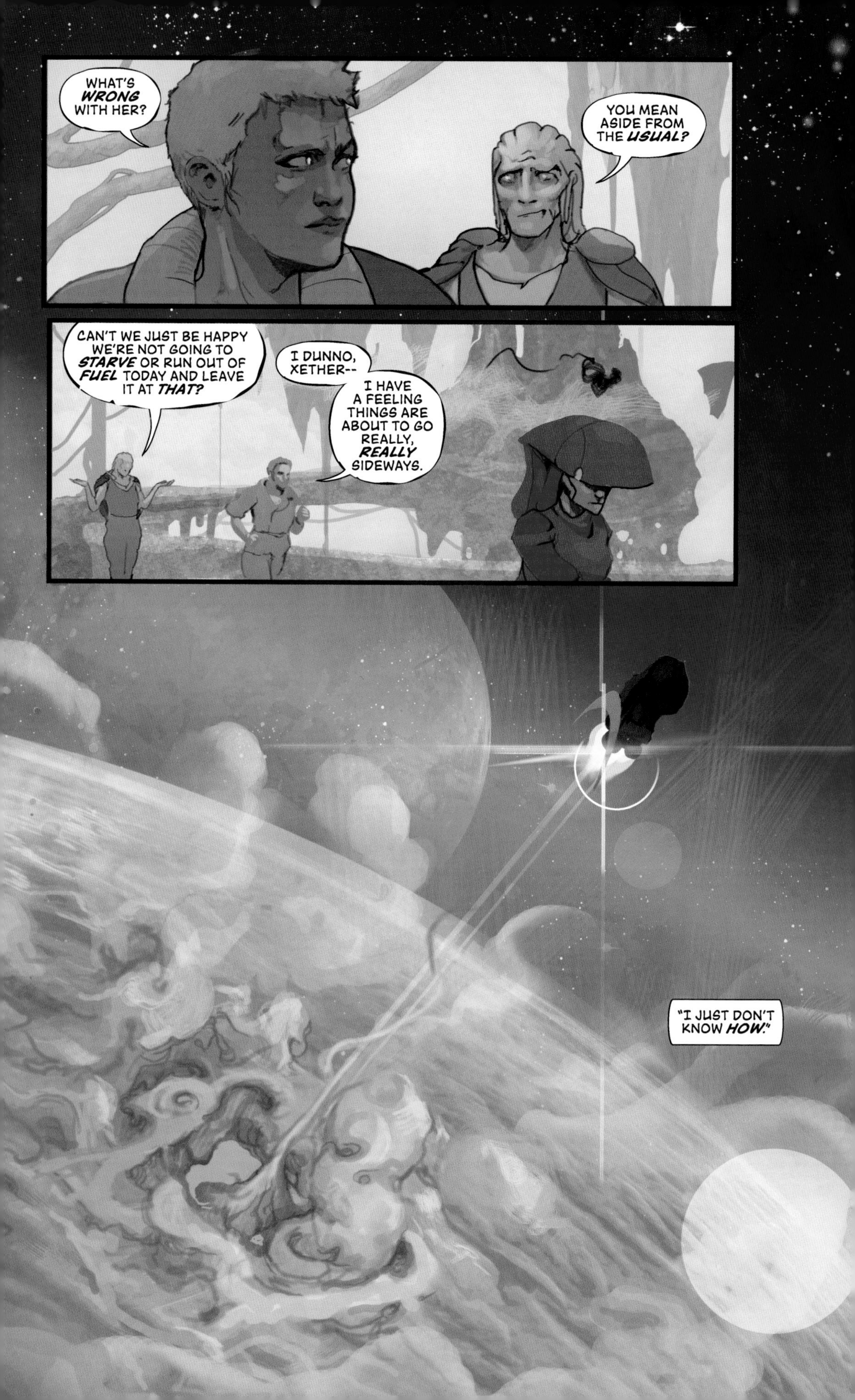
WHAT'S WRONG WITH HER?
YOU MEAN ASIDE FROM THE USUAL?
CAN'T WE JUST BE HAPPY WE'RE NOT GOING TO STARVE OR RUN OUT OF FUEL TODAY AND LEAVE IT AT THAT?
I DUNNO, XETHER--
I HAVE A FEELING THINGS ARE ABOUT TO GO REALLY, REALLY SIDEWAYS.
"I JUST DON'T KNOW HOW."

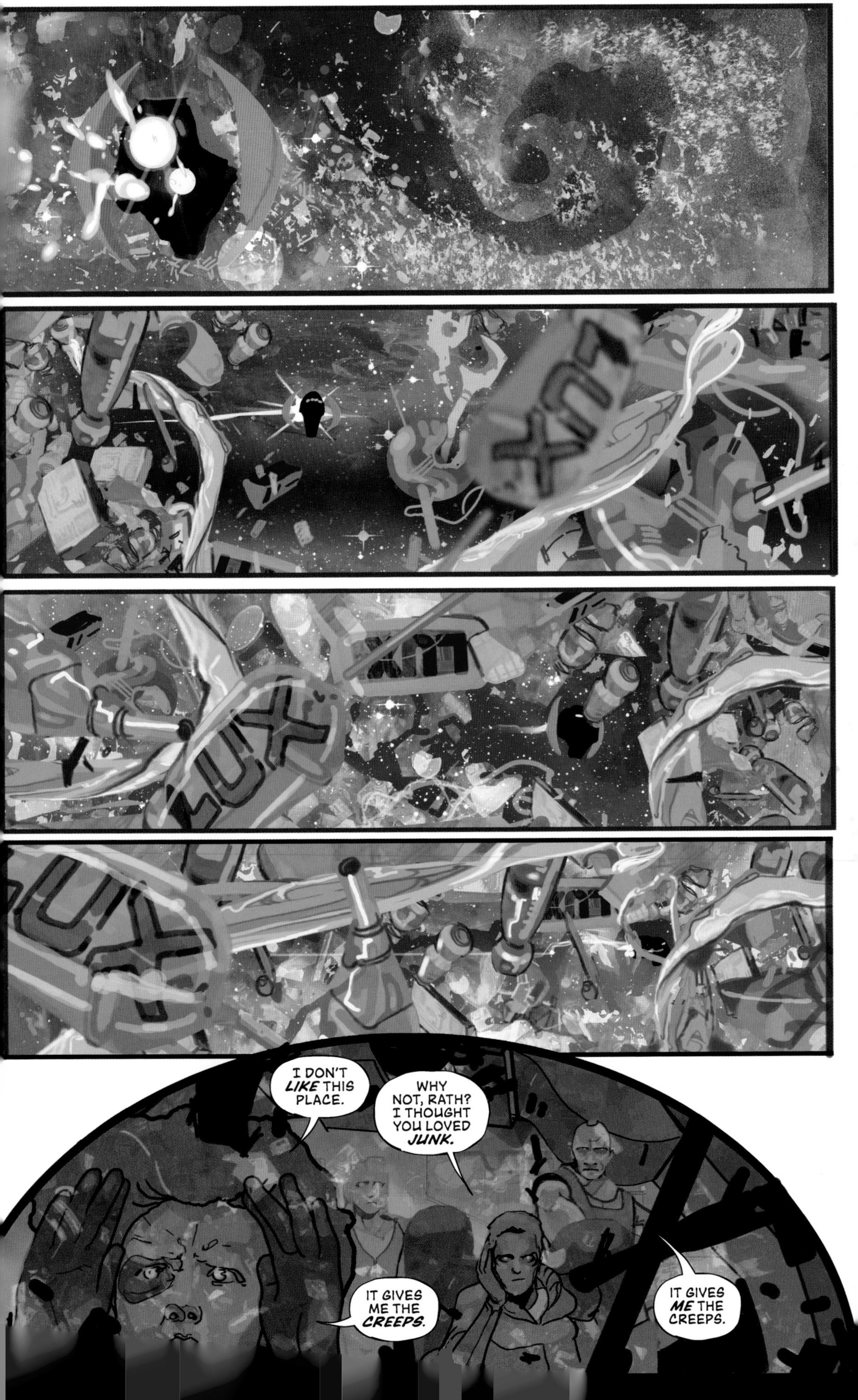

I DON'T *LIKE* THIS PLACE.
WHY NOT, RATH? I THOUGHT YOU LOVED *JUNK.*
IT GIVES ME THE *CREEPS.*
IT GIVES *ME* THE CREEPS.

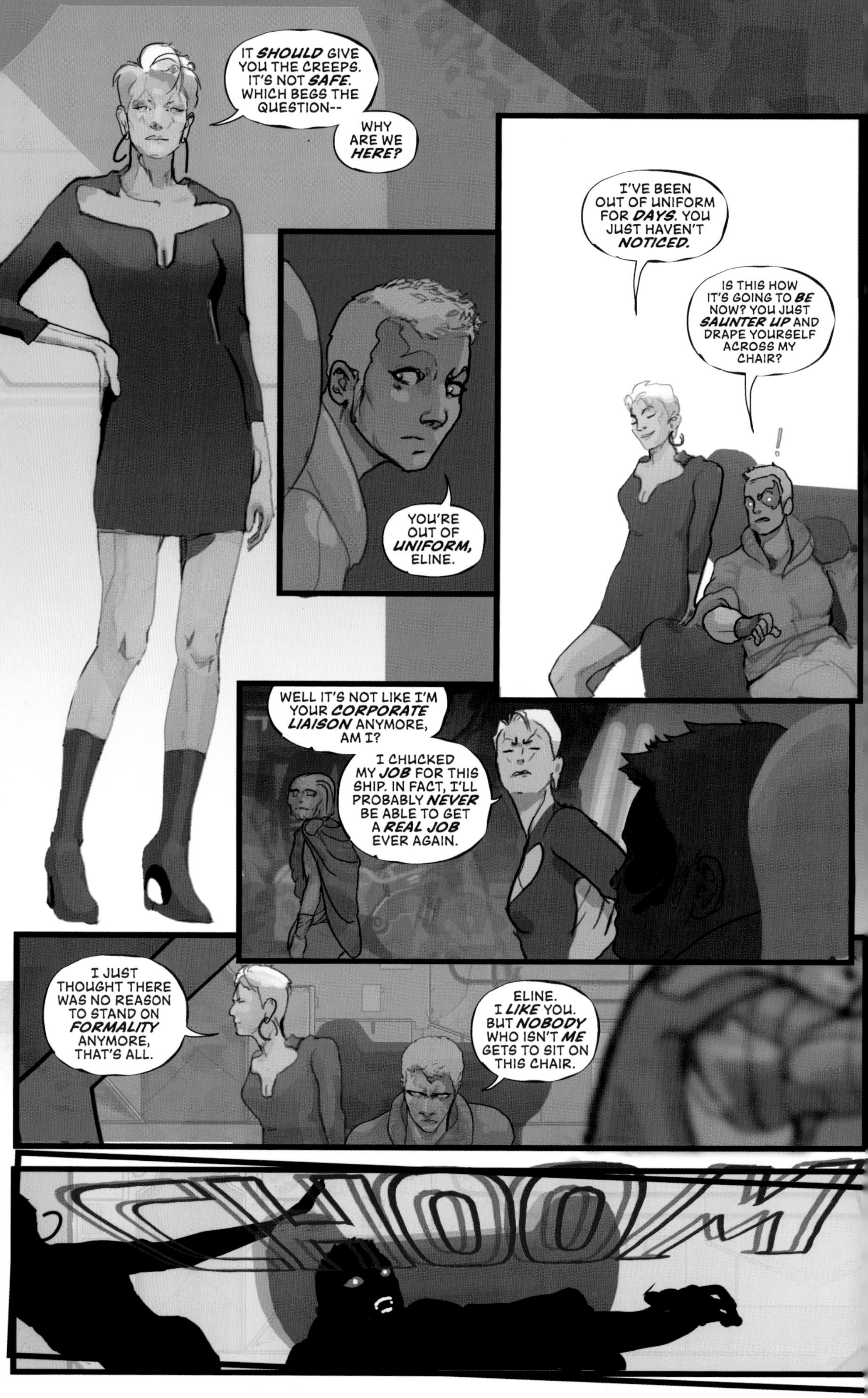
IT *SHOULD* GIVE YOU THE CREEPS. IT'S NOT *SAFE*. WHICH BEGS THE QUESTION--
WHY ARE WE *HERE?*
YOU'RE OUT OF *UNIFORM,* ELINE.
I'VE BEEN OUT OF UNIFORM FOR *DAYS*. YOU JUST HAVEN'T *NOTICED.*
IS THIS HOW IT'S GOING TO *BE* NOW? YOU JUST *SAUNTER UP* AND DRAPE YOURSELF ACROSS MY CHAIR?
!
WELL IT'S NOT LIKE I'M YOUR *CORPORATE LIAISON* ANYMORE, AM I?
I CHUCKED MY *JOB* FOR THIS SHIP. IN FACT, I'LL PROBABLY *NEVER* BE ABLE TO GET A *REAL JOB* EVER AGAIN.
I JUST THOUGHT THERE WAS NO REASON TO STAND ON *FORMALITY* ANYMORE, THAT'S ALL.
ELINE. I *LIKE* YOU. BUT *NOBODY* WHO ISN'T *ME* GETS TO SIT ON THIS CHAIR.

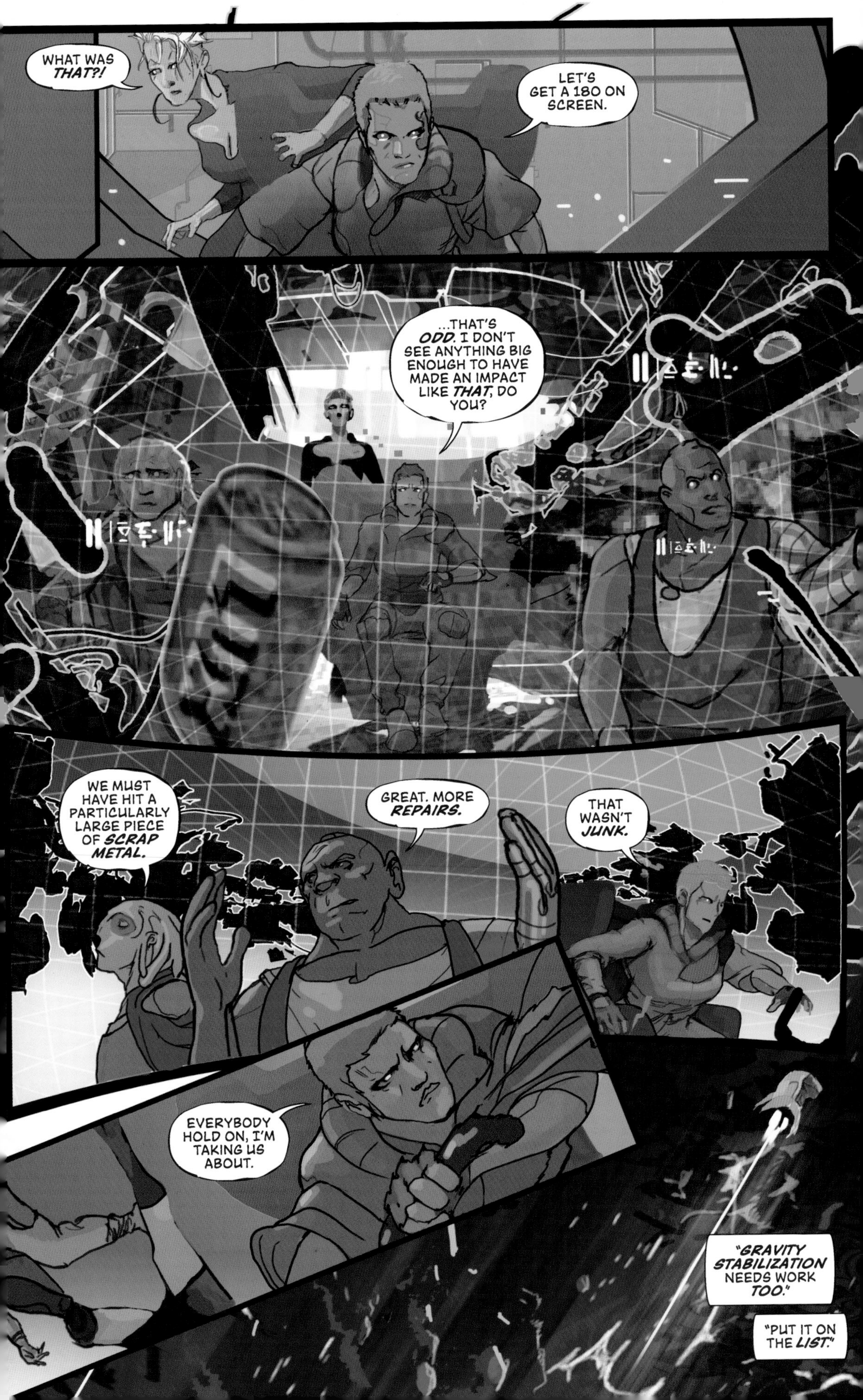
WHAT WAS THAT?!
LET'S GET A 180 ON SCREEN.
...THAT'S ODD. I DON'T SEE ANYTHING BIG ENOUGH TO HAVE MADE AN IMPACT LIKE THAT, DO YOU?
WE MUST HAVE HIT A PARTICULARLY LARGE PIECE OF SCRAP METAL.
GREAT. MORE REPAIRS.
THAT WASN'T JUNK.
EVERYBODY HOLD ON, I'M TAKING US ABOUT.
"GRAVITY STABILIZATION NEEDS WORK TOO."
"PUT IT ON THE LIST."

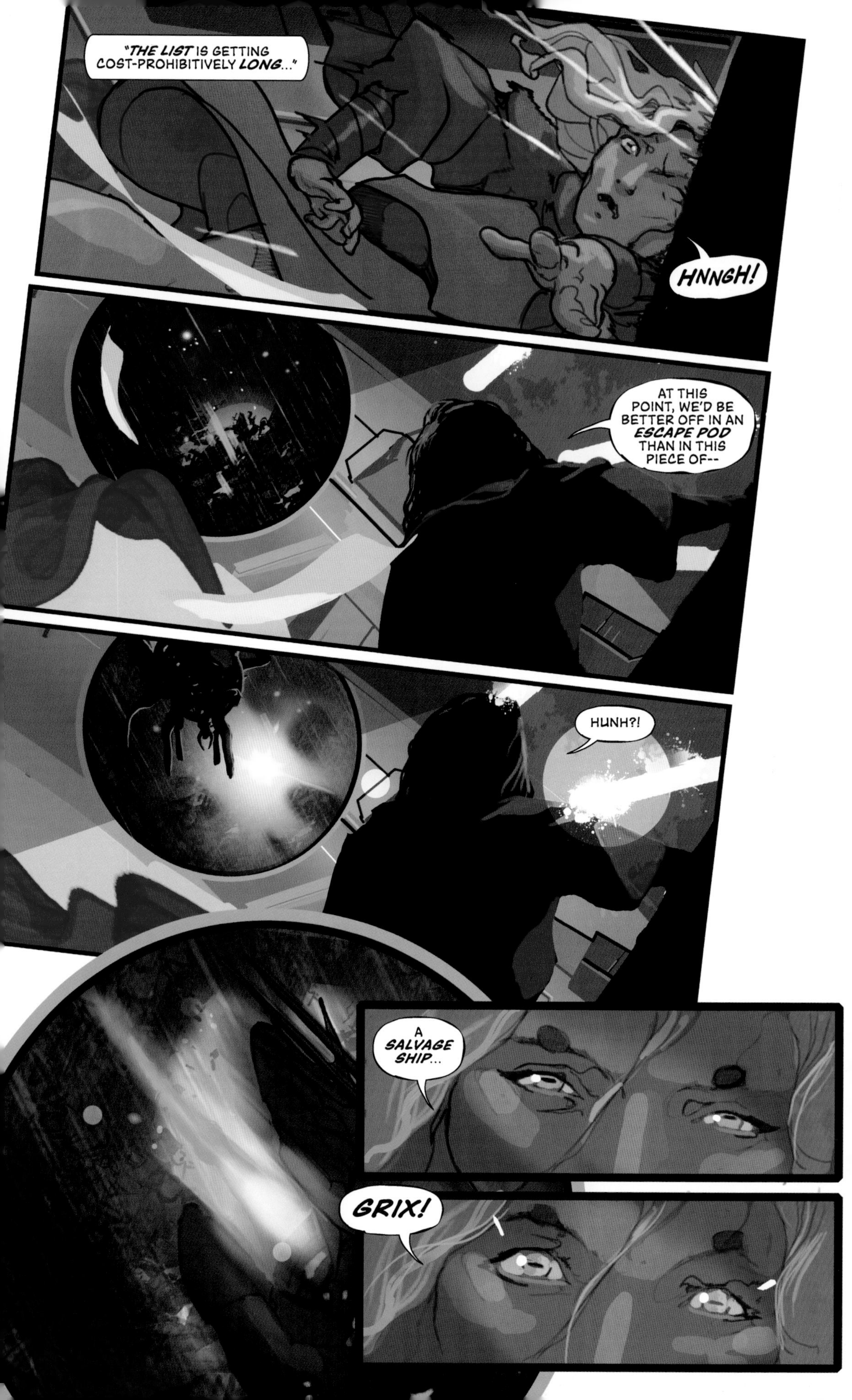
"THE LIST IS GETTING COST-PROHIBITIVELY LONG..."
HNNGH!
AT THIS POINT, WE'D BE BETTER OFF IN AN ESCAPE POD THAN IN THIS PIECE OF--
HUNH?!
A SALVAGE SHIP...
GRIX!

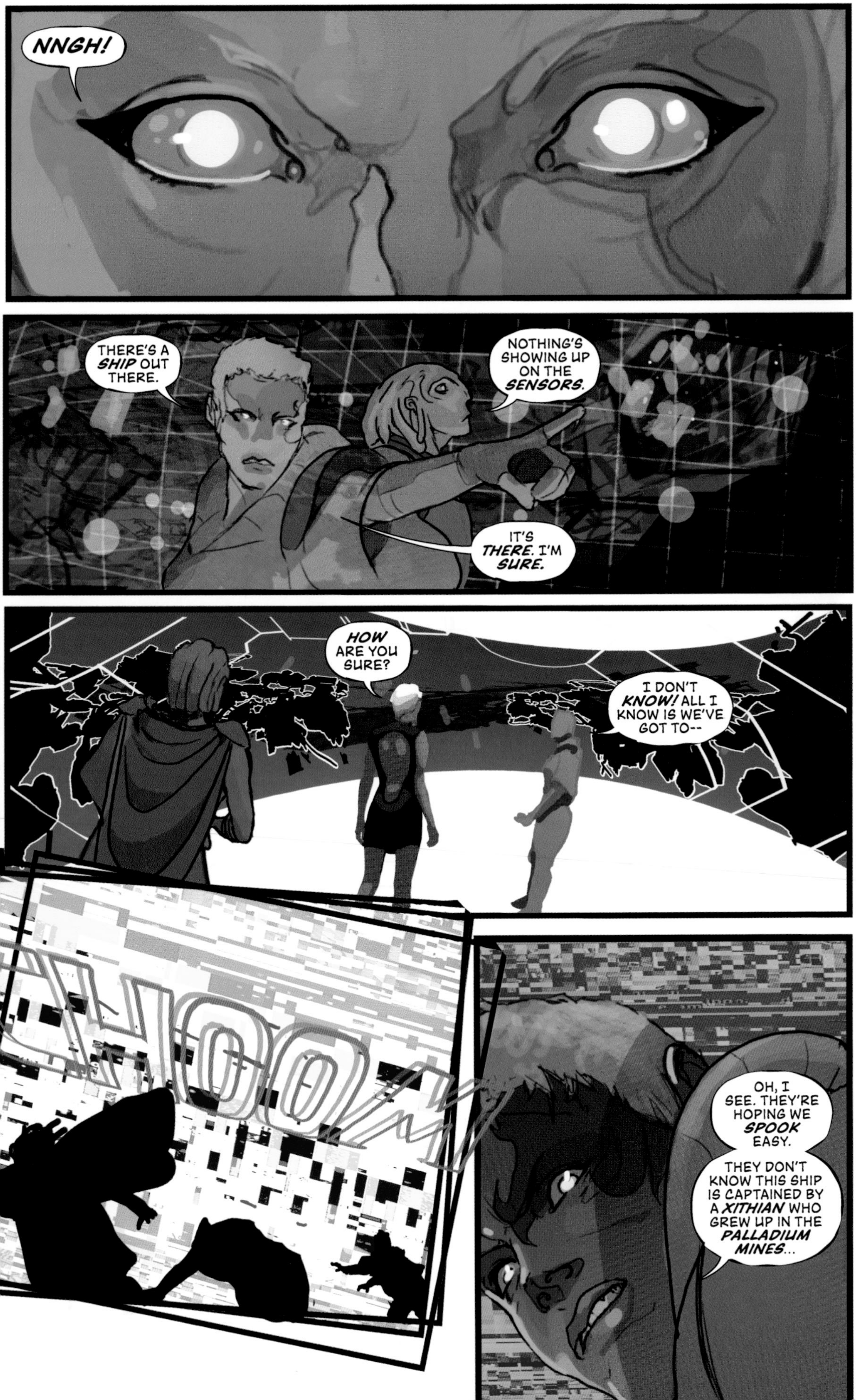
NNGH!
THERE'S A SHIP OUT THERE.
NOTHING'S SHOWING UP ON THE SENSORS.
IT'S THERE. I'M SURE.
HOW ARE YOU SURE?
I DON'T KNOW! ALL I KNOW IS WE'VE GOT TO--
OH, I SEE. THEY'RE HOPING WE SPOOK EASY.
THEY DON'T KNOW THIS SHIP IS CAPTAINED BY A XITHIAN WHO GREW UP IN THE PALLADIUM MINES...

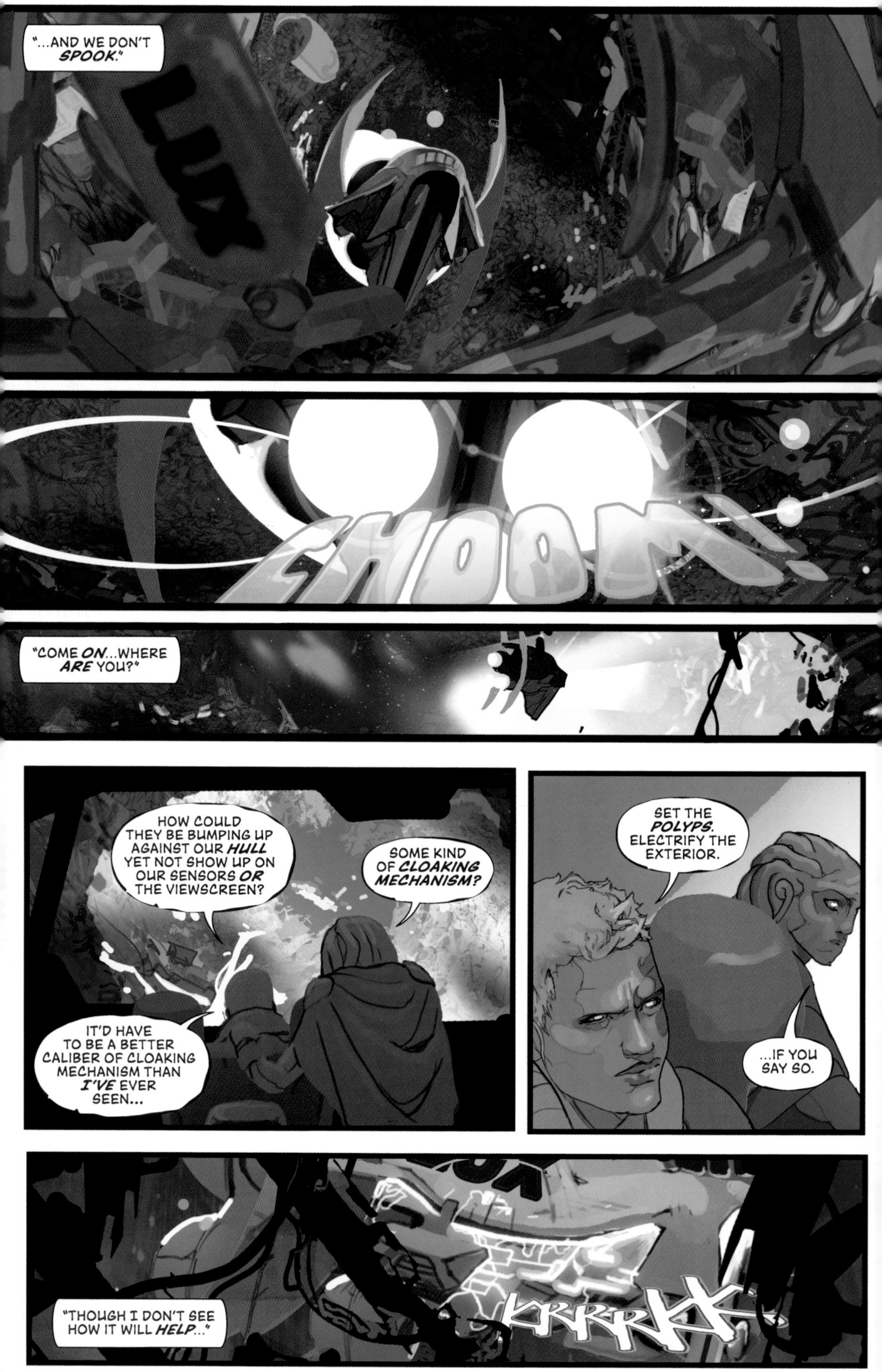
"...AND WE DON'T *SPOOK*."
CHOOM!
"COME *ON*...WHERE *ARE* YOU?"
HOW COULD THEY BE BUMPING UP AGAINST OUR *HULL* YET NOT SHOW UP ON OUR SENSORS *OR* THE VIEWSCREEN?
SOME KIND OF *CLOAKING MECHANISM?*
IT'D HAVE TO BE A BETTER CALIBER OF CLOAKING MECHANISM THAN *I'VE* EVER SEEN...
SET THE *POLYPS*. ELECTRIFY THE EXTERIOR.
...IF YOU SAY SO.
"THOUGH I DON'T SEE HOW IT WILL *HELP*..."
KRRRKK

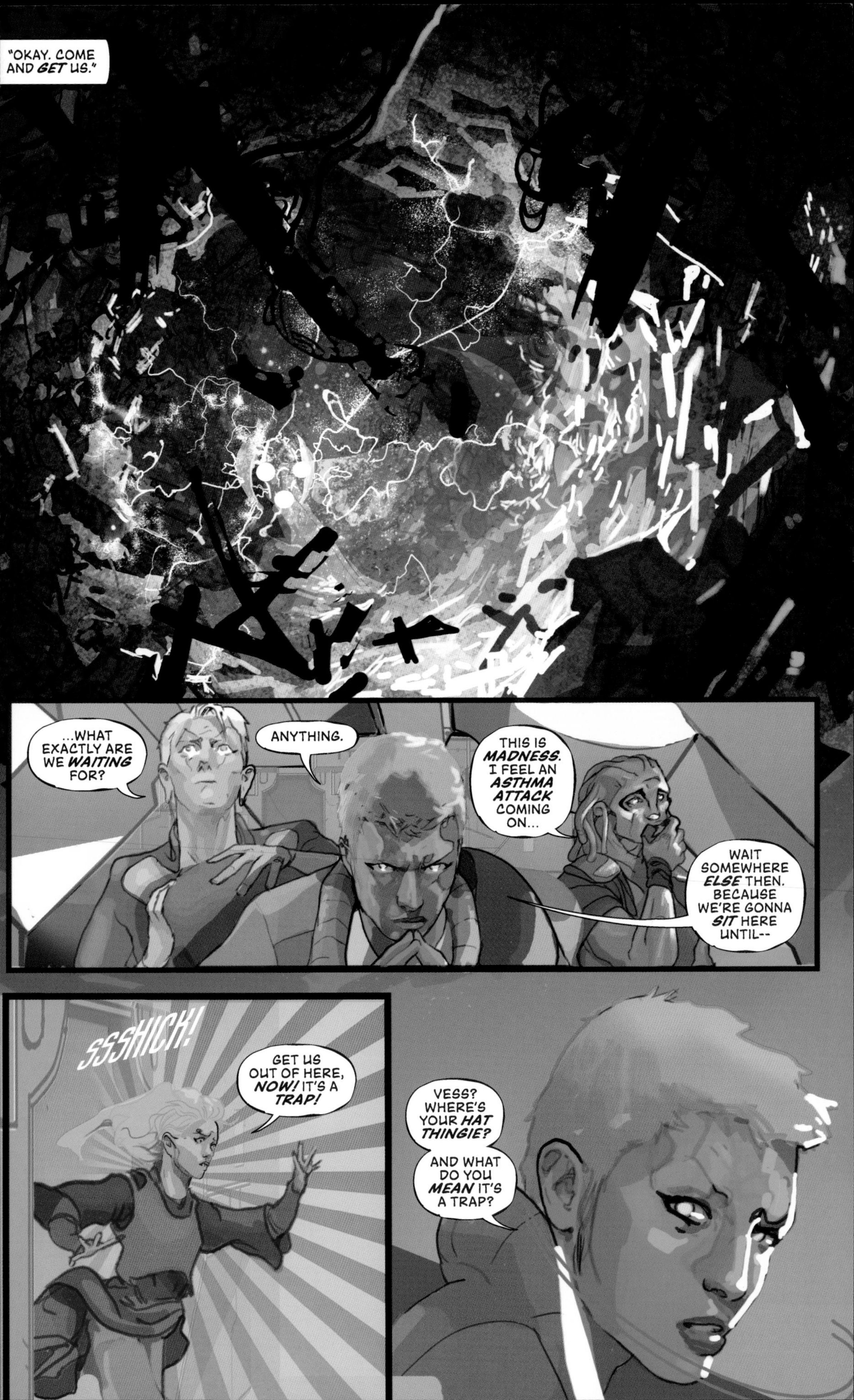
"OKAY. COME AND GET US."
...WHAT EXACTLY ARE WE WAITING FOR?
ANYTHING.
THIS IS MADNESS. I FEEL AN ASTHMA ATTACK COMING ON...
WAIT SOMEWHERE ELSE THEN. BECAUSE WE'RE GONNA SIT HERE UNTIL--
SSSHICK!
GET US OUT OF HERE, NOW! IT'S A TRAP!
VESS? WHERE'S YOUR HAT THINGIE?
AND WHAT DO YOU MEAN IT'S A TRAP?

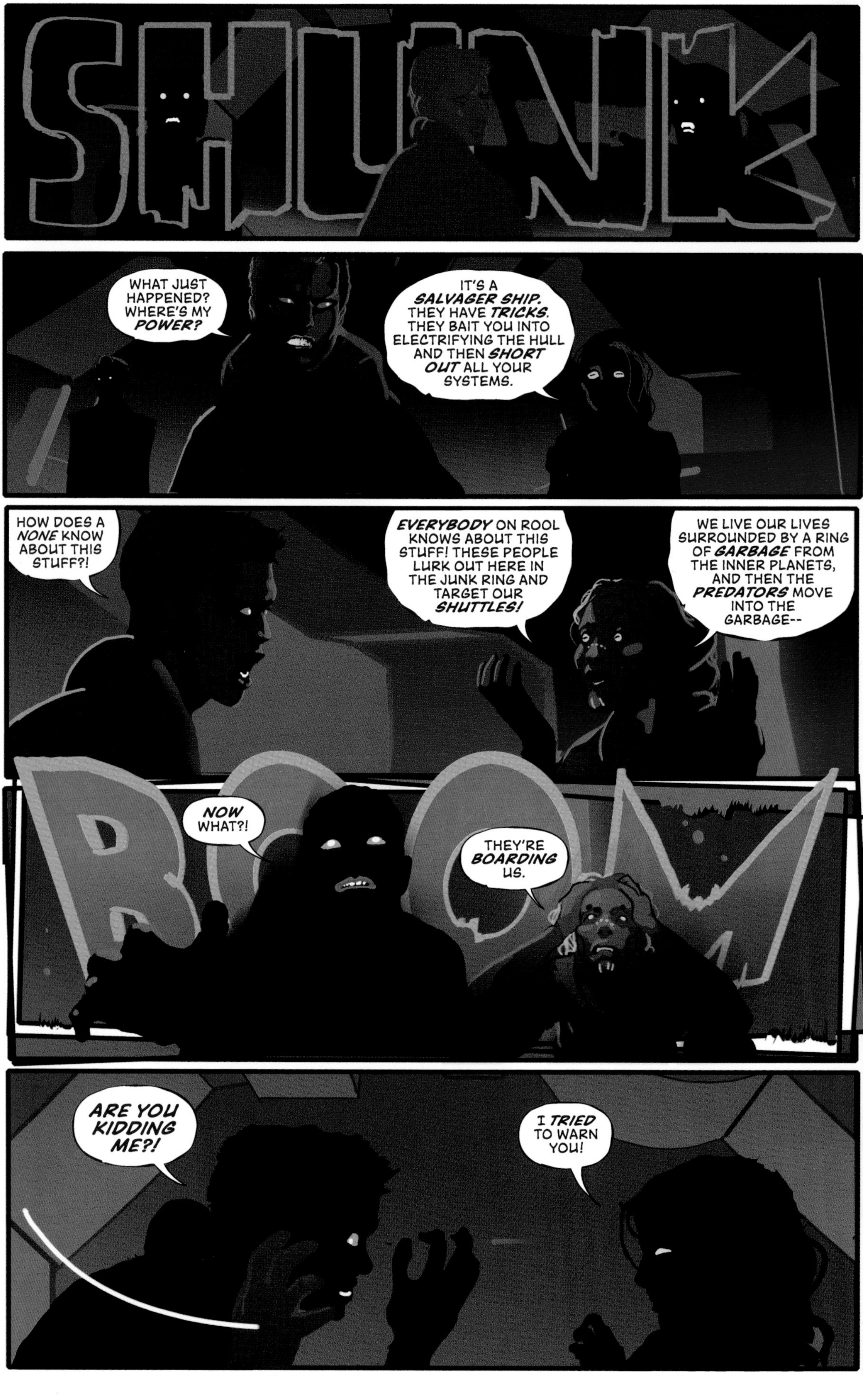
SHUNK
WHAT JUST HAPPENED? WHERE'S MY POWER?
IT'S A SALVAGER SHIP. THEY HAVE TRICKS. THEY BAIT YOU INTO ELECTRIFYING THE HULL AND THEN SHORT OUT ALL YOUR SYSTEMS.
HOW DOES A NONE KNOW ABOUT THIS STUFF?!
EVERYBODY ON ROOL KNOWS ABOUT THIS STUFF! THESE PEOPLE LURK OUT HERE IN THE JUNK RING AND TARGET OUR SHUTTLES!
WE LIVE OUR LIVES SURROUNDED BY A RING OF GARBAGE FROM THE INNER PLANETS, AND THEN THE PREDATORS MOVE INTO THE GARBAGE--
BOOM
NOW WHAT?!
THEY'RE BOARDING US.
ARE YOU KIDDING ME?!
I TRIED TO WARN YOU!

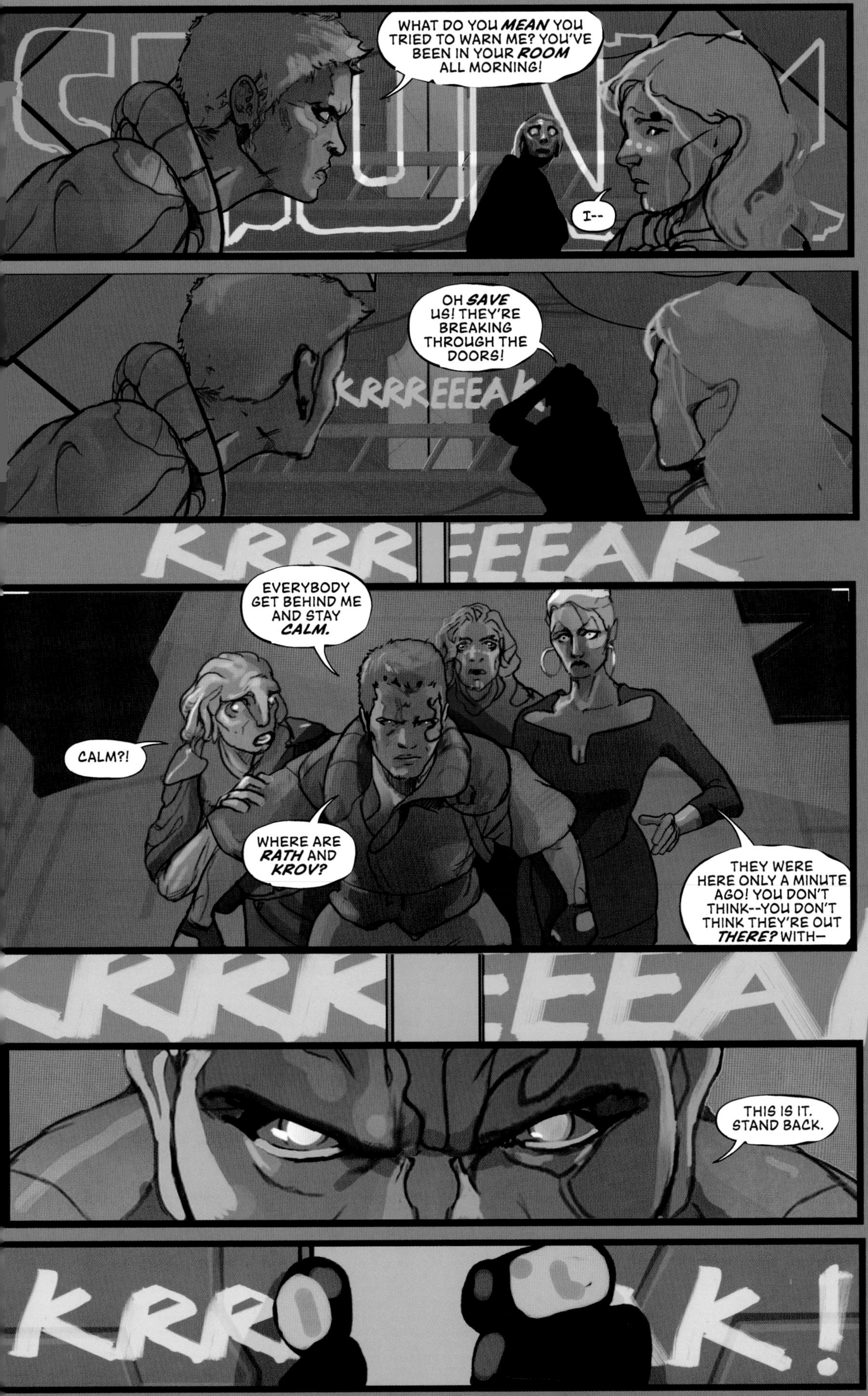
WHAT DO YOU MEAN YOU TRIED TO WARN ME? YOU'VE BEEN IN YOUR ROOM ALL MORNING!
I--
OH SAVE US! THEY'RE BREAKING THROUGH THE DOORS!
KRRREEEAK
KRRREEEAK
EVERYBODY GET BEHIND ME AND STAY CALM.
CALM?!
WHERE ARE RATH AND KROV?
THEY WERE HERE ONLY A MINUTE AGO! YOU DON'T THINK--YOU DON'T THINK THEY'RE OUT THERE? WITH—
THIS IS IT. STAND BACK.
K!

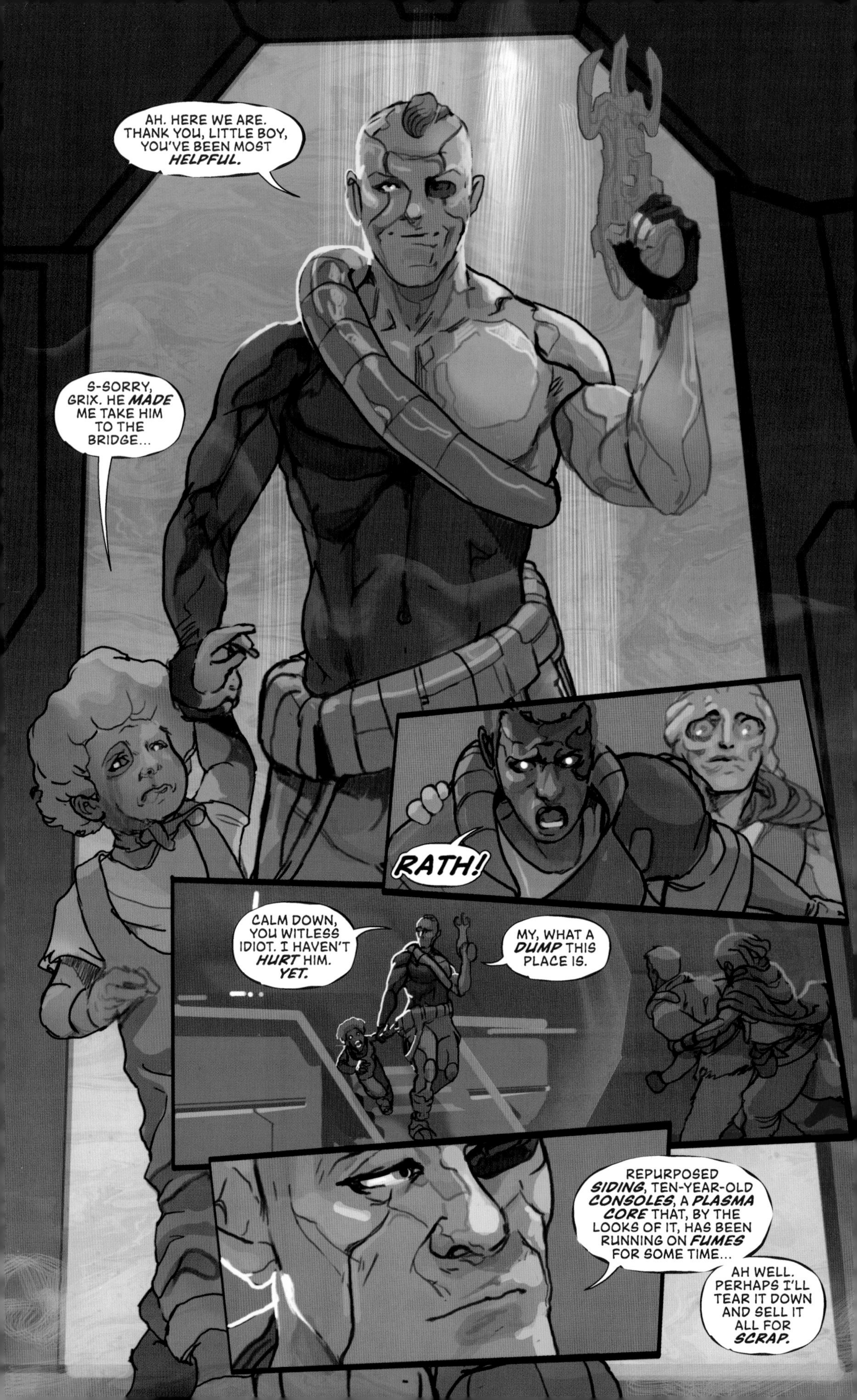
AH. HERE WE ARE. THANK YOU, LITTLE BOY, YOU'VE BEEN MOST HELPFUL.
S-SORRY, GRIX. HE MADE ME TAKE HIM TO THE BRIDGE...
RATH!
CALM DOWN, YOU WITLESS IDIOT. I HAVEN'T HURT HIM. YET.
MY, WHAT A DUMP THIS PLACE IS.
REPURPOSED SIDING, TEN-YEAR-OLD CONSOLES, A PLASMA CORE THAT, BY THE LOOKS OF IT, HAS BEEN RUNNING ON FUMES FOR SOME TIME...
AH WELL. PERHAPS I'LL TEAR IT DOWN AND SELL IT ALL FOR SCRAP.

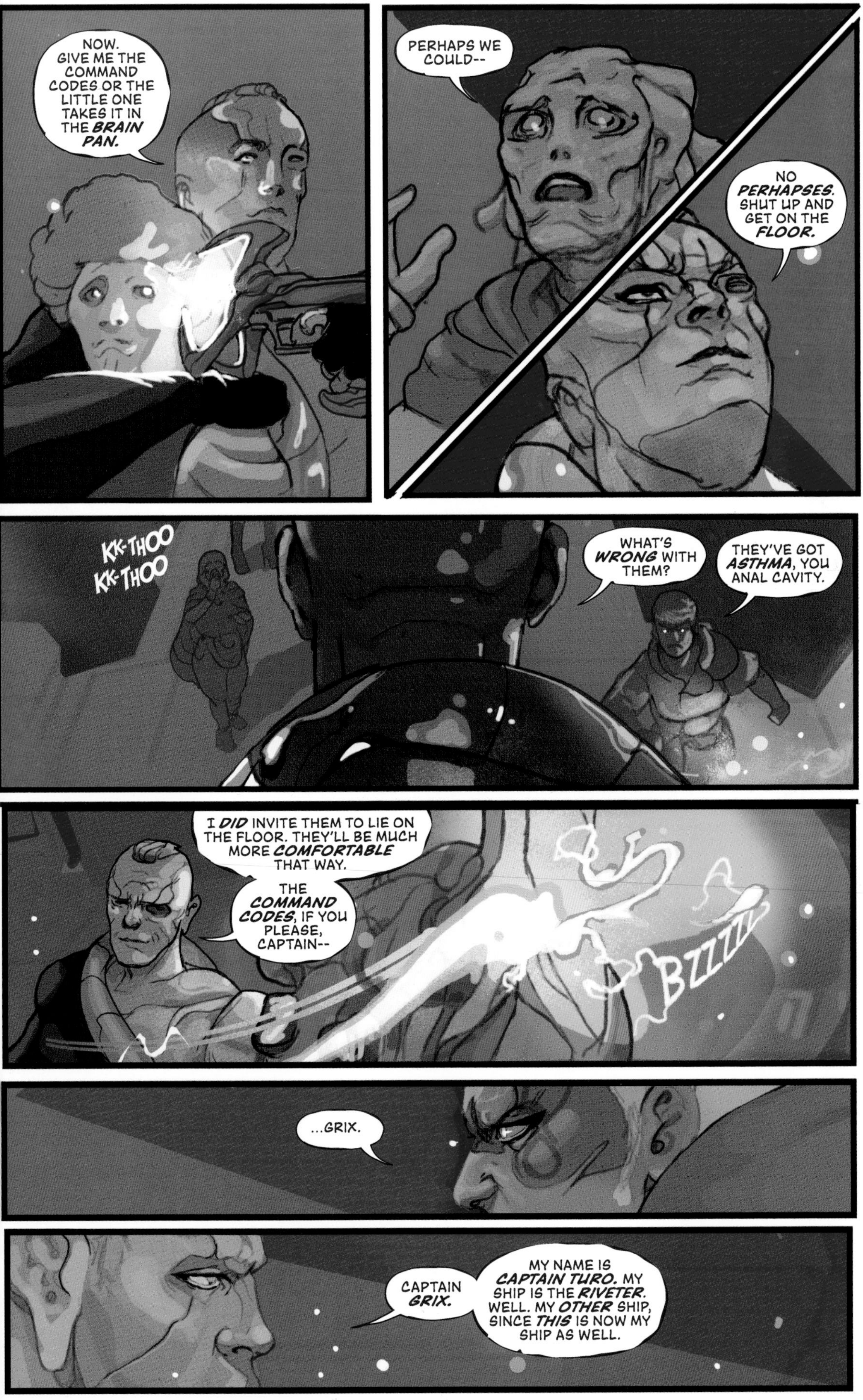
NOW. GIVE ME THE COMMAND CODES OR THE LITTLE ONE TAKES IT IN THE BRAIN PAN.
PERHAPS WE COULD--
NO PERHAPSES. SHUT UP AND GET ON THE FLOOR.
KK-THOO KK-THOO
WHAT'S WRONG WITH THEM?
THEY'VE GOT ASTHMA, YOU ANAL CAVITY.
I DID INVITE THEM TO LIE ON THE FLOOR. THEY'LL BE MUCH MORE COMFORTABLE THAT WAY.
THE COMMAND CODES, IF YOU PLEASE, CAPTAIN--
BZZZZ
...GRIX.
CAPTAIN GRIX.
MY NAME IS CAPTAIN TURO. MY SHIP IS THE RIVETER. WELL. MY OTHER SHIP, SINCE THIS IS NOW MY SHIP AS WELL.

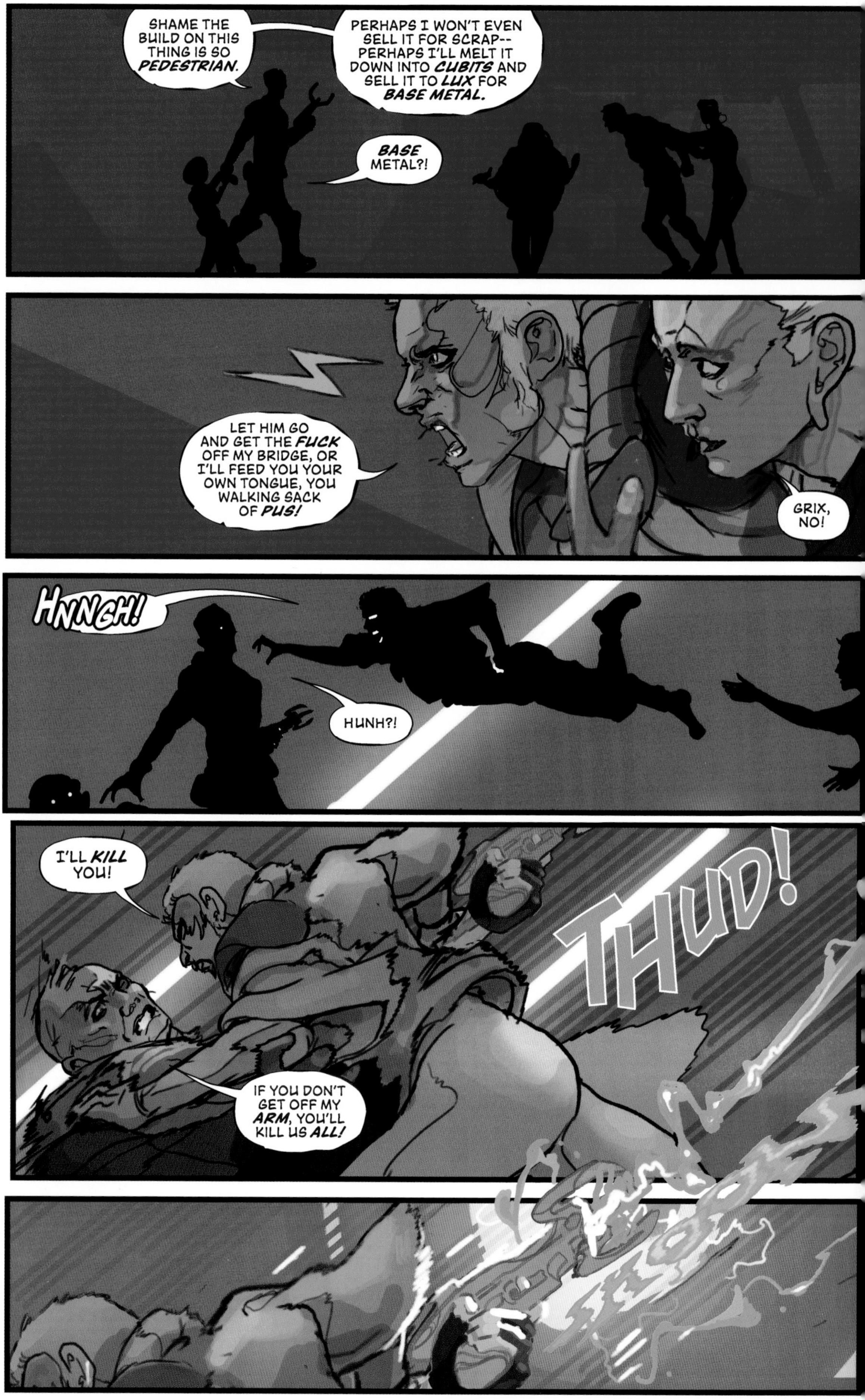
SHAME THE BUILD ON THIS THING IS SO *PEDESTRIAN.*
PERHAPS I WON'T EVEN SELL IT FOR SCRAP-- PERHAPS I'LL MELT IT DOWN INTO *CUBITS* AND SELL IT TO *LUX* FOR *BASE METAL.*
BASE METAL?!
LET HIM GO AND GET THE *FUCK* OFF MY BRIDGE, OR I'LL FEED YOU YOUR OWN TONGUE, YOU WALKING SACK OF *PUS!*
GRIX, NO!
HNNGH!
HUNH?!
I'LL *KILL* YOU!
THUD!
IF YOU DON'T GET OFF MY *ARM*, YOU'LL KILL US *ALL!*

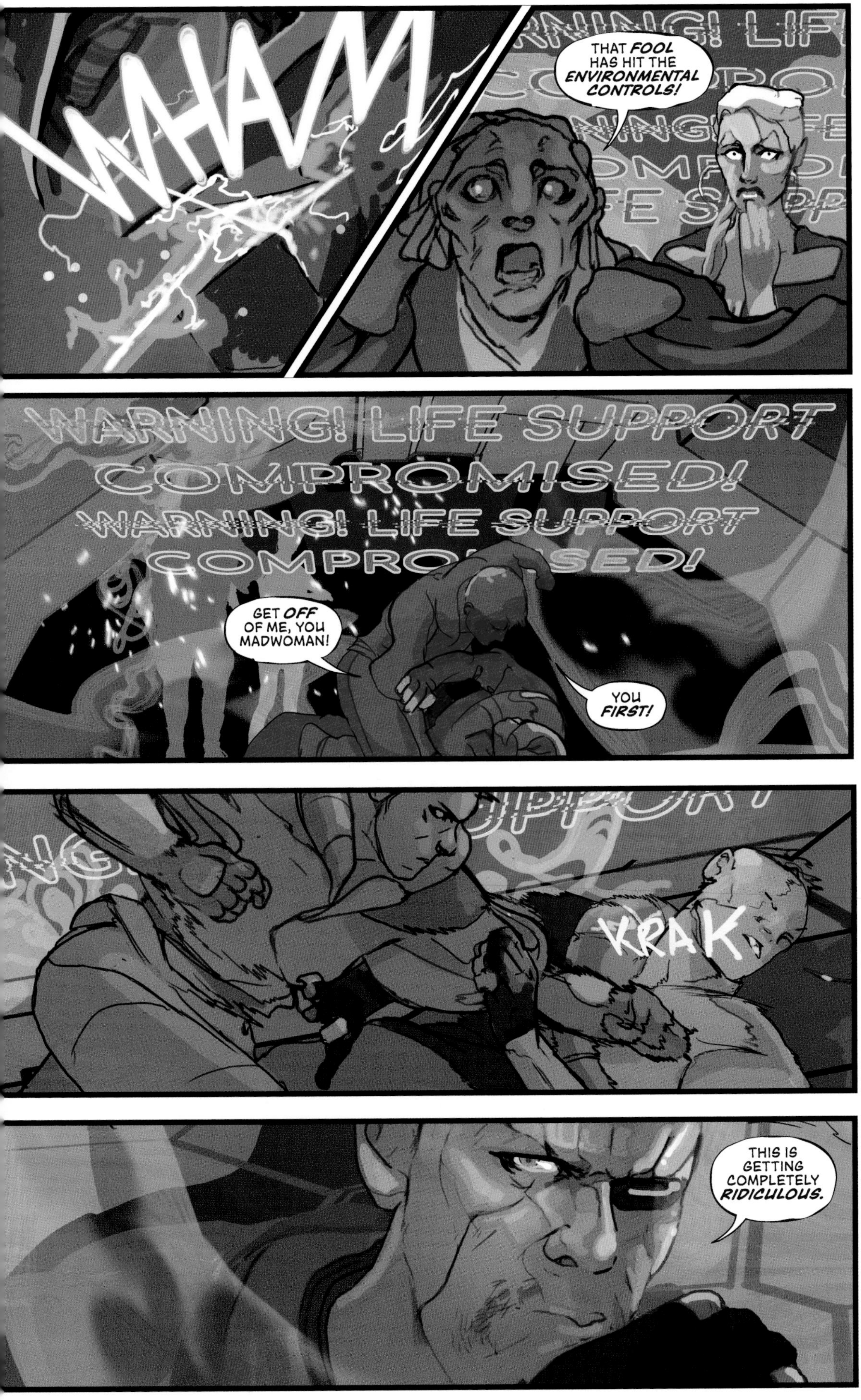
WHAM
THAT FOOL HAS HIT THE ENVIRONMENTAL CONTROLS!
WARNING! LIFE SUPPORT COMPROMISED!
WARNING! LIFE SUPPORT COMPROMISED!
GET OFF OF ME, YOU MADWOMAN!
YOU FIRST!
KRAK
THIS IS GETTING COMPLETELY RIDICULOUS.

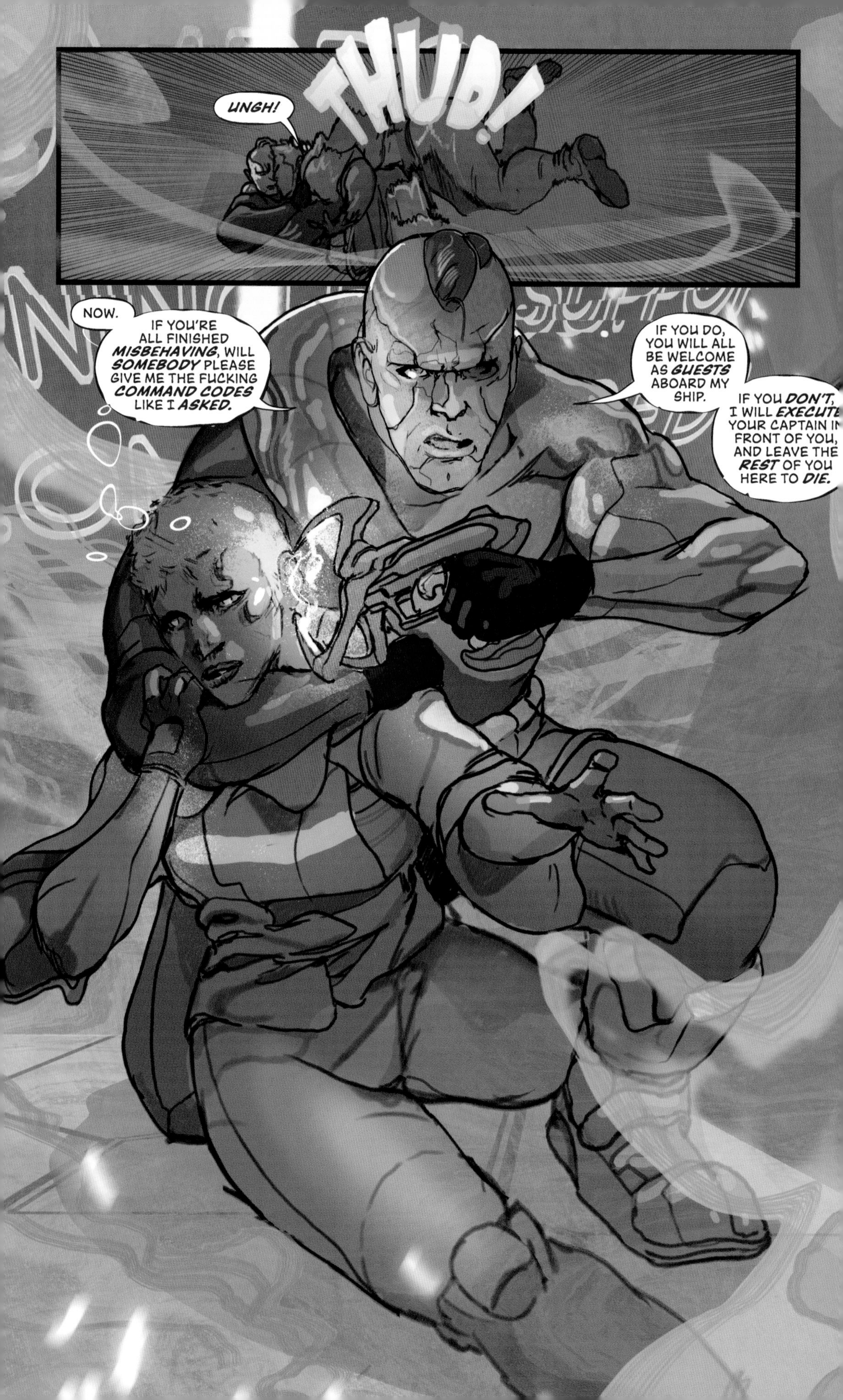

UNGH!
THUD!
NOW.
IF YOU'RE ALL FINISHED MISBEHAVING, WILL SOMEBODY PLEASE GIVE ME THE FUCKING COMMAND CODES LIKE I ASKED.
IF YOU DO, YOU WILL ALL BE WELCOME AS GUESTS ABOARD MY SHIP.
IF YOU DON'T, I WILL EXECUTE YOUR CAPTAIN IN FRONT OF YOU, AND LEAVE THE REST OF YOU HERE TO DIE.

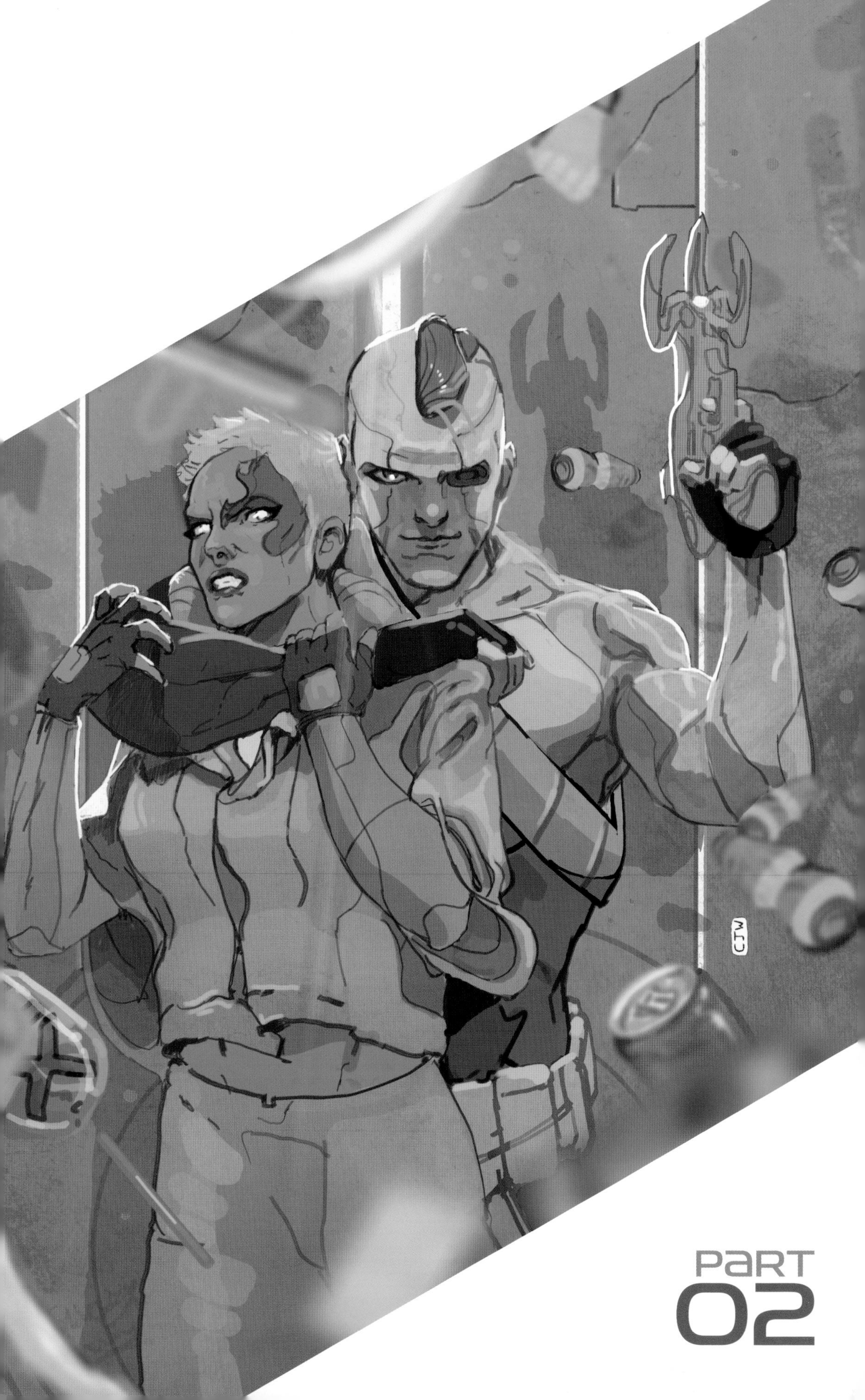

PART 02

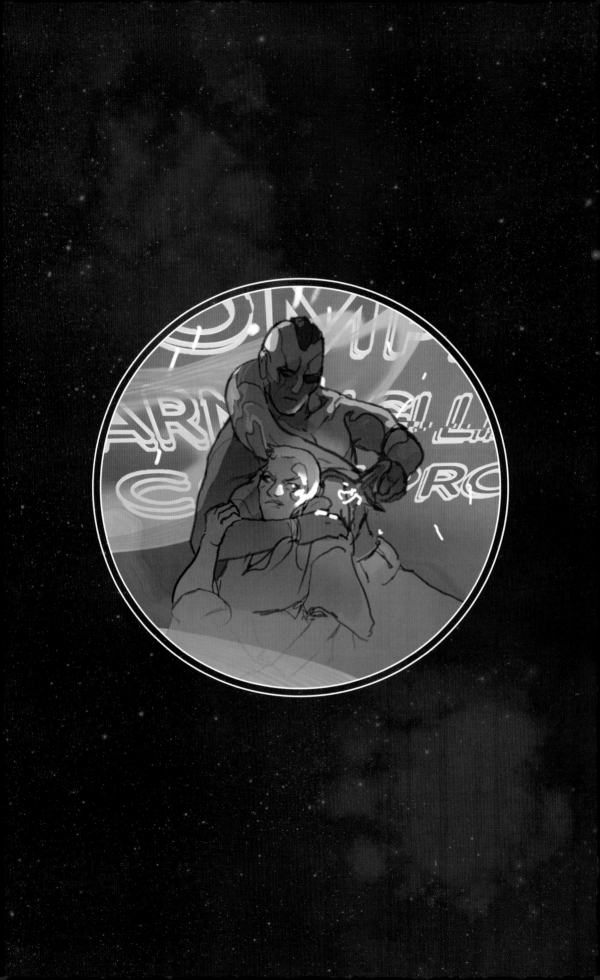

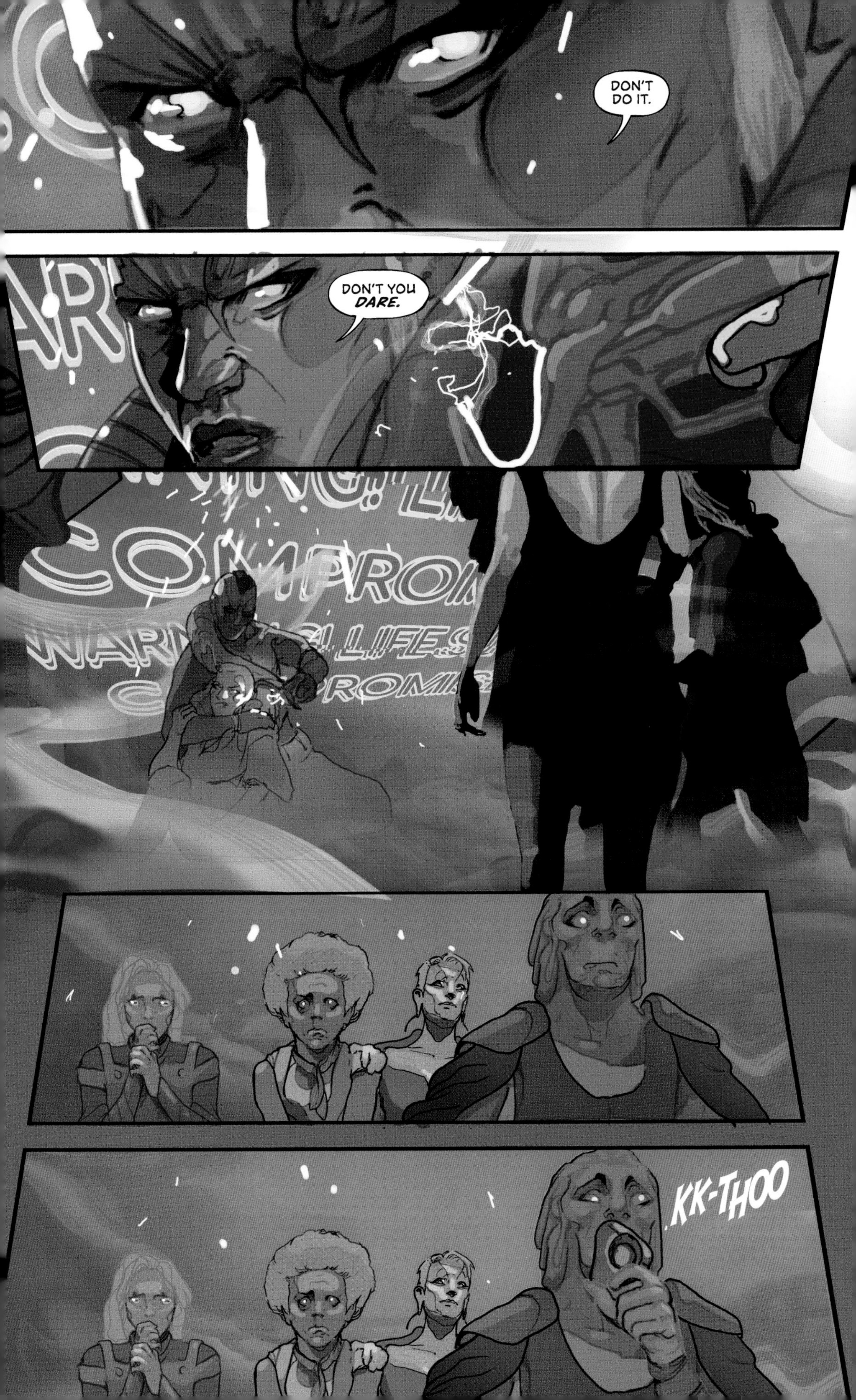
DON'T DO IT.
DON'T YOU *DARE.*
KK-THOO

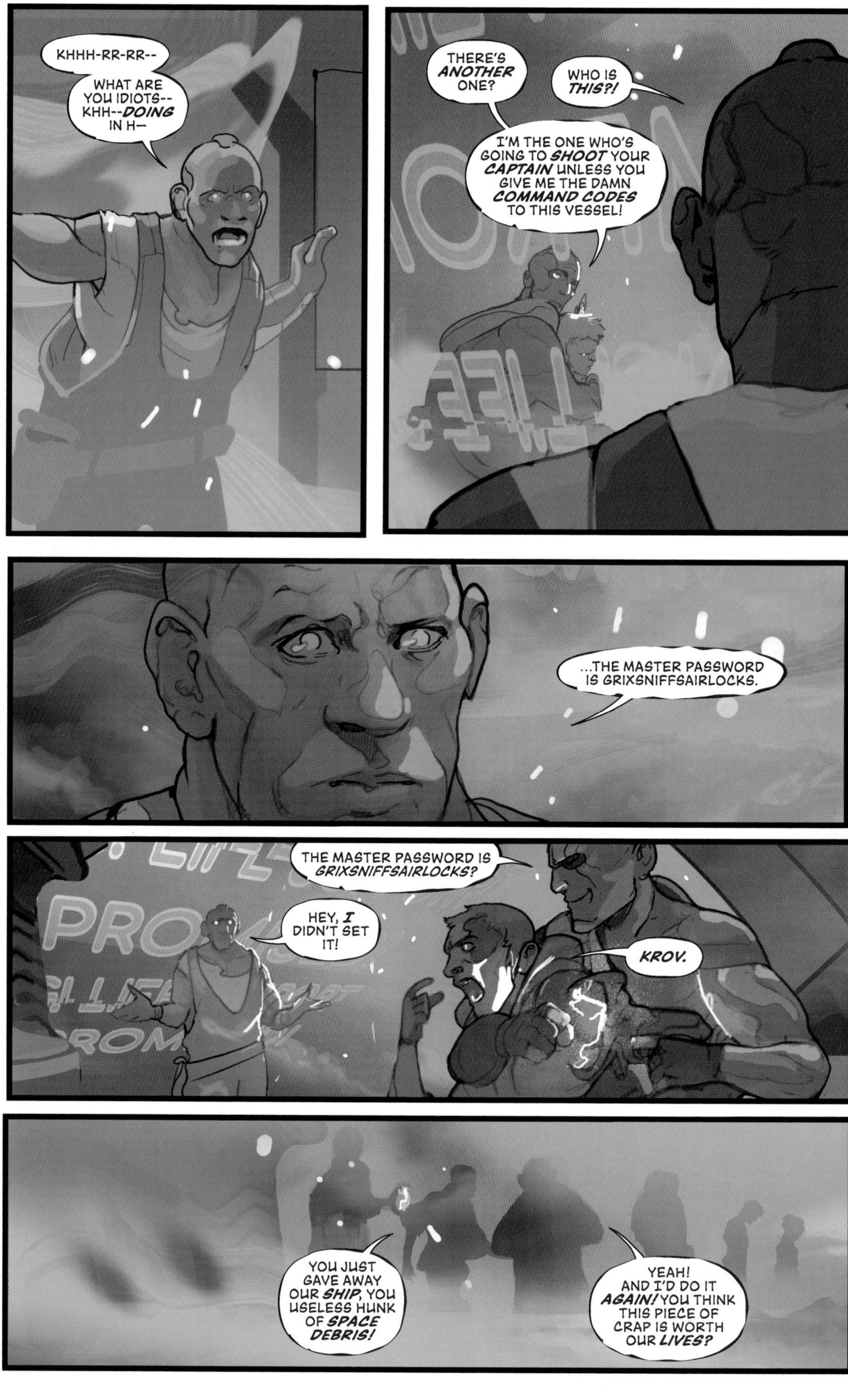
KHHH-RR-RR--
WHAT ARE YOU IDIOTS-- KHH--DOING IN H—
THERE'S ANOTHER ONE?
WHO IS THIS?!
I'M THE ONE WHO'S GOING TO SHOOT YOUR CAPTAIN UNLESS YOU GIVE ME THE DAMN COMMAND CODES TO THIS VESSEL!
...THE MASTER PASSWORD IS GRIXSNIFFSAIRLOCKS.
THE MASTER PASSWORD IS GRIXSNIFFSAIRLOCKS?
HEY, I DIDN'T SET IT!
KROV.
YOU JUST GAVE AWAY OUR SHIP, YOU USELESS HUNK OF SPACE DEBRIS!
YEAH! AND I'D DO IT AGAIN! YOU THINK THIS PIECE OF CRAP IS WORTH OUR LIVES?

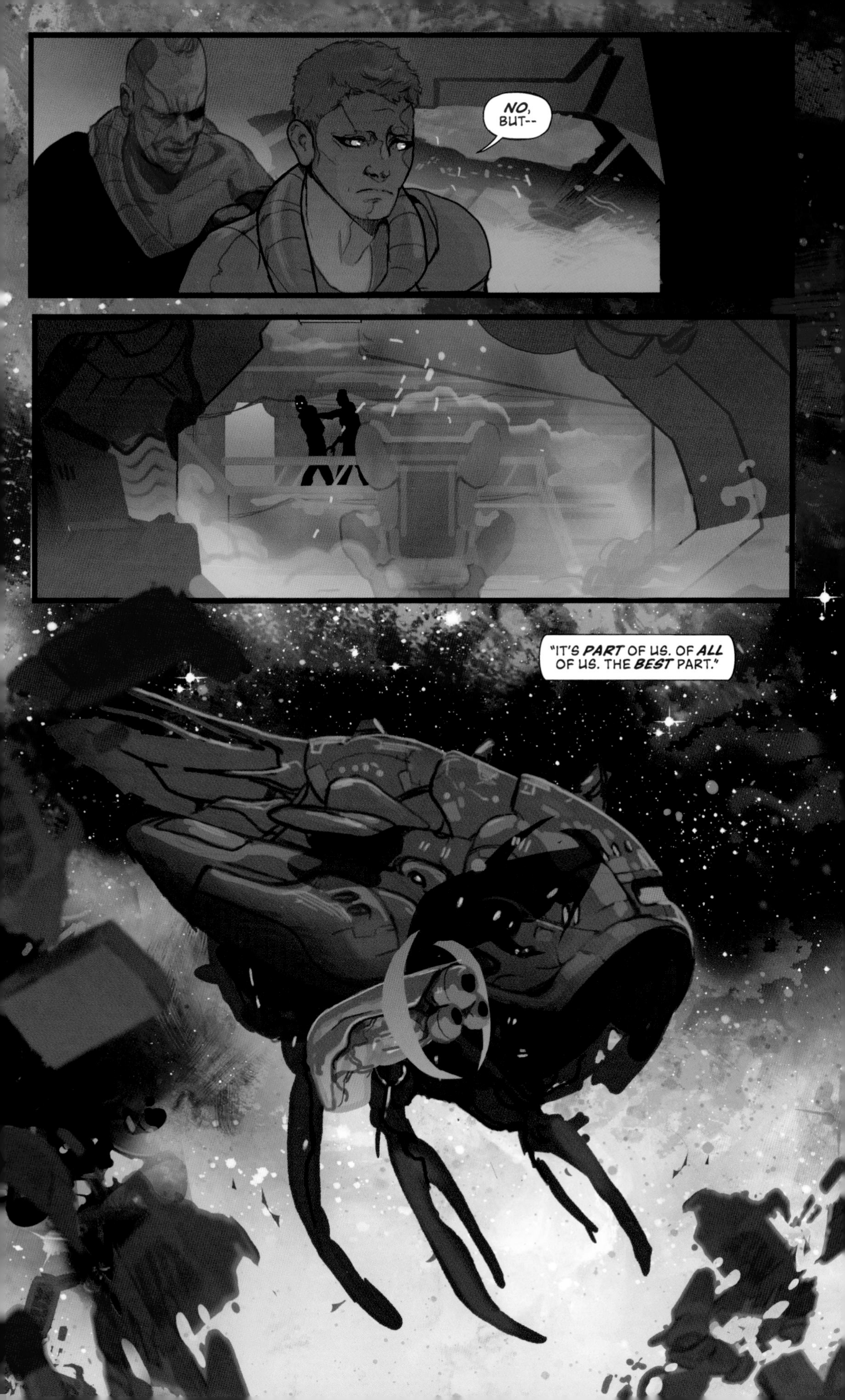
NO, BUT--
"IT'S PART OF US. OF ALL OF US. THE BEST PART."

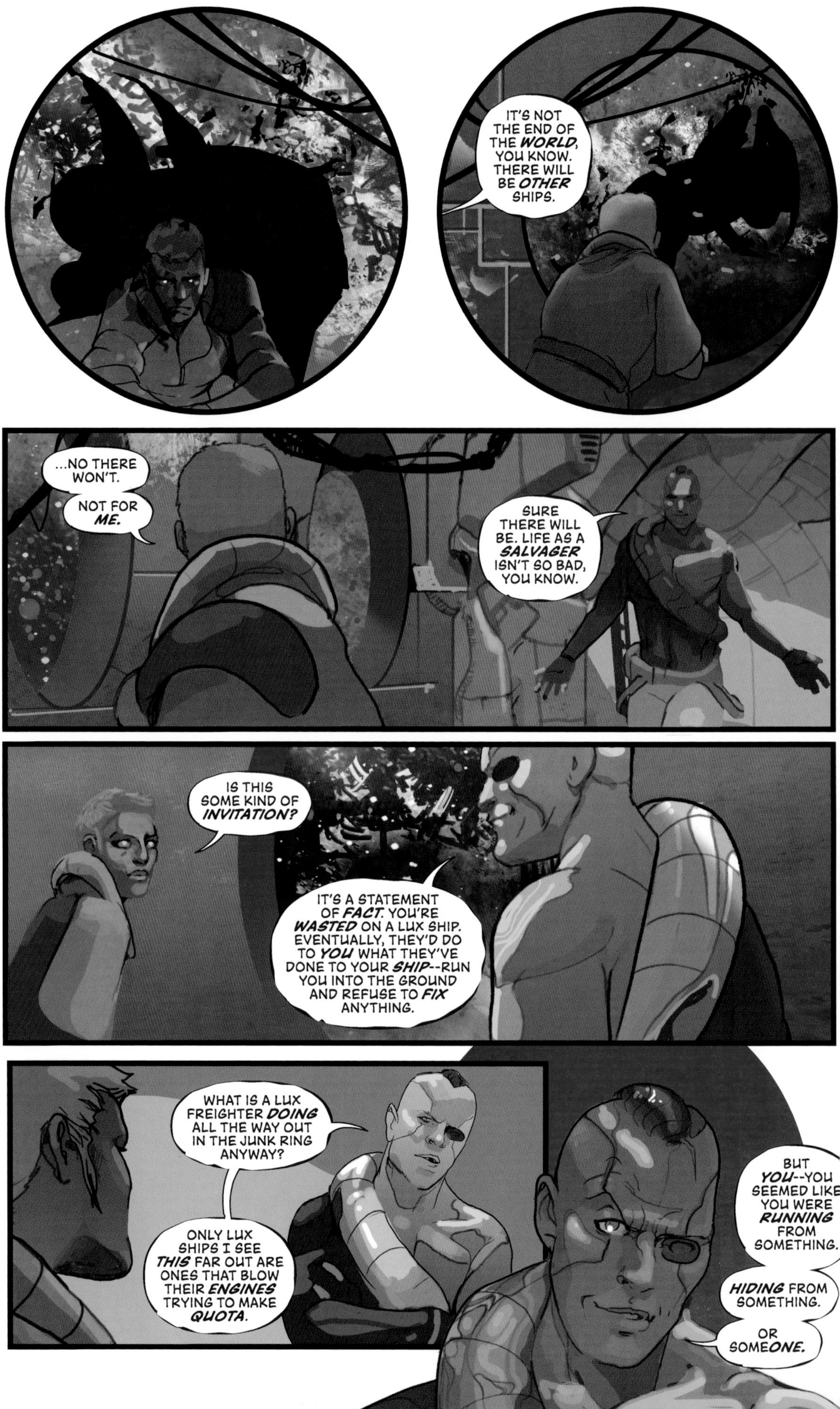
IT'S NOT THE END OF THE WORLD, YOU KNOW. THERE WILL BE OTHER SHIPS.
...NO THERE WON'T.
NOT FOR ME.
SURE THERE WILL BE. LIFE AS A SALVAGER ISN'T SO BAD, YOU KNOW.
IS THIS SOME KIND OF INVITATION?
IT'S A STATEMENT OF FACT. YOU'RE WASTED ON A LUX SHIP. EVENTUALLY, THEY'D DO TO YOU WHAT THEY'VE DONE TO YOUR SHIP--RUN YOU INTO THE GROUND AND REFUSE TO FIX ANYTHING.
WHAT IS A LUX FREIGHTER DOING ALL THE WAY OUT IN THE JUNK RING ANYWAY?
ONLY LUX SHIPS I SEE THIS FAR OUT ARE ONES THAT BLOW THEIR ENGINES TRYING TO MAKE QUOTA.
BUT YOU--YOU SEEMED LIKE YOU WERE RUNNING FROM SOMETHING.
HIDING FROM SOMETHING.
OR SOMEONE.

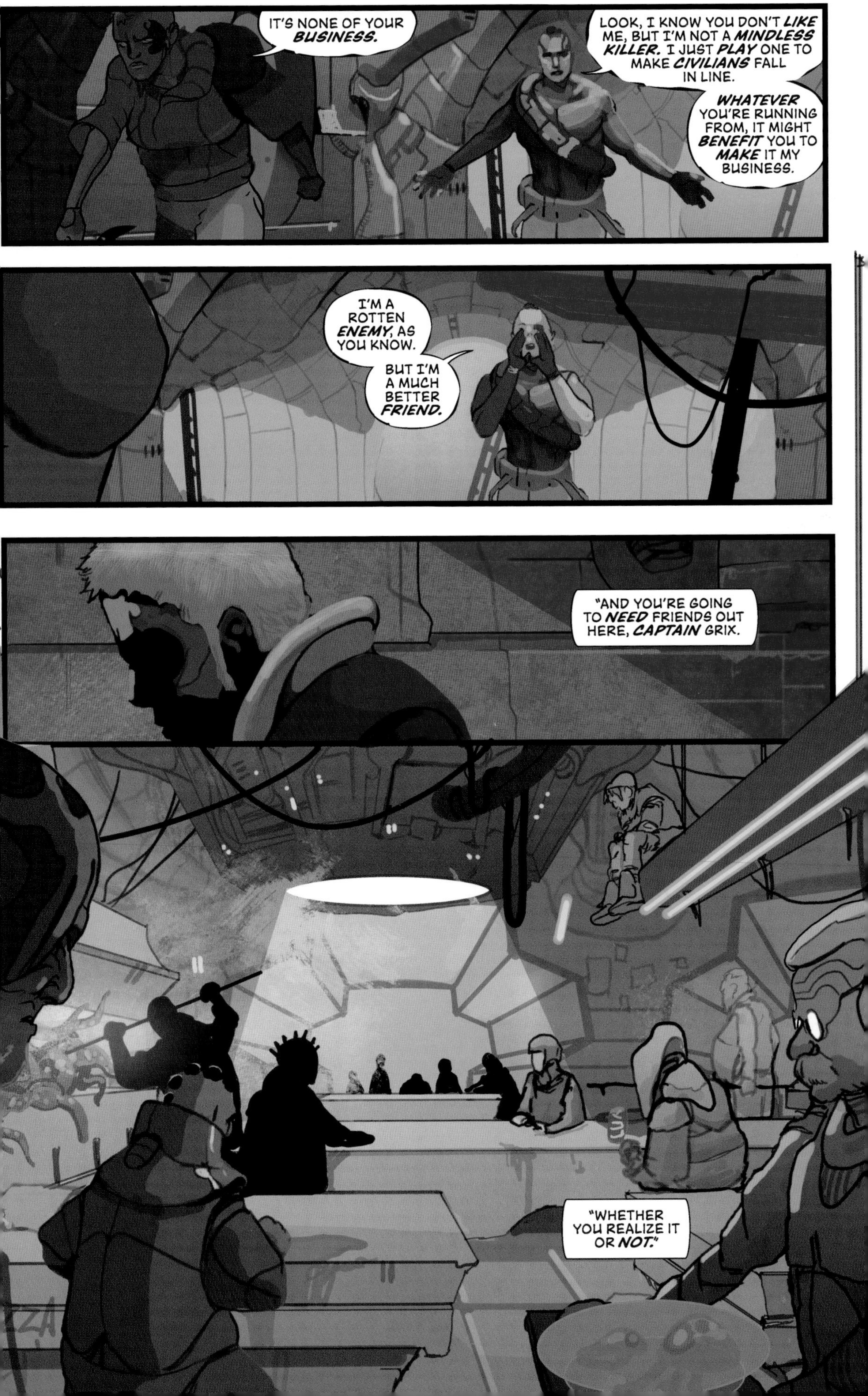
IT'S NONE OF YOUR BUSINESS.
LOOK, I KNOW YOU DON'T LIKE ME, BUT I'M NOT A MINDLESS KILLER. I JUST PLAY ONE TO MAKE CIVILIANS FALL IN LINE.
WHATEVER YOU'RE RUNNING FROM, IT MIGHT BENEFIT YOU TO MAKE IT MY BUSINESS.
I'M A ROTTEN ENEMY, AS YOU KNOW.
BUT I'M A MUCH BETTER FRIEND.
"AND YOU'RE GOING TO NEED FRIENDS OUT HERE, CAPTAIN GRIX.
"WHETHER YOU REALIZE IT OR NOT."

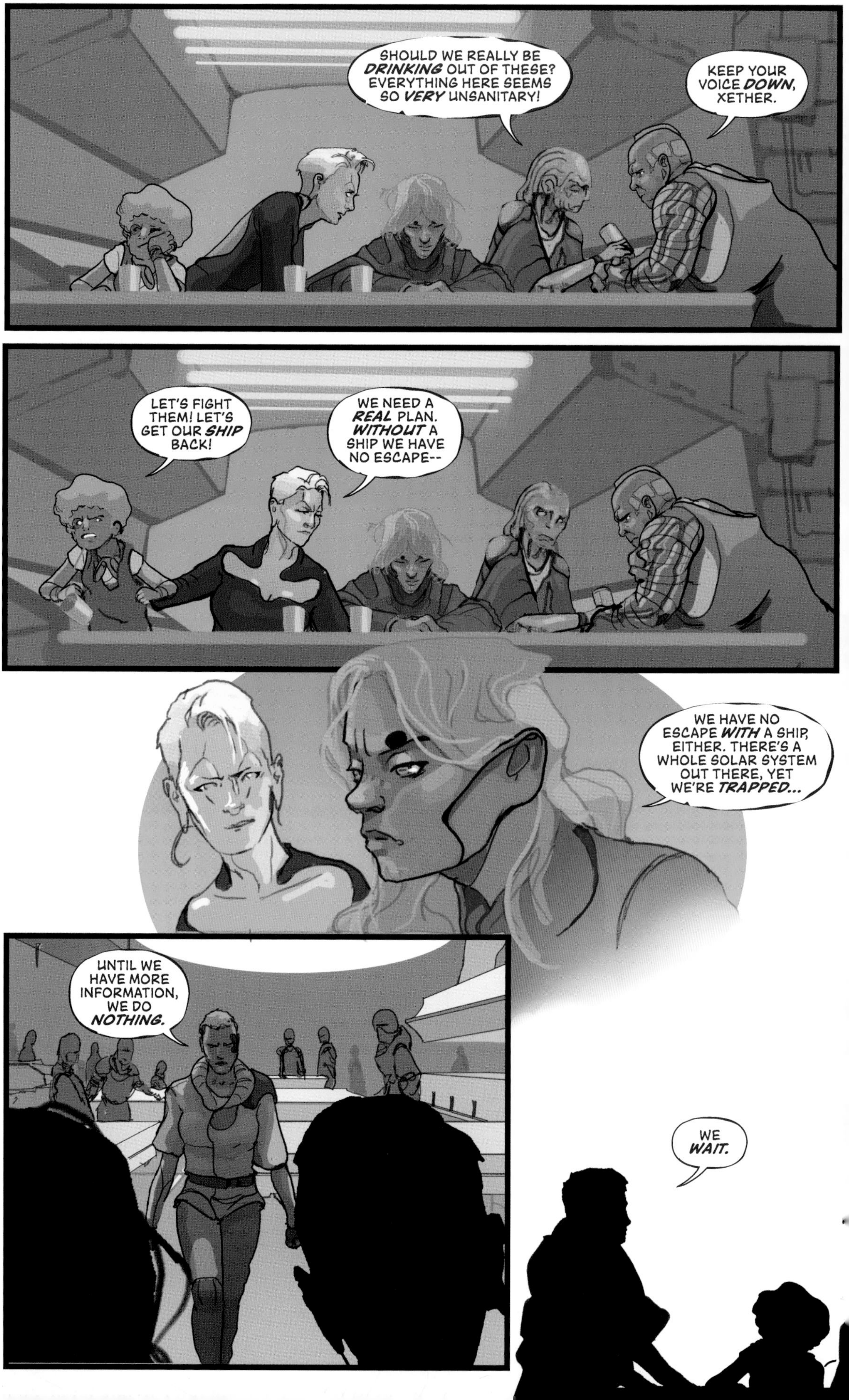
SHOULD WE REALLY BE DRINKING OUT OF THESE? EVERYTHING HERE SEEMS SO VERY UNSANITARY!
KEEP YOUR VOICE DOWN, XETHER.
LET'S FIGHT THEM! LET'S GET OUR SHIP BACK!
WE NEED A REAL PLAN. WITHOUT A SHIP WE HAVE NO ESCAPE--
WE HAVE NO ESCAPE WITH A SHIP, EITHER. THERE'S A WHOLE SOLAR SYSTEM OUT THERE, YET WE'RE TRAPPED...
UNTIL WE HAVE MORE INFORMATION, WE DO NOTHING.
WE WAIT.

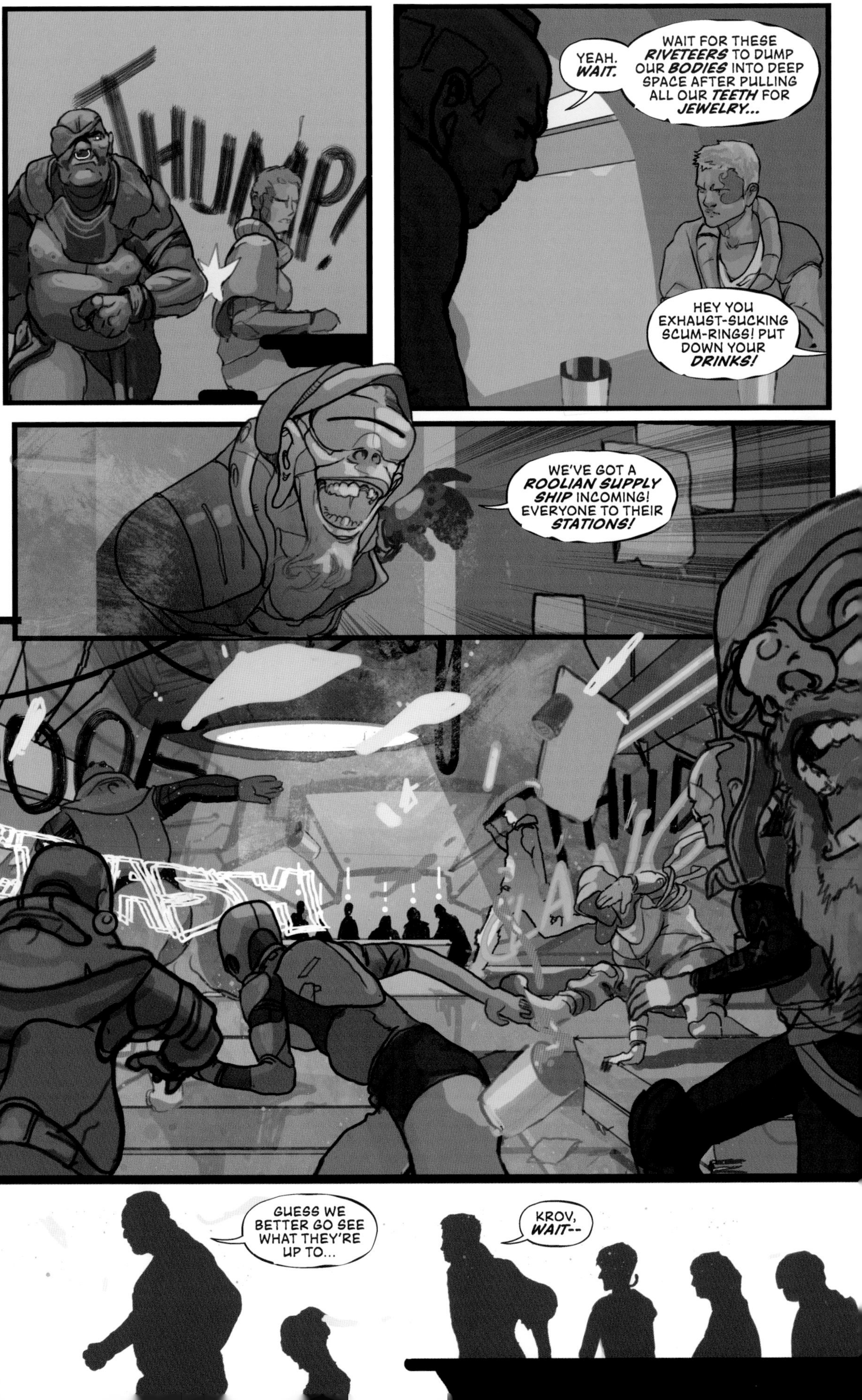
THUMP!
YEAH. WAIT.
WAIT FOR THESE RIVETEERS TO DUMP OUR BODIES INTO DEEP SPACE AFTER PULLING ALL OUR TEETH FOR JEWELRY...
HEY YOU EXHAUST-SUCKING SCUM-RINGS! PUT DOWN YOUR DRINKS!
WE'VE GOT A ROOLIAN SUPPLY SHIP INCOMING! EVERYONE TO THEIR STATIONS!
GUESS WE BETTER GO SEE WHAT THEY'RE UP TO...
KROV, WAIT--

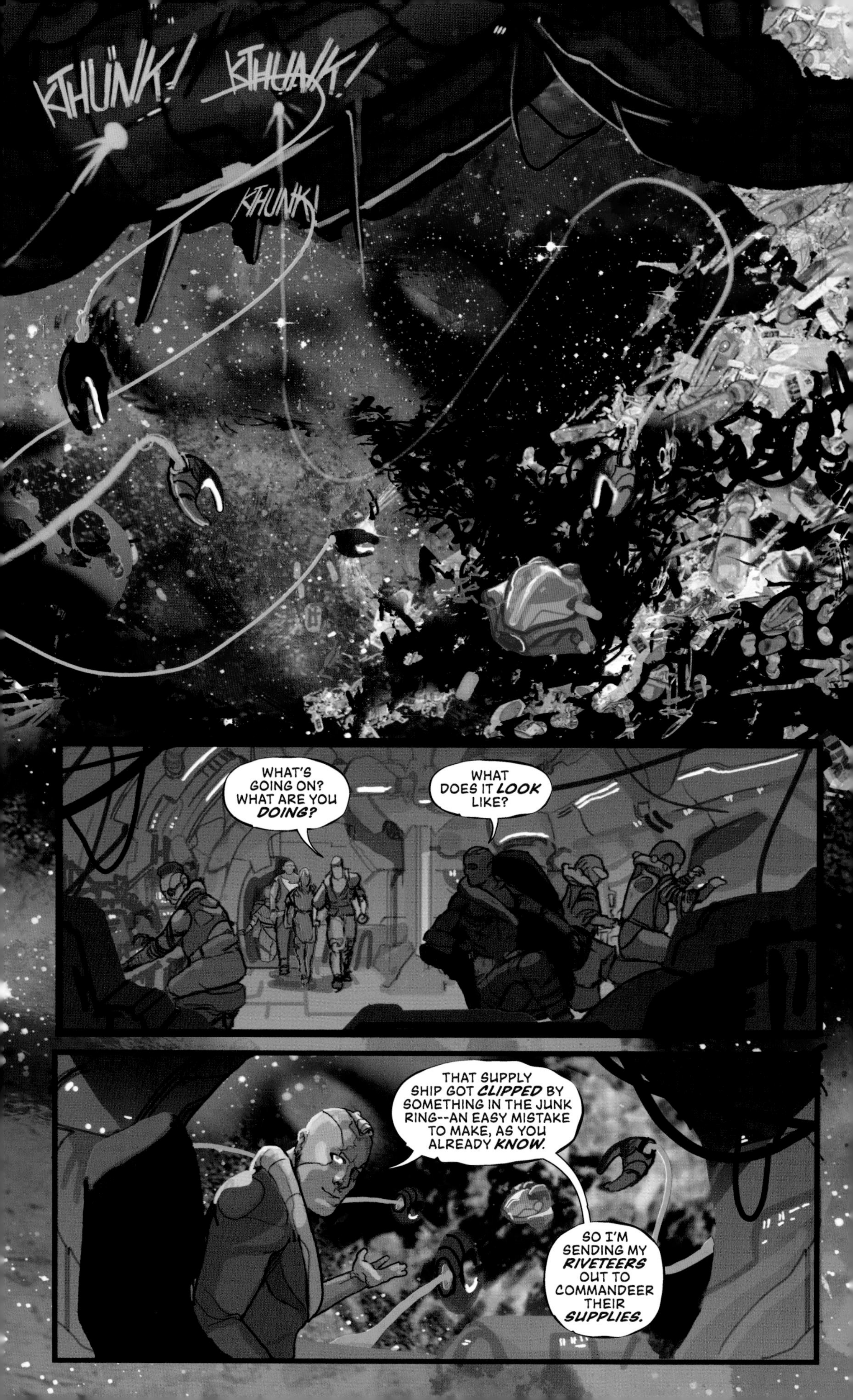
KTHUNK! KTHUNK!
KTHUNK!
WHAT'S GOING ON? WHAT ARE YOU *DOING?*
WHAT DOES IT *LOOK* LIKE?
THAT SUPPLY SHIP GOT *CLIPPED* BY SOMETHING IN THE JUNK RING--AN EASY MISTAKE TO MAKE, AS YOU ALREADY *KNOW*.
SO I'M SENDING MY *RIVETEERS* OUT TO COMMANDEER THEIR *SUPPLIES*.

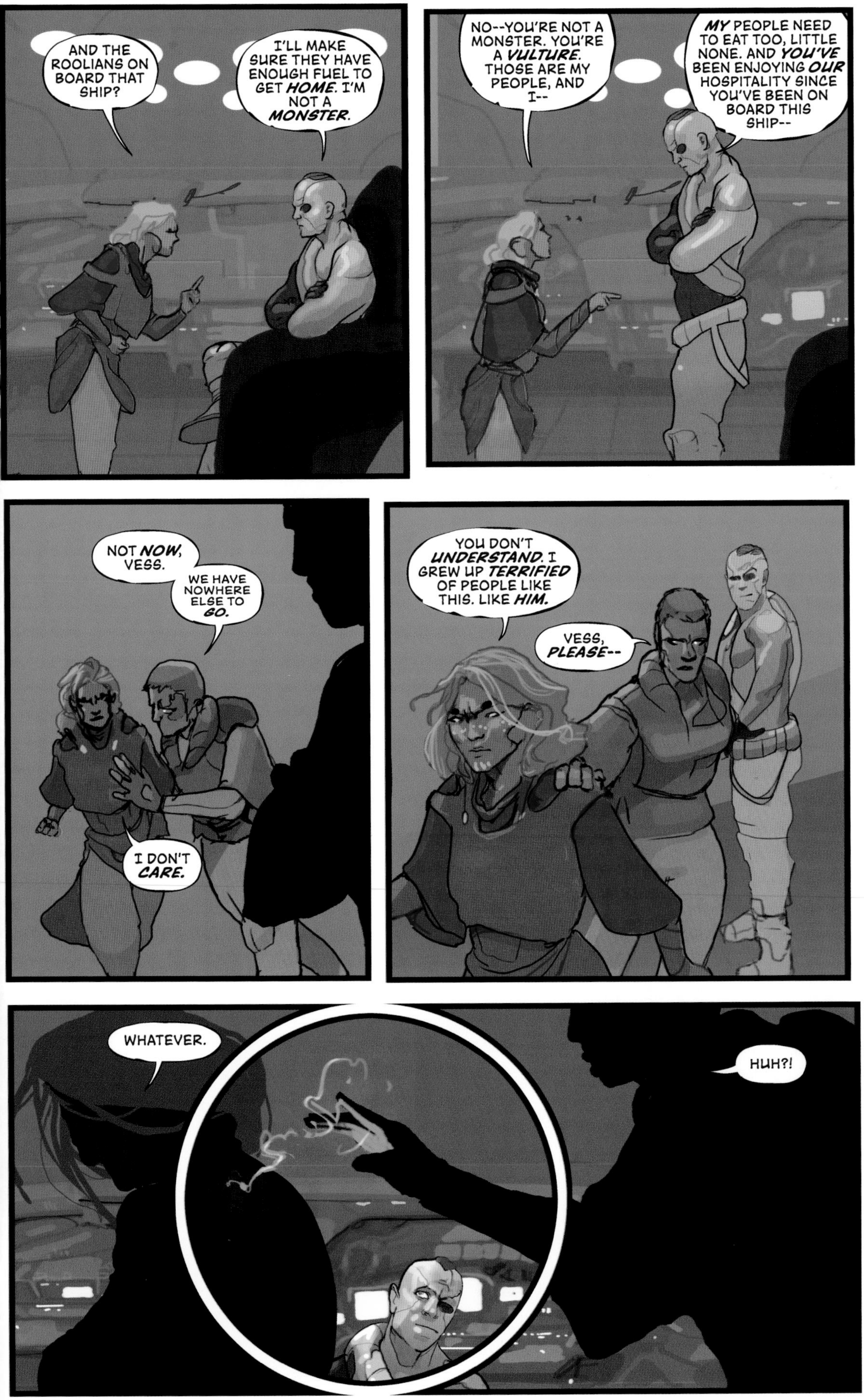
AND THE ROOLIANS ON BOARD THAT SHIP?
I'LL MAKE SURE THEY HAVE ENOUGH FUEL TO GET HOME. I'M NOT A MONSTER.
NO--YOU'RE NOT A MONSTER. YOU'RE A VULTURE. THOSE ARE MY PEOPLE, AND I--
MY PEOPLE NEED TO EAT TOO, LITTLE NONE. AND YOU'VE BEEN ENJOYING OUR HOSPITALITY SINCE YOU'VE BEEN ON BOARD THIS SHIP--
NOT NOW, VESS.
WE HAVE NOWHERE ELSE TO GO.
I DON'T CARE.
YOU DON'T UNDERSTAND. I GREW UP TERRIFIED OF PEOPLE LIKE THIS. LIKE HIM.
VESS, PLEASE--
WHATEVER.
HUH?!

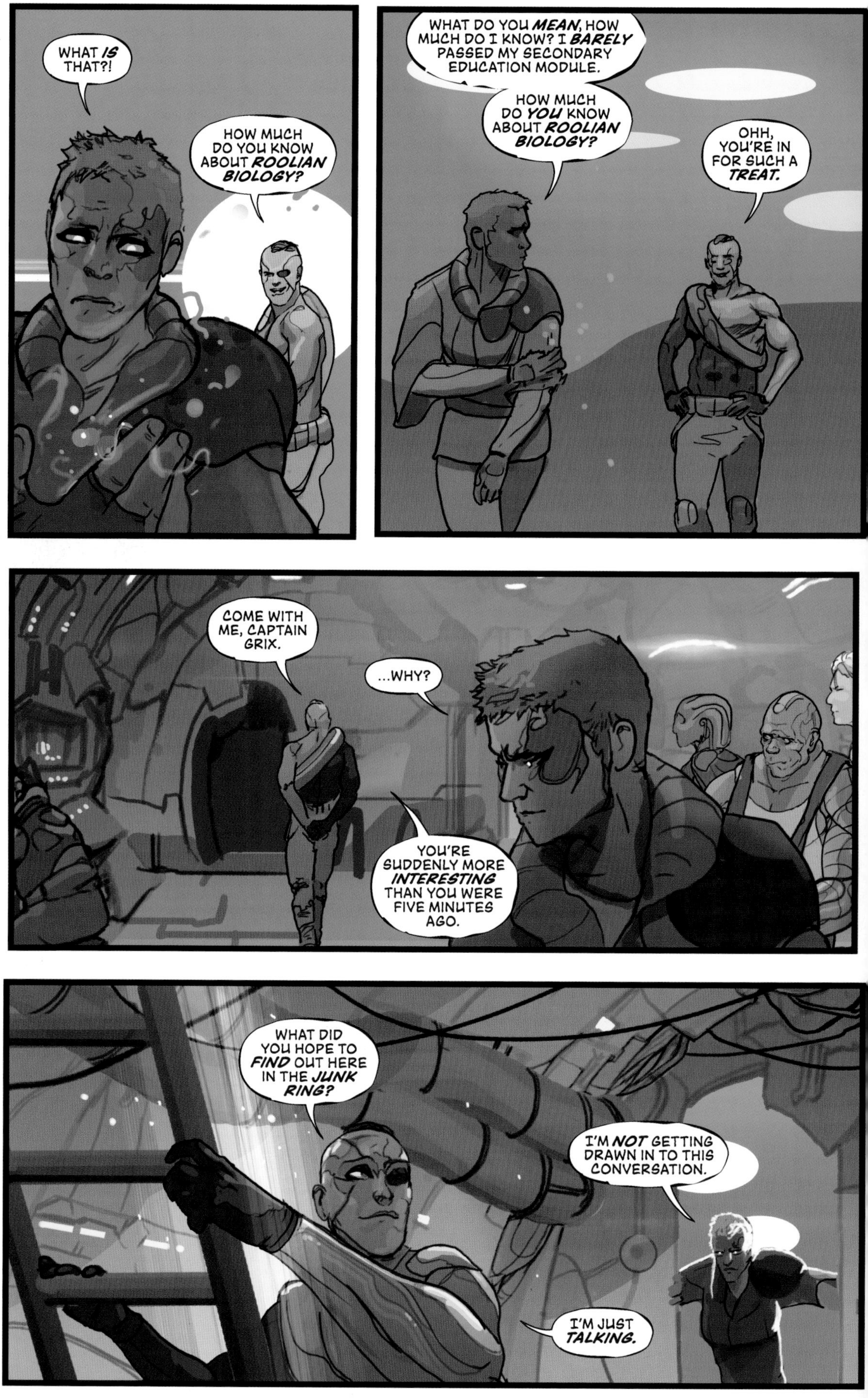
WHAT IS THAT?!
HOW MUCH DO YOU KNOW ABOUT ROOLIAN BIOLOGY?
WHAT DO YOU MEAN, HOW MUCH DO I KNOW? I BARELY PASSED MY SECONDARY EDUCATION MODULE.
HOW MUCH DO YOU KNOW ABOUT ROOLIAN BIOLOGY?
OHH, YOU'RE IN FOR SUCH A TREAT.
COME WITH ME, CAPTAIN GRIX.
...WHY?
YOU'RE SUDDENLY MORE INTERESTING THAN YOU WERE FIVE MINUTES AGO.
WHAT DID YOU HOPE TO FIND OUT HERE IN THE JUNK RING?
I'M NOT GETTING DRAWN IN TO THIS CONVERSATION.
I'M JUST TALKING.

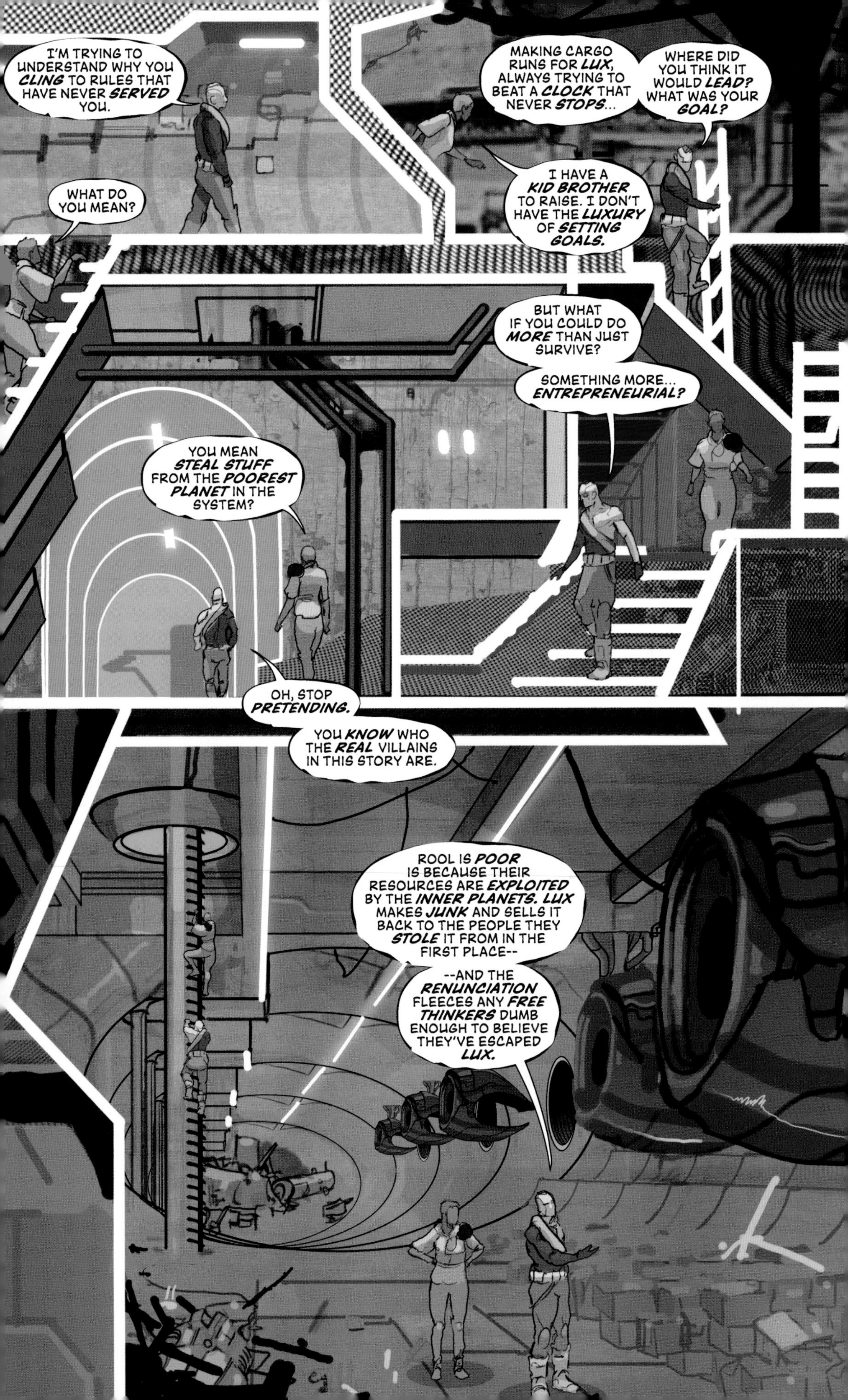
I'M TRYING TO UNDERSTAND WHY YOU CLING TO RULES THAT HAVE NEVER SERVED YOU.
WHAT DO YOU MEAN?
MAKING CARGO RUNS FOR LUX, ALWAYS TRYING TO BEAT A CLOCK THAT NEVER STOPS...
WHERE DID YOU THINK IT WOULD LEAD? WHAT WAS YOUR GOAL?
I HAVE A KID BROTHER TO RAISE. I DON'T HAVE THE LUXURY OF SETTING GOALS.
BUT WHAT IF YOU COULD DO MORE THAN JUST SURVIVE?
SOMETHING MORE... ENTREPRENEURIAL?
YOU MEAN STEAL STUFF FROM THE POOREST PLANET IN THE SYSTEM?
OH, STOP PRETENDING.
YOU KNOW WHO THE REAL VILLAINS IN THIS STORY ARE.
ROOL IS POOR IS BECAUSE THEIR RESOURCES ARE EXPLOITED BY THE INNER PLANETS. LUX MAKES JUNK AND SELLS IT BACK TO THE PEOPLE THEY STOLE IT FROM IN THE FIRST PLACE--
--AND THE RENUNCIATION FLEECES ANY FREE THINKERS DUMB ENOUGH TO BELIEVE THEY'VE ESCAPED LUX.

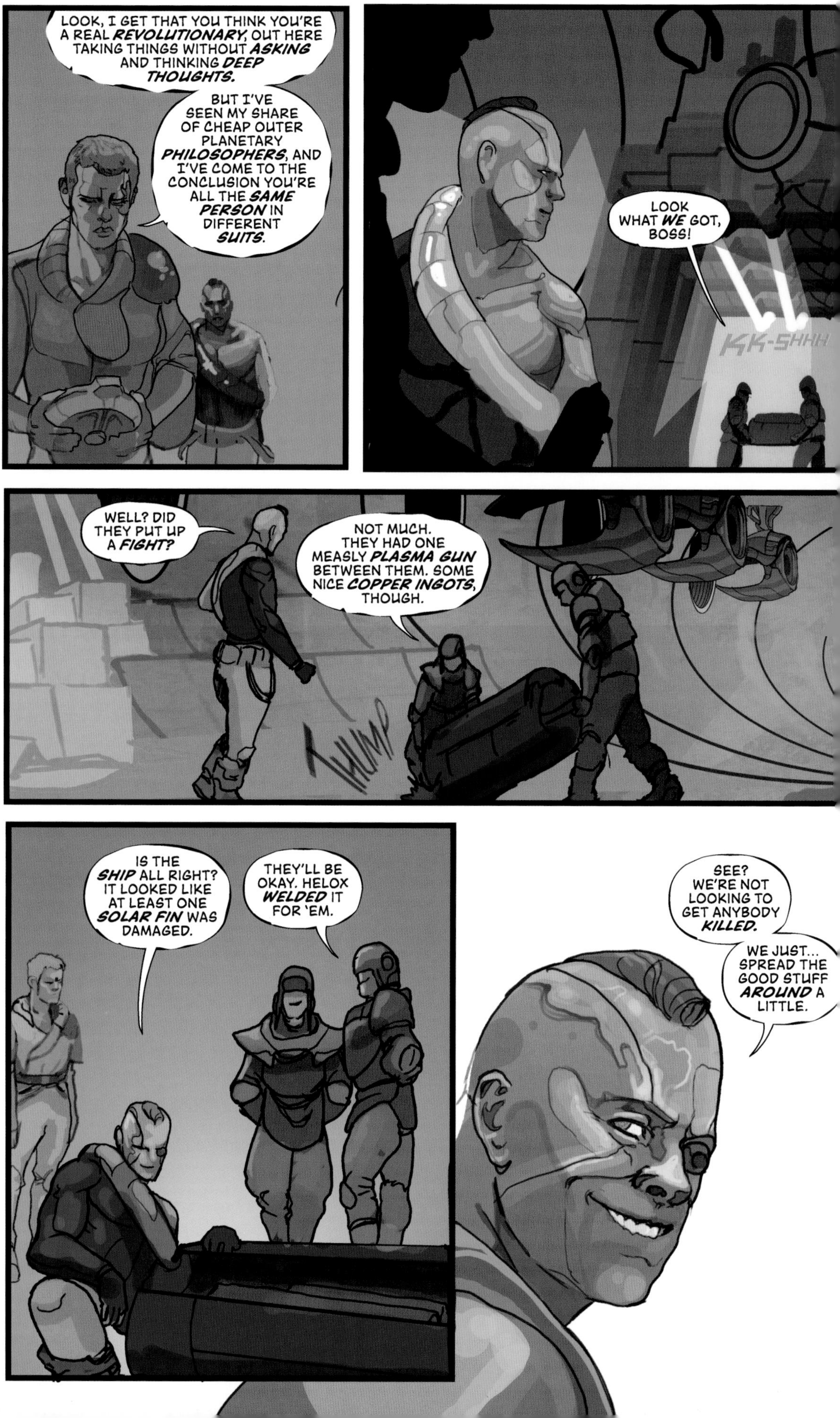

LOOK, I GET THAT YOU THINK YOU'RE A REAL REVOLUTIONARY, OUT HERE TAKING THINGS WITHOUT ASKING AND THINKING DEEP THOUGHTS.
BUT I'VE SEEN MY SHARE OF CHEAP OUTER PLANETARY PHILOSOPHERS, AND I'VE COME TO THE CONCLUSION YOU'RE ALL THE SAME PERSON IN DIFFERENT SUITS.
LOOK WHAT WE GOT, BOSS!
KK-SHHH
WELL? DID THEY PUT UP A FIGHT?
NOT MUCH. THEY HAD ONE MEASLY PLASMA GUN BETWEEN THEM. SOME NICE COPPER INGOTS, THOUGH.
THUMP
IS THE SHIP ALL RIGHT? IT LOOKED LIKE AT LEAST ONE SOLAR FIN WAS DAMAGED.
THEY'LL BE OKAY. HELOX WELDED IT FOR 'EM.
SEE? WE'RE NOT LOOKING TO GET ANYBODY KILLED.
WE JUST... SPREAD THE GOOD STUFF AROUND A LITTLE.

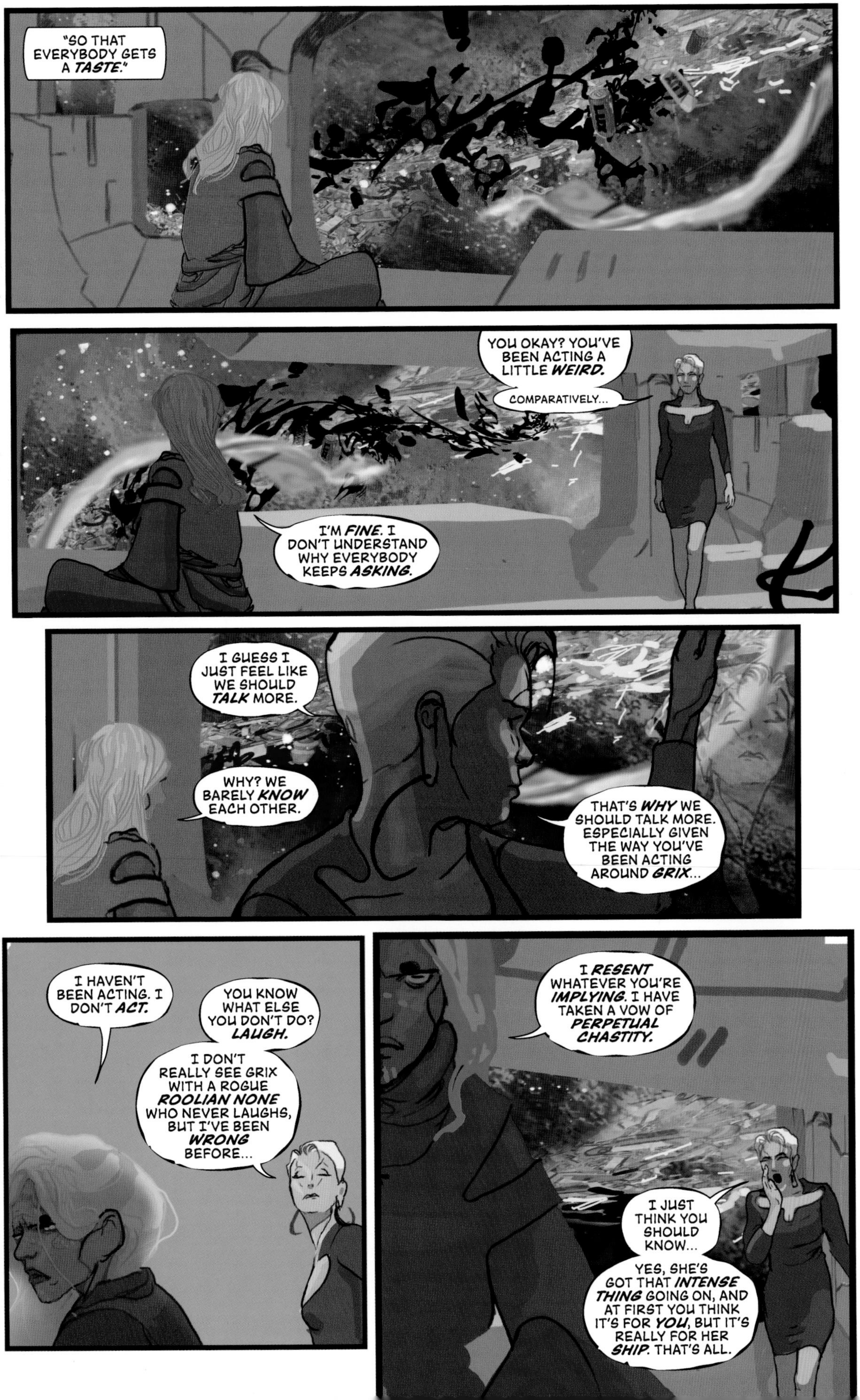
"SO THAT EVERYBODY GETS A *TASTE.*"
YOU OKAY? YOU'VE BEEN ACTING A LITTLE *WEIRD.*
COMPARATIVELY...
I'M *FINE*. I DON'T UNDERSTAND WHY EVERYBODY KEEPS *ASKING.*
I GUESS I JUST FEEL LIKE WE SHOULD *TALK* MORE.
WHY? WE BARELY *KNOW* EACH OTHER.
THAT'S *WHY* WE SHOULD TALK MORE. ESPECIALLY GIVEN THE WAY YOU'VE BEEN ACTING AROUND *GRIX*...
I HAVEN'T BEEN ACTING. I DON'T *ACT.*
YOU KNOW WHAT ELSE YOU DON'T DO? *LAUGH.*
I DON'T REALLY SEE GRIX WITH A ROGUE *ROOLIAN NONE* WHO NEVER LAUGHS, BUT I'VE BEEN *WRONG* BEFORE...
I *RESENT* WHATEVER YOU'RE *IMPLYING*. I HAVE TAKEN A VOW OF *PERPETUAL CHASTITY.*
I JUST THINK YOU SHOULD KNOW...
YES, SHE'S GOT THAT *INTENSE THING* GOING ON, AND AT FIRST *YOU* THINK IT'S FOR *YOU*, BUT IT'S REALLY FOR HER *SHIP*. THAT'S ALL.

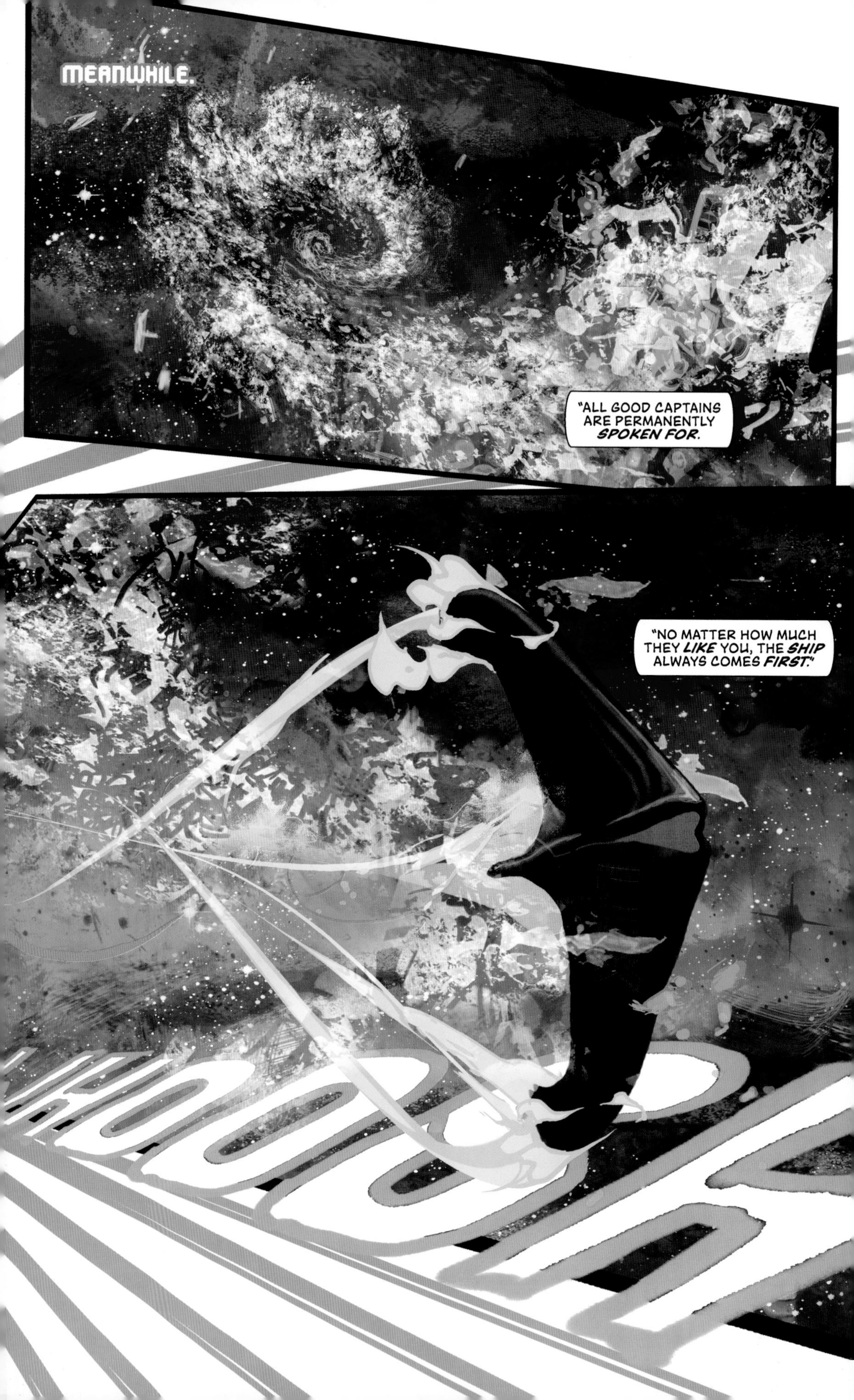
MEANWHILE.
"ALL GOOD CAPTAINS ARE PERMANENTLY SPOKEN FOR.
"NO MATTER HOW MUCH THEY LIKE YOU, THE SHIP ALWAYS COMES FIRST."

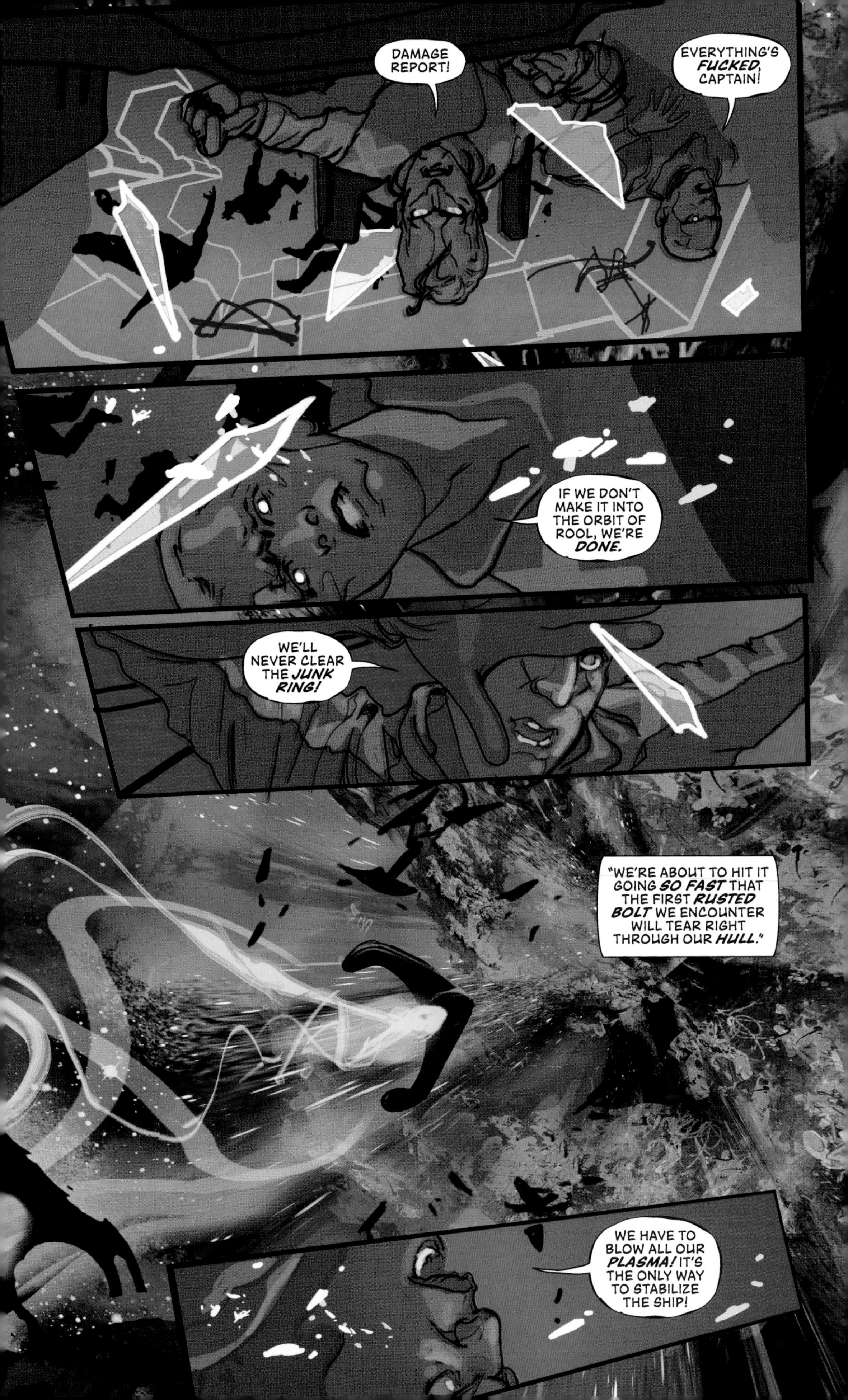

DAMAGE REPORT!
EVERYTHING'S **FUCKED**, CAPTAIN!
IF WE DON'T MAKE IT INTO THE ORBIT OF ROOL, WE'RE **DONE.**
WE'LL NEVER CLEAR THE **JUNK RING!**
"WE'RE ABOUT TO HIT IT GOING **SO FAST** THAT THE FIRST **RUSTED BOLT** WE ENCOUNTER WILL TEAR RIGHT THROUGH OUR **HULL**."
WE HAVE TO BLOW ALL OUR **PLASMA!** IT'S THE ONLY WAY TO STABILIZE THE SHIP!

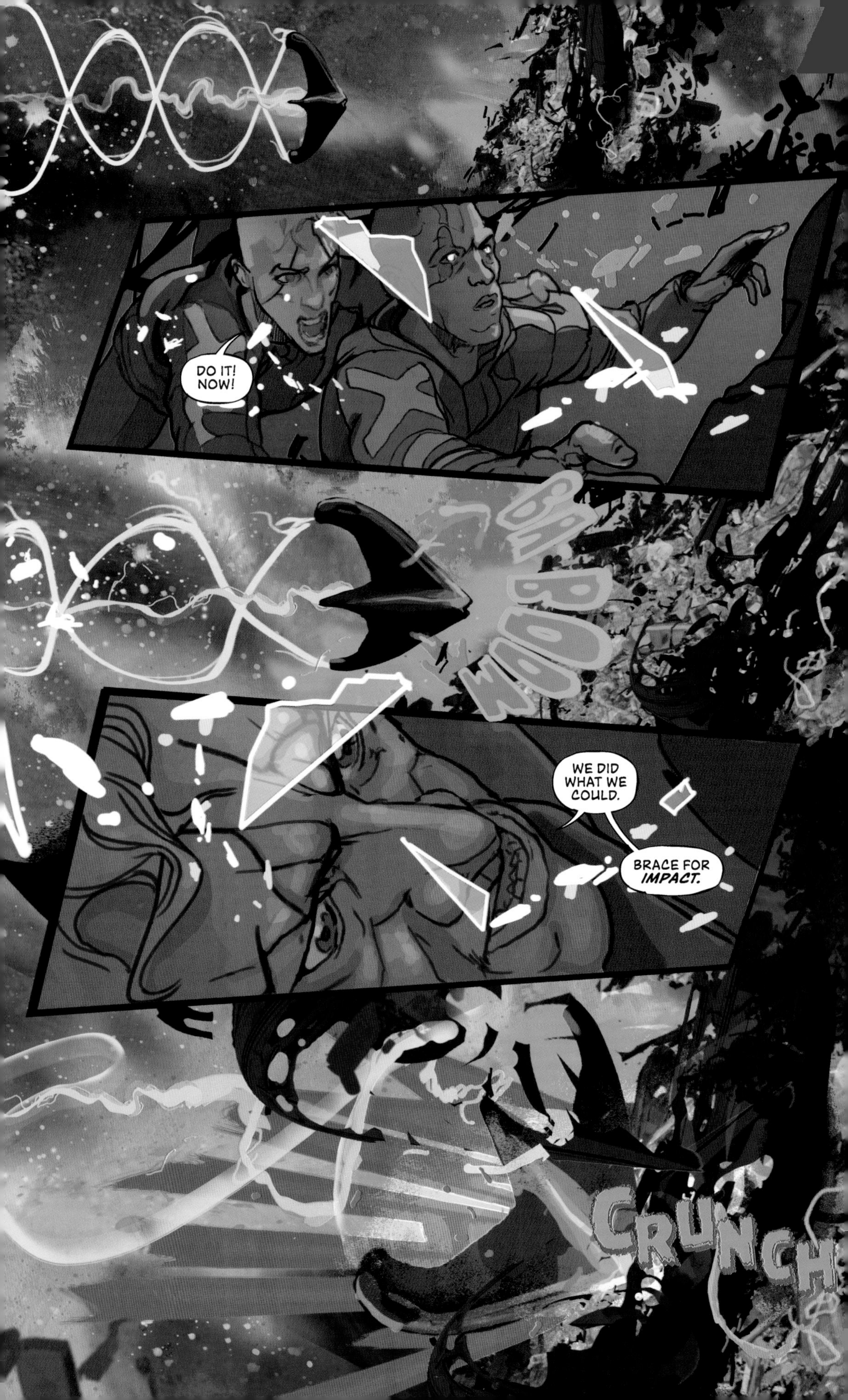
DO IT! NOW!
BOOM
WE DID WHAT WE COULD.
BRACE FOR *IMPACT.*
CRUNCH

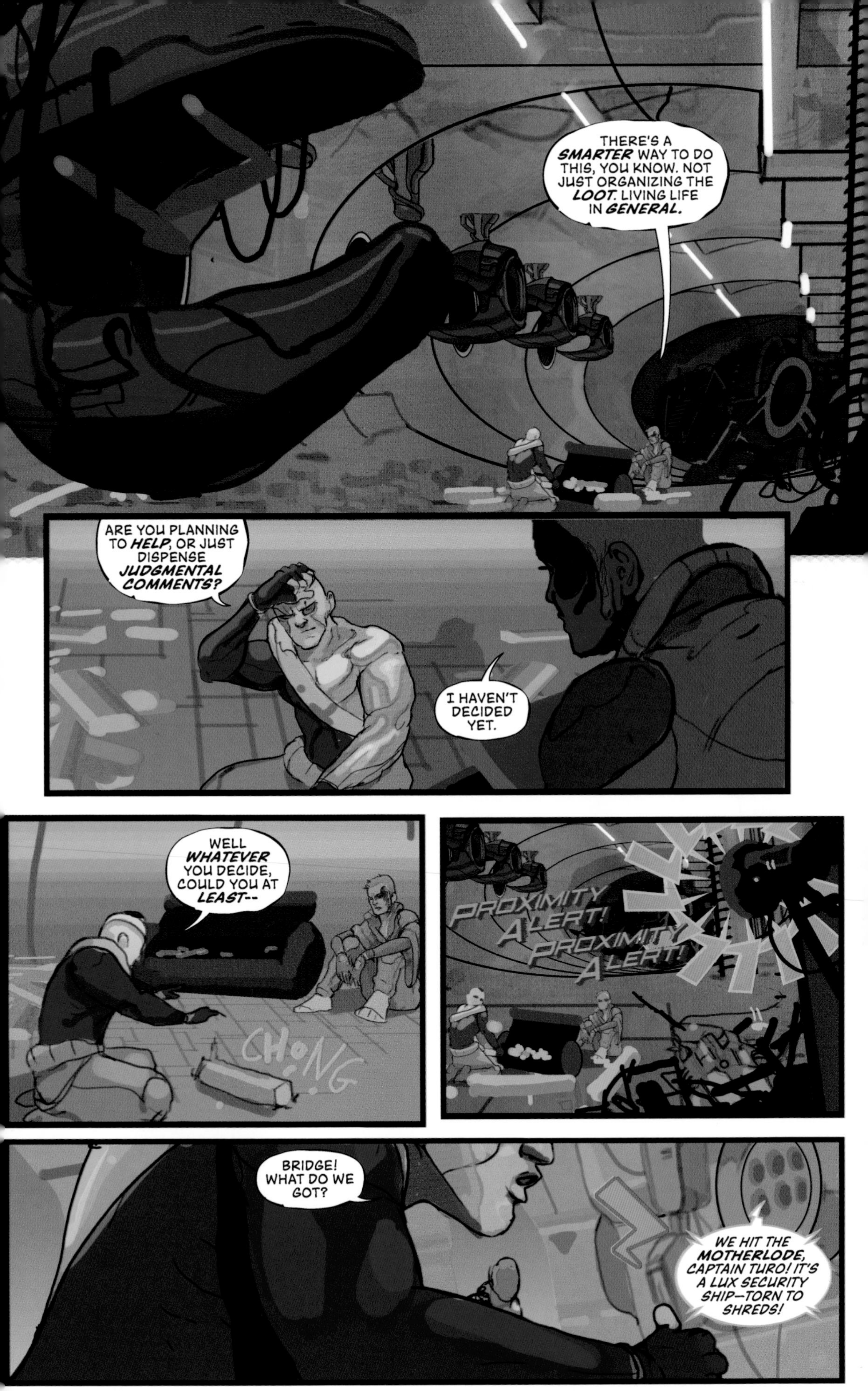
THERE'S A SMARTER WAY TO DO THIS, YOU KNOW. NOT JUST ORGANIZING THE LOOT. LIVING LIFE IN GENERAL.
ARE YOU PLANNING TO HELP, OR JUST DISPENSE JUDGMENTAL COMMENTS?
I HAVEN'T DECIDED YET.
WELL WHATEVER YOU DECIDE, COULD YOU AT LEAST--
CHONG
PROXIMITY ALERT! PROXIMITY ALERT!
BRIDGE! WHAT DO WE GOT?
WE HIT THE MOTHERLODE, CAPTAIN TURO! IT'S A LUX SECURITY SHIP—TORN TO SHREDS!

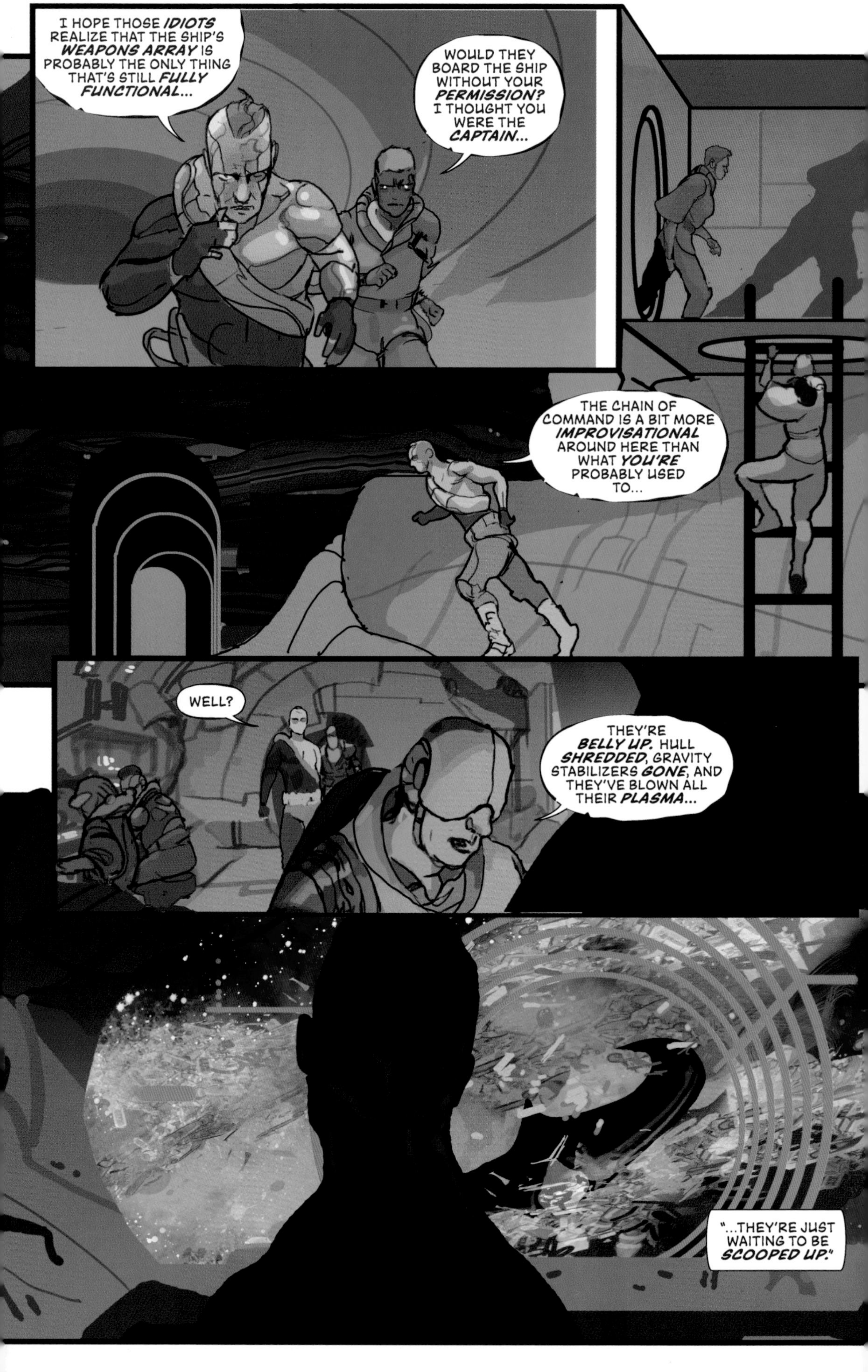
I HOPE THOSE IDIOTS REALIZE THAT THE SHIP'S WEAPONS ARRAY IS PROBABLY THE ONLY THING THAT'S STILL FULLY FUNCTIONAL...
WOULD THEY BOARD THE SHIP WITHOUT YOUR PERMISSION? I THOUGHT YOU WERE THE CAPTAIN...
THE CHAIN OF COMMAND IS A BIT MORE IMPROVISATIONAL AROUND HERE THAN WHAT YOU'RE PROBABLY USED TO...
WELL?
THEY'RE BELLY UP. HULL SHREDDED, GRAVITY STABILIZERS GONE, AND THEY'VE BLOWN ALL THEIR PLASMA...
"...THEY'RE JUST WAITING TO BE SCOOPED UP."

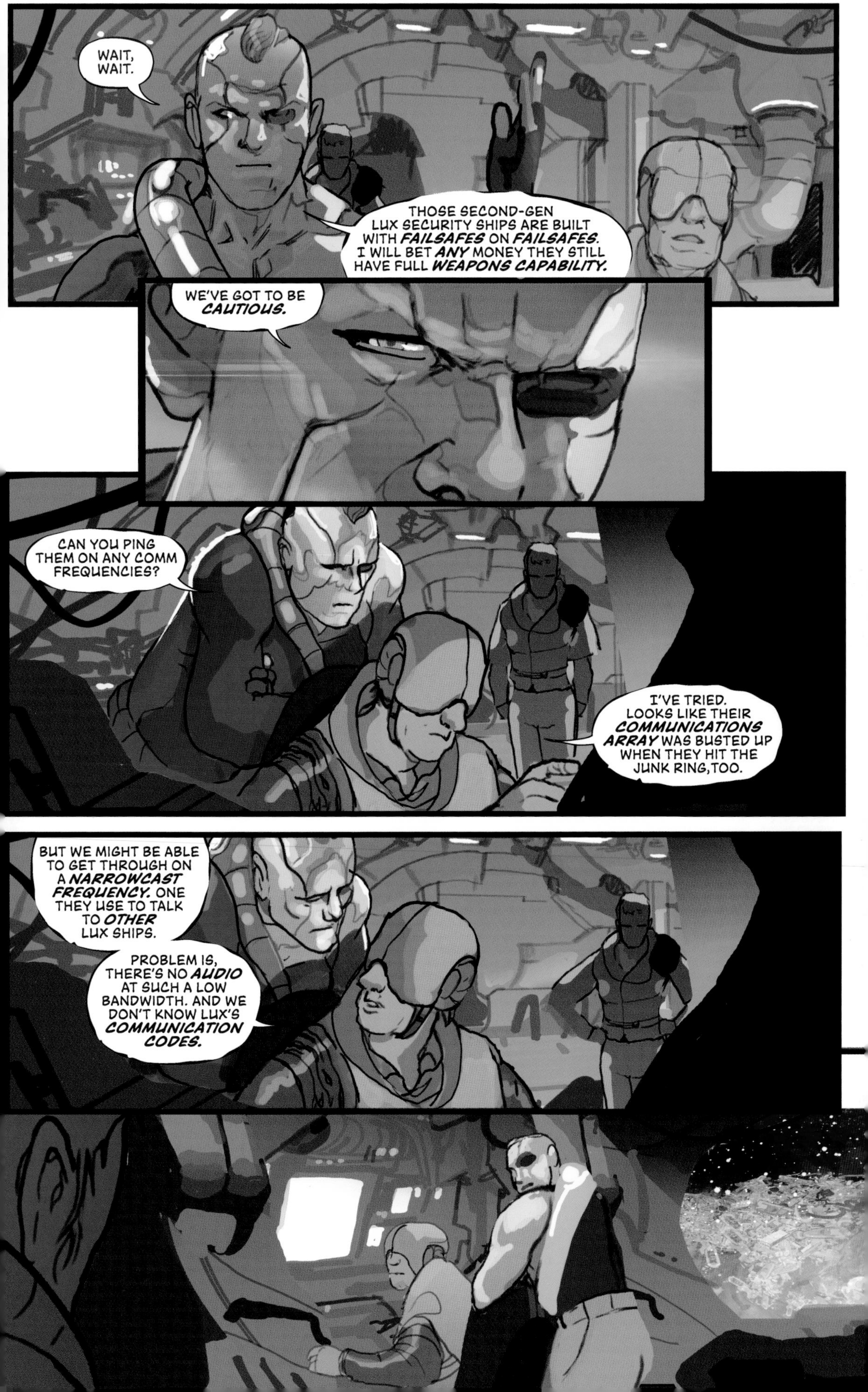
WAIT, WAIT.
THOSE SECOND-GEN LUX SECURITY SHIPS ARE BUILT WITH FAILSAFES ON FAILSAFES. I WILL BET ANY MONEY THEY STILL HAVE FULL WEAPONS CAPABILITY.
WE'VE GOT TO BE CAUTIOUS.
CAN YOU PING THEM ON ANY COMM FREQUENCIES?
I'VE TRIED. LOOKS LIKE THEIR COMMUNICATIONS ARRAY WAS BUSTED UP WHEN THEY HIT THE JUNK RING,TOO.
BUT WE MIGHT BE ABLE TO GET THROUGH ON A NARROWCAST FREQUENCY. ONE THEY USE TO TALK TO OTHER LUX SHIPS.
PROBLEM IS, THERE'S NO AUDIO AT SUCH A LOW BANDWIDTH. AND WE DON'T KNOW LUX'S COMMUNICATION CODES.

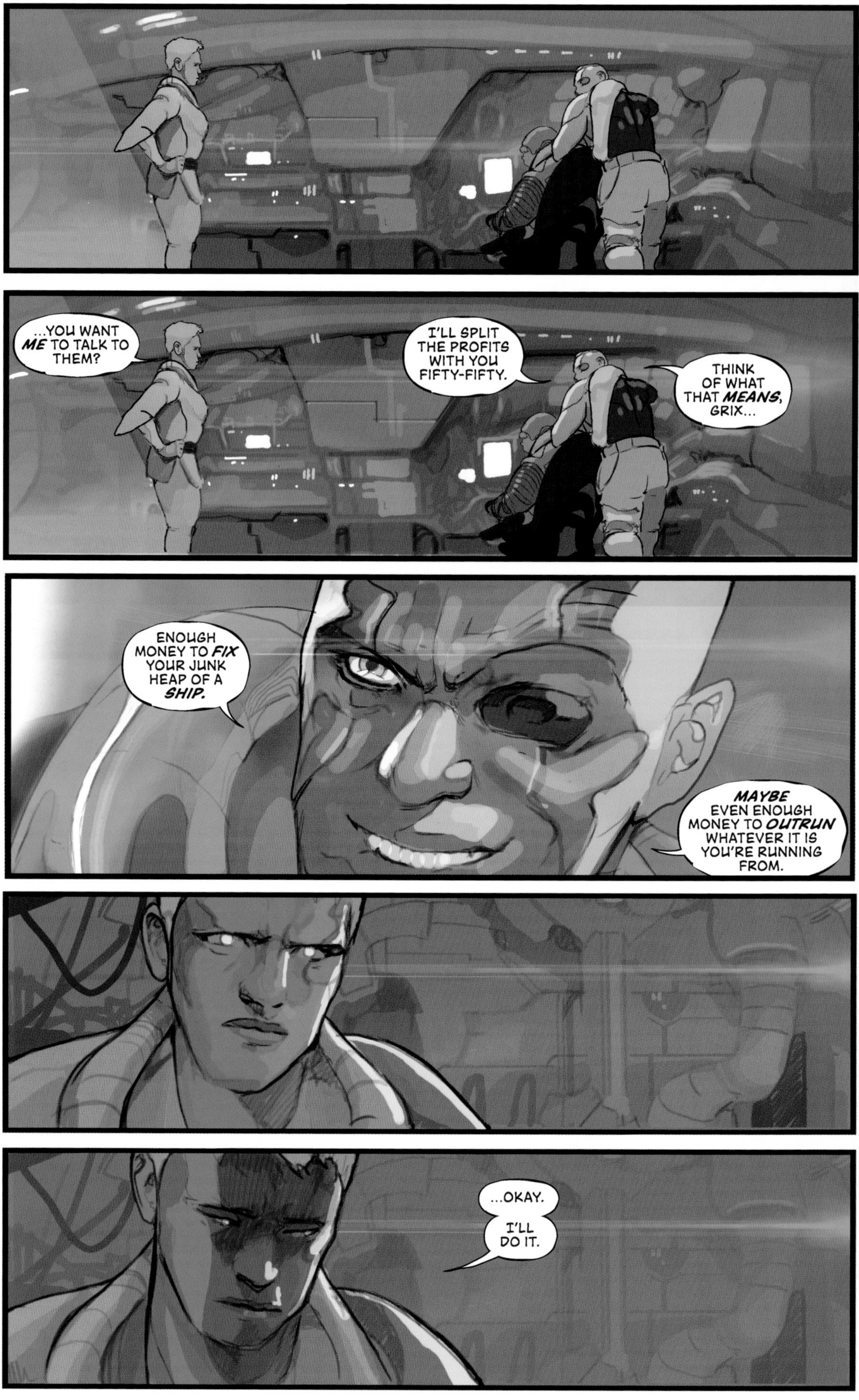
...YOU WANT ME TO TALK TO THEM?
I'LL SPLIT THE PROFITS WITH YOU FIFTY-FIFTY.
THINK OF WHAT THAT MEANS, GRIX...
ENOUGH MONEY TO FIX YOUR JUNK HEAP OF A SHIP.
MAYBE EVEN ENOUGH MONEY TO OUTRUN WHATEVER IT IS YOU'RE RUNNING FROM.
...OKAY.
I'LL DO IT.

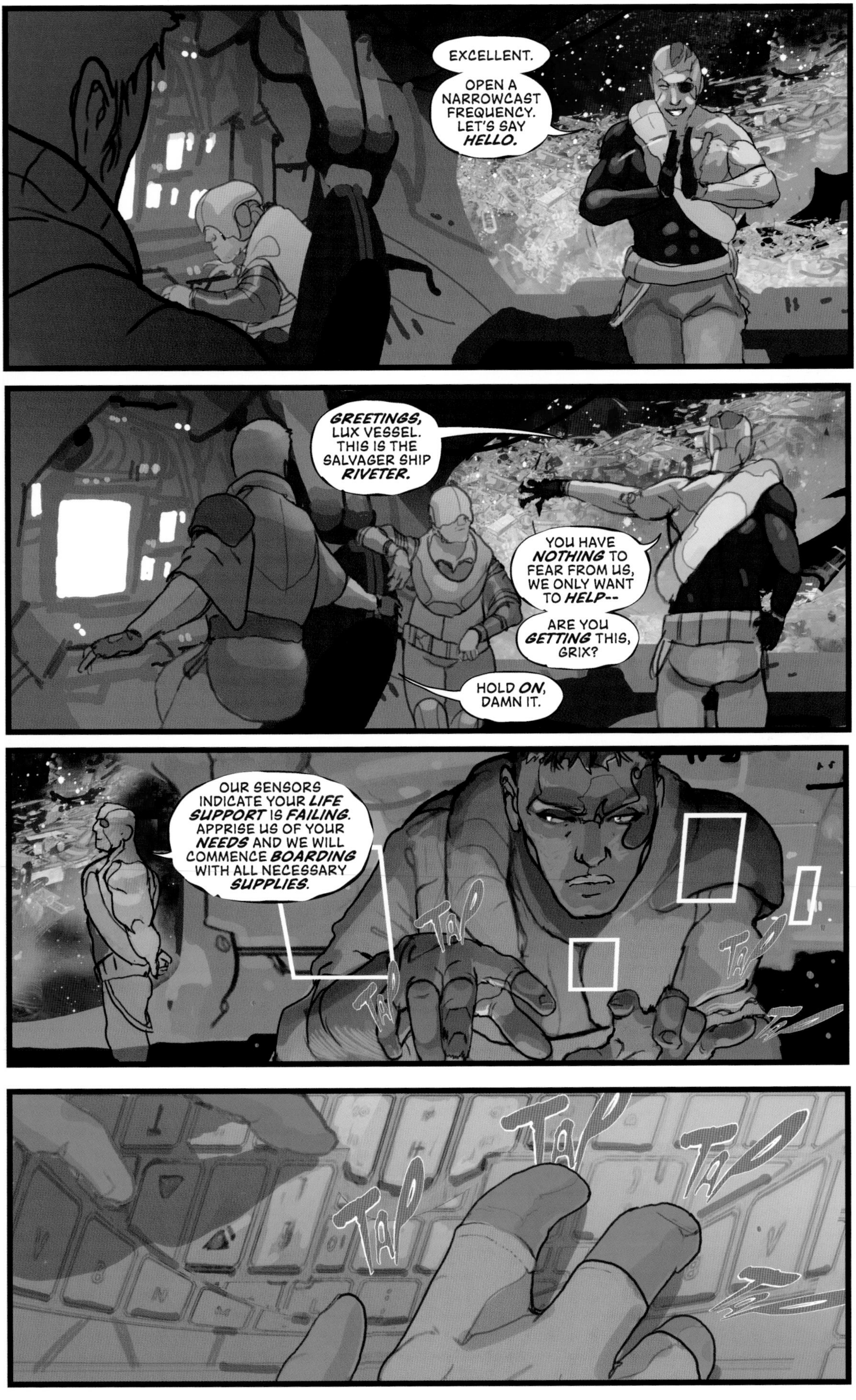
EXCELLENT.
OPEN A NARROWCAST FREQUENCY. LET'S SAY HELLO.
GREETINGS, LUX VESSEL. THIS IS THE SALVAGER SHIP RIVETER.
YOU HAVE NOTHING TO FEAR FROM US, WE ONLY WANT TO HELP--
ARE YOU GETTING THIS, GRIX?
HOLD ON, DAMN IT.
OUR SENSORS INDICATE YOUR LIFE SUPPORT IS FAILING. APPRISE US OF YOUR NEEDS AND WE WILL COMMENCE BOARDING WITH ALL NECESSARY SUPPLIES.
TAP TAP TAP
TAP TAP TAP

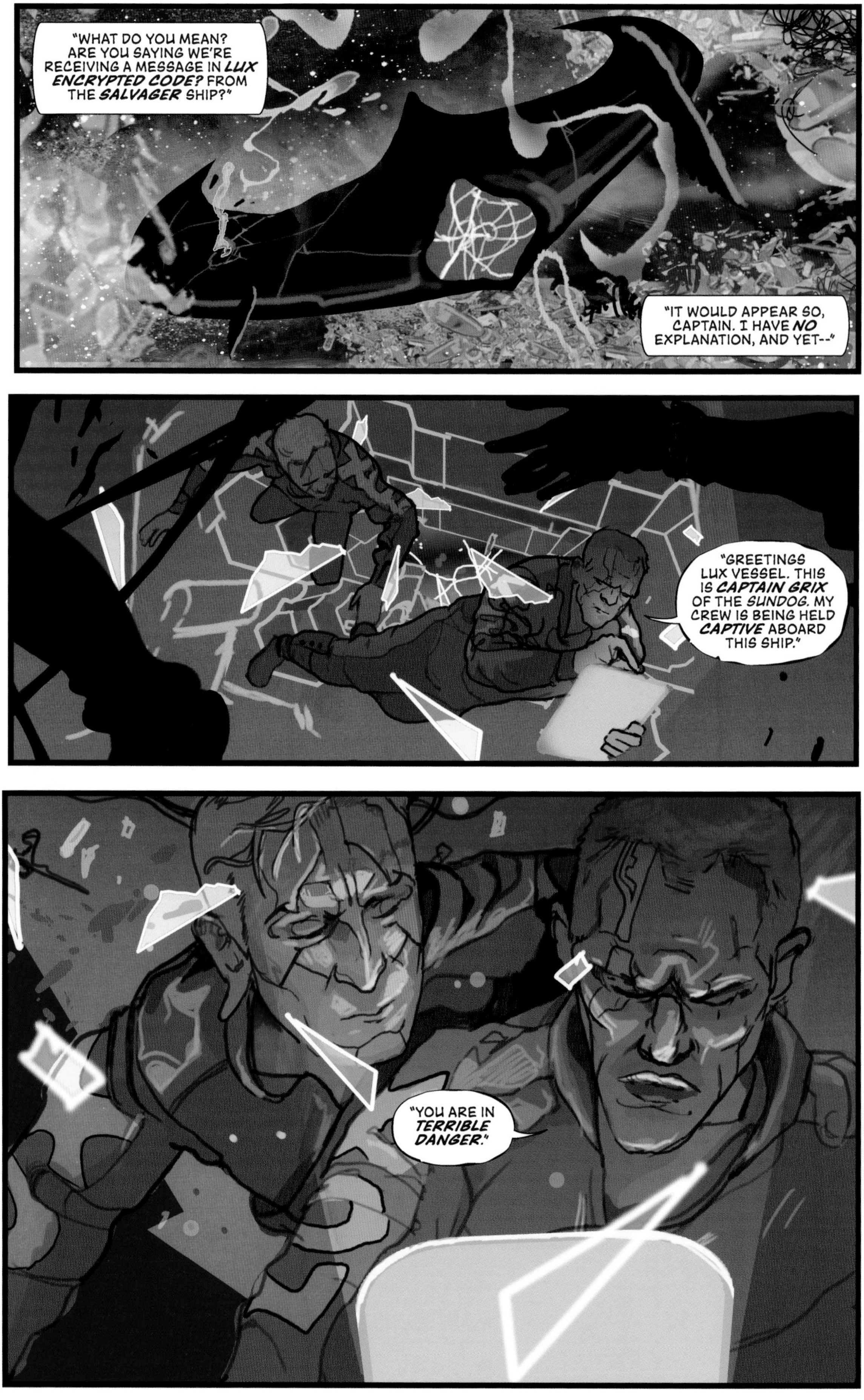
"WHAT DO YOU MEAN? ARE YOU SAYING WE'RE RECEIVING A MESSAGE IN ***LUX ENCRYPTED CODE?*** FROM THE ***SALVAGER*** SHIP?"
"IT WOULD APPEAR SO, CAPTAIN. I HAVE ***NO*** EXPLANATION, AND YET--"
"GREETINGS LUX VESSEL. THIS IS ***CAPTAIN GRIX*** OF THE *SUNDOG*. MY CREW IS BEING HELD ***CAPTIVE*** ABOARD THIS SHIP."
"YOU ARE IN ***TERRIBLE DANGER.***"

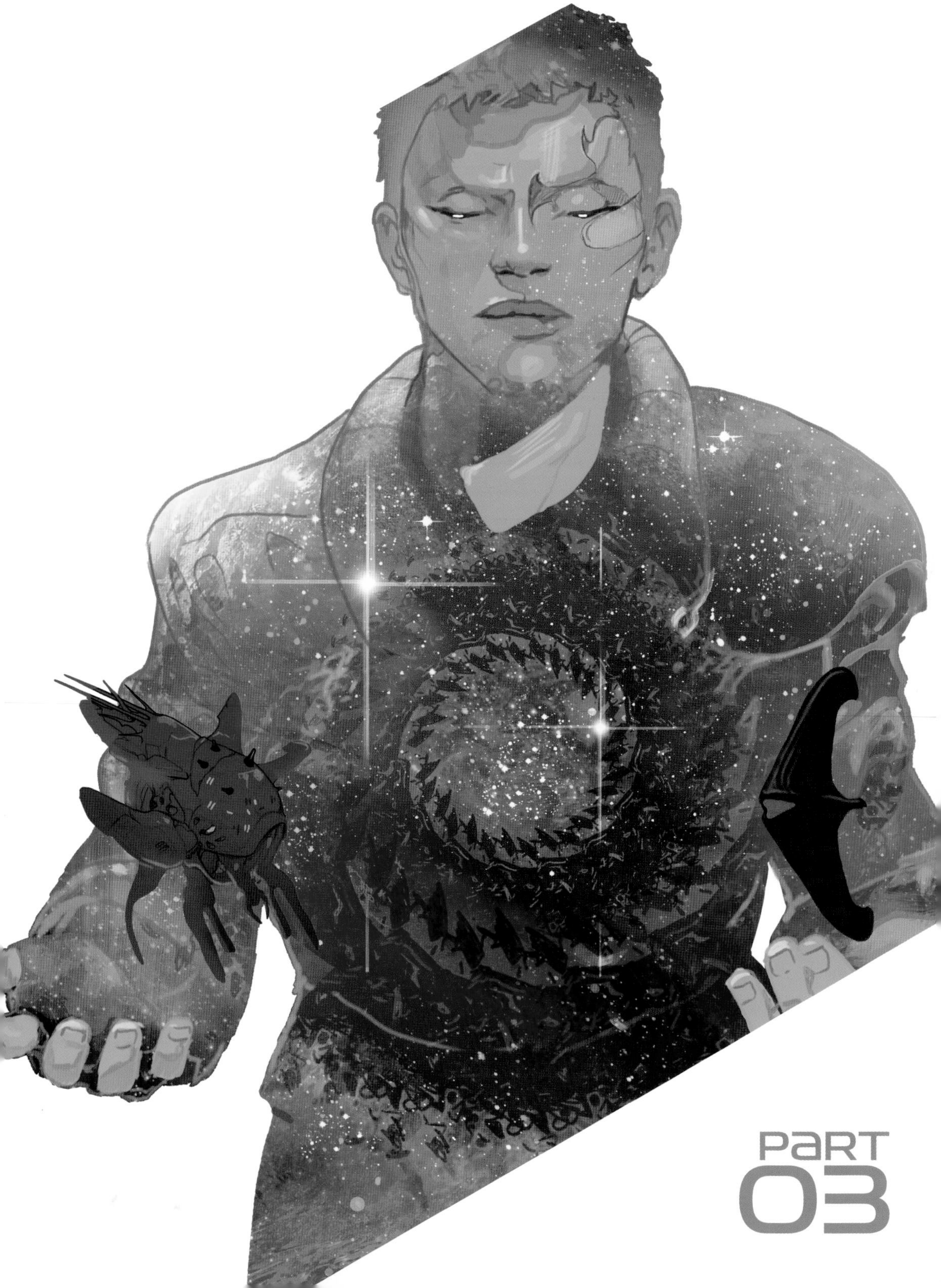

PART 03

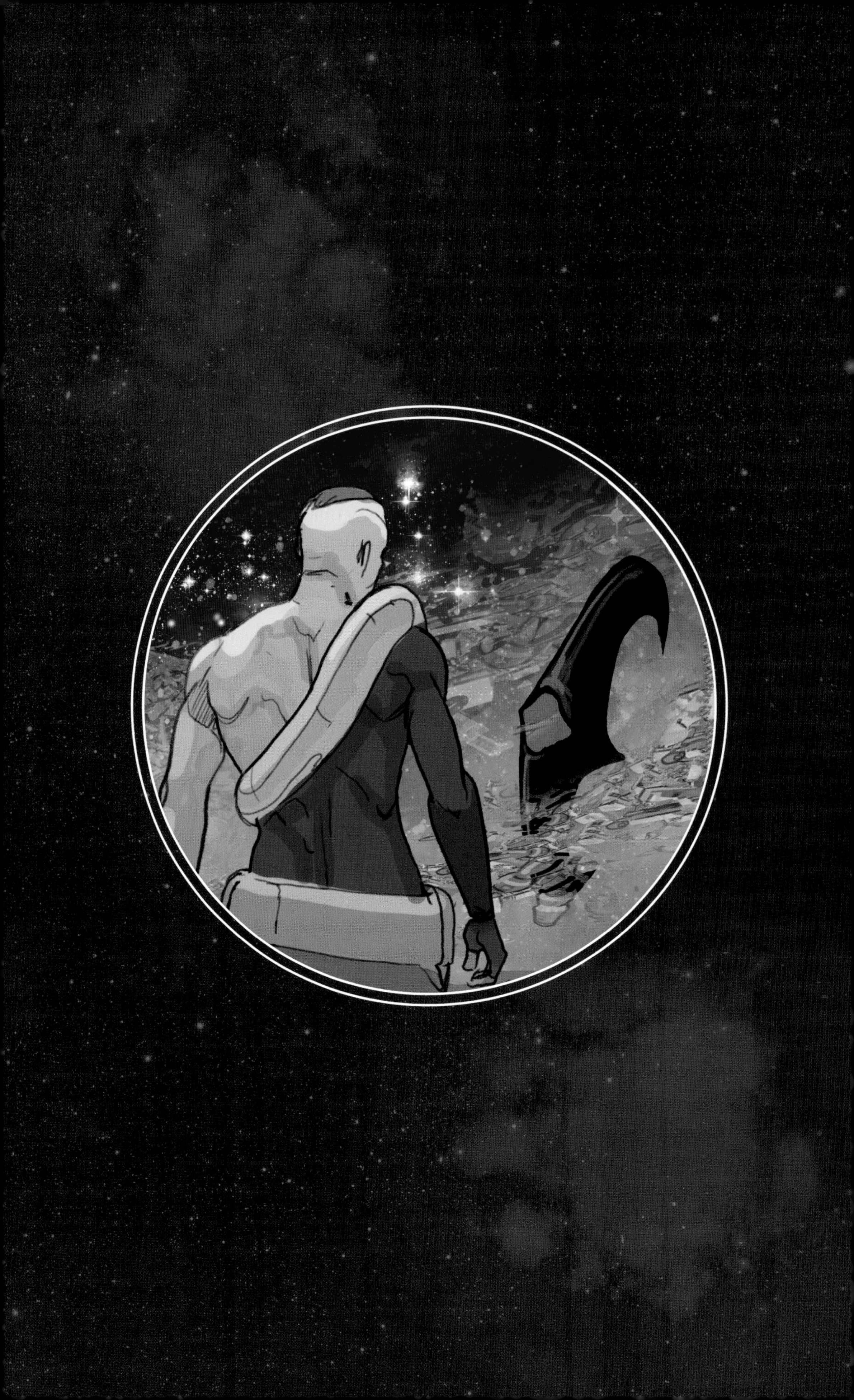

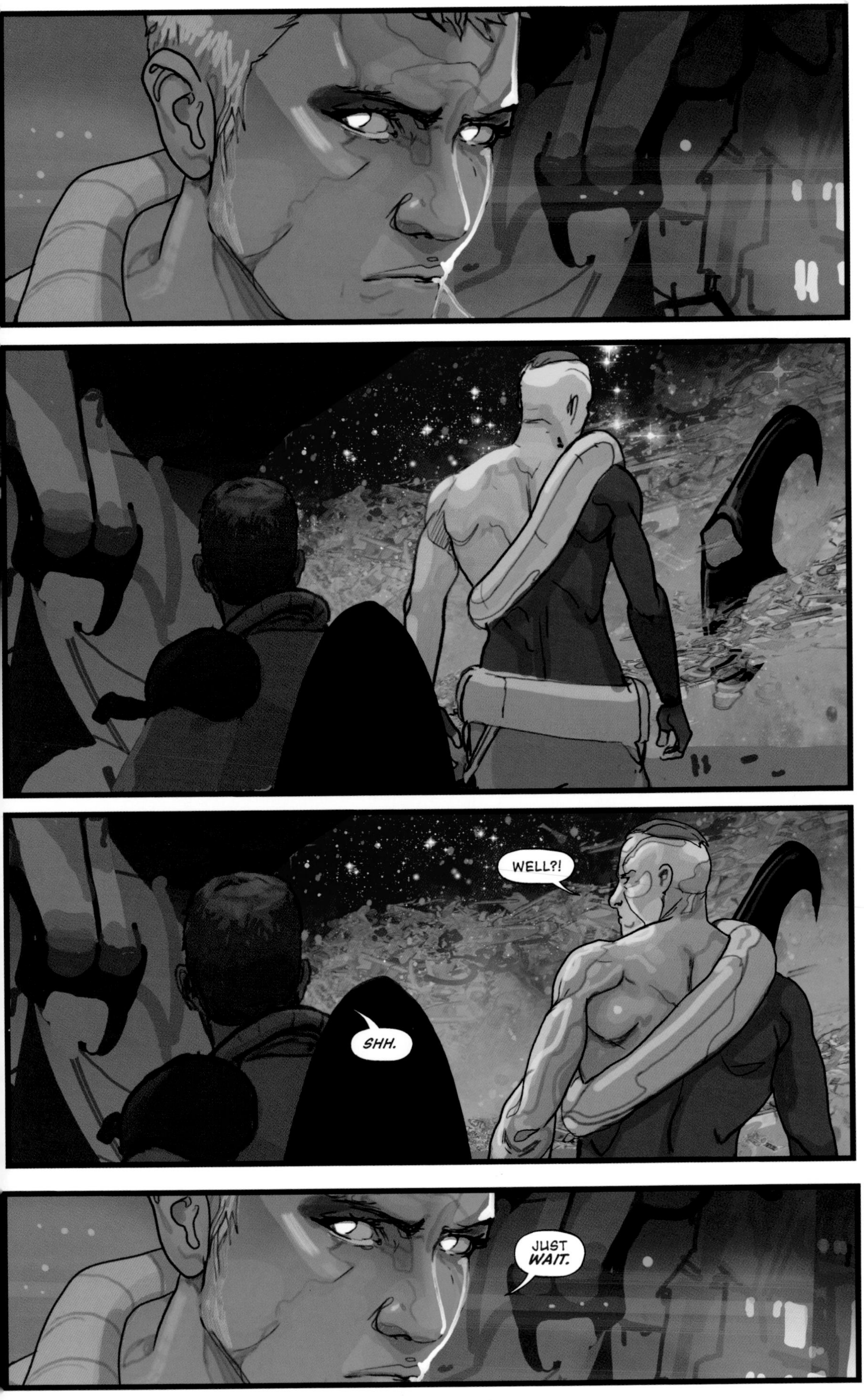
WELL?!
SHH.
JUST WAIT.

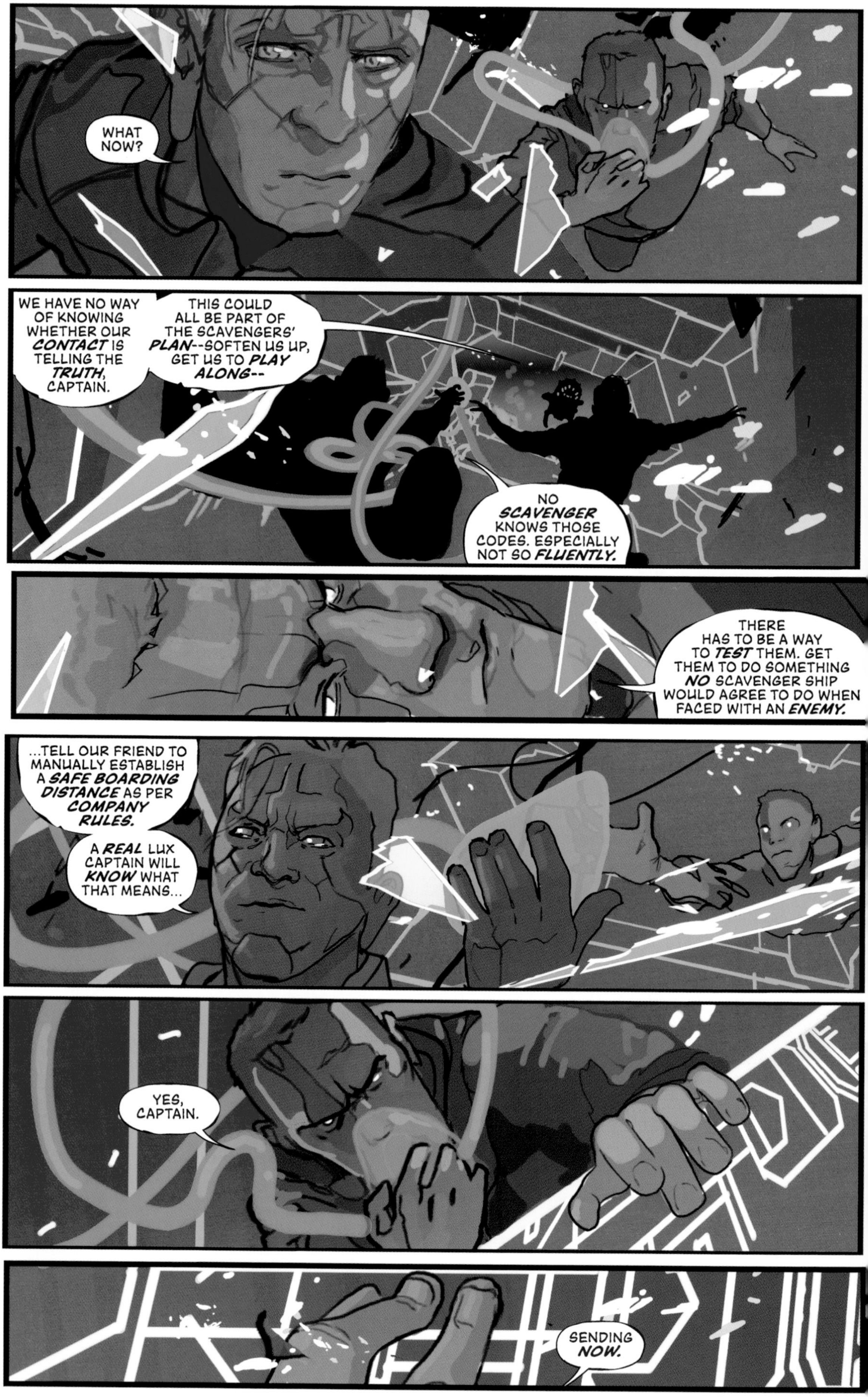
WHAT NOW?
WE HAVE NO WAY OF KNOWING WHETHER OUR CONTACT IS TELLING THE TRUTH, CAPTAIN.
THIS COULD ALL BE PART OF THE SCAVENGERS' PLAN--SOFTEN US UP, GET US TO PLAY ALONG--
NO SCAVENGER KNOWS THOSE CODES. ESPECIALLY NOT SO FLUENTLY.
THERE HAS TO BE A WAY TO TEST THEM. GET THEM TO DO SOMETHING NO SCAVENGER SHIP WOULD AGREE TO DO WHEN FACED WITH AN ENEMY.
...TELL OUR FRIEND TO MANUALLY ESTABLISH A SAFE BOARDING DISTANCE AS PER COMPANY RULES.
A REAL LUX CAPTAIN WILL KNOW WHAT THAT MEANS...
YES, CAPTAIN.
SENDING NOW.

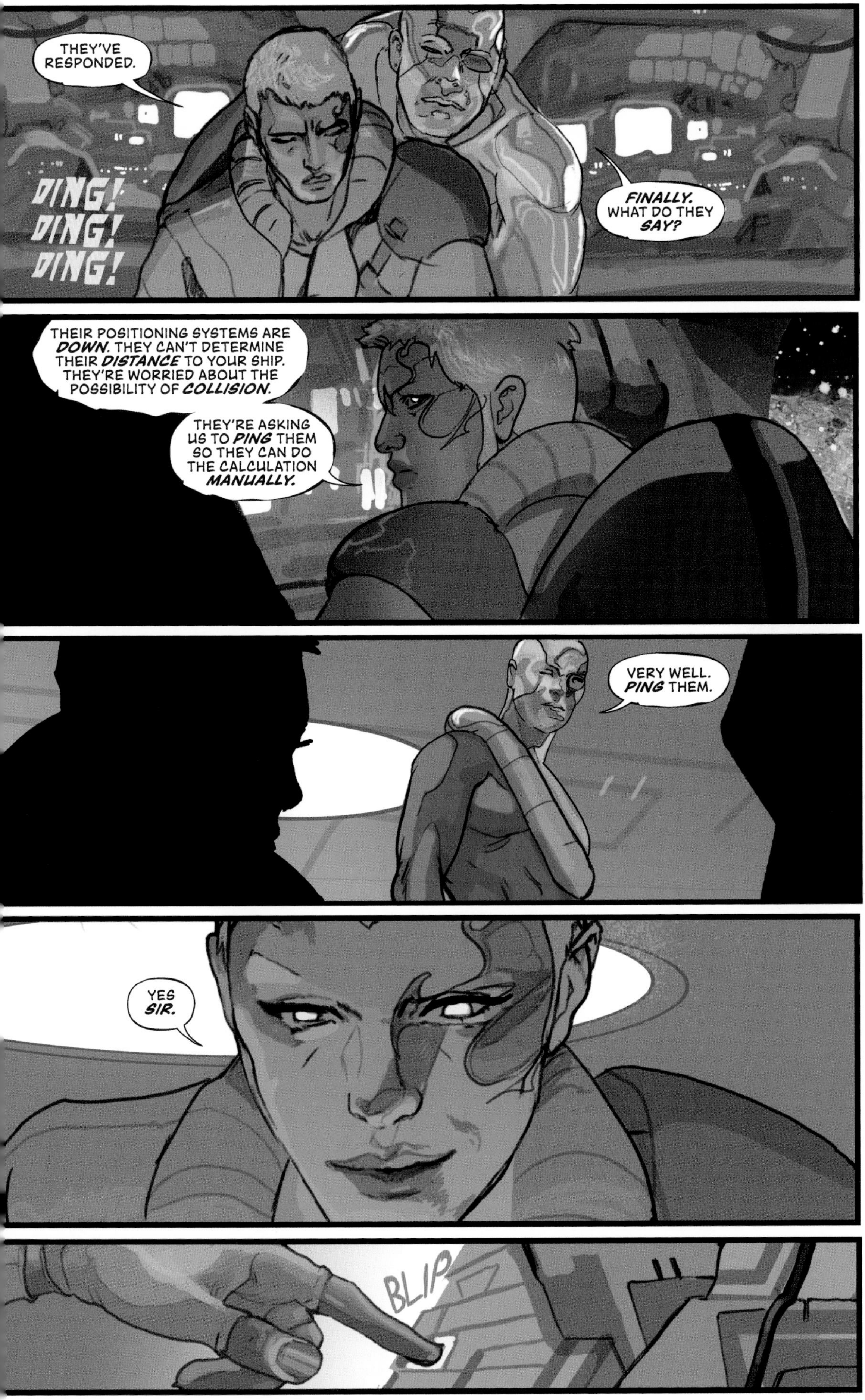

THEY'VE RESPONDED.
DING! DING! DING!
FINALLY. WHAT DO THEY SAY?
THEIR POSITIONING SYSTEMS ARE DOWN. THEY CAN'T DETERMINE THEIR DISTANCE TO YOUR SHIP. THEY'RE WORRIED ABOUT THE POSSIBILITY OF COLLISION.
THEY'RE ASKING US TO PING THEM SO THEY CAN DO THE CALCULATION MANUALLY.
VERY WELL. PING THEM.
YES SIR.
BLIP

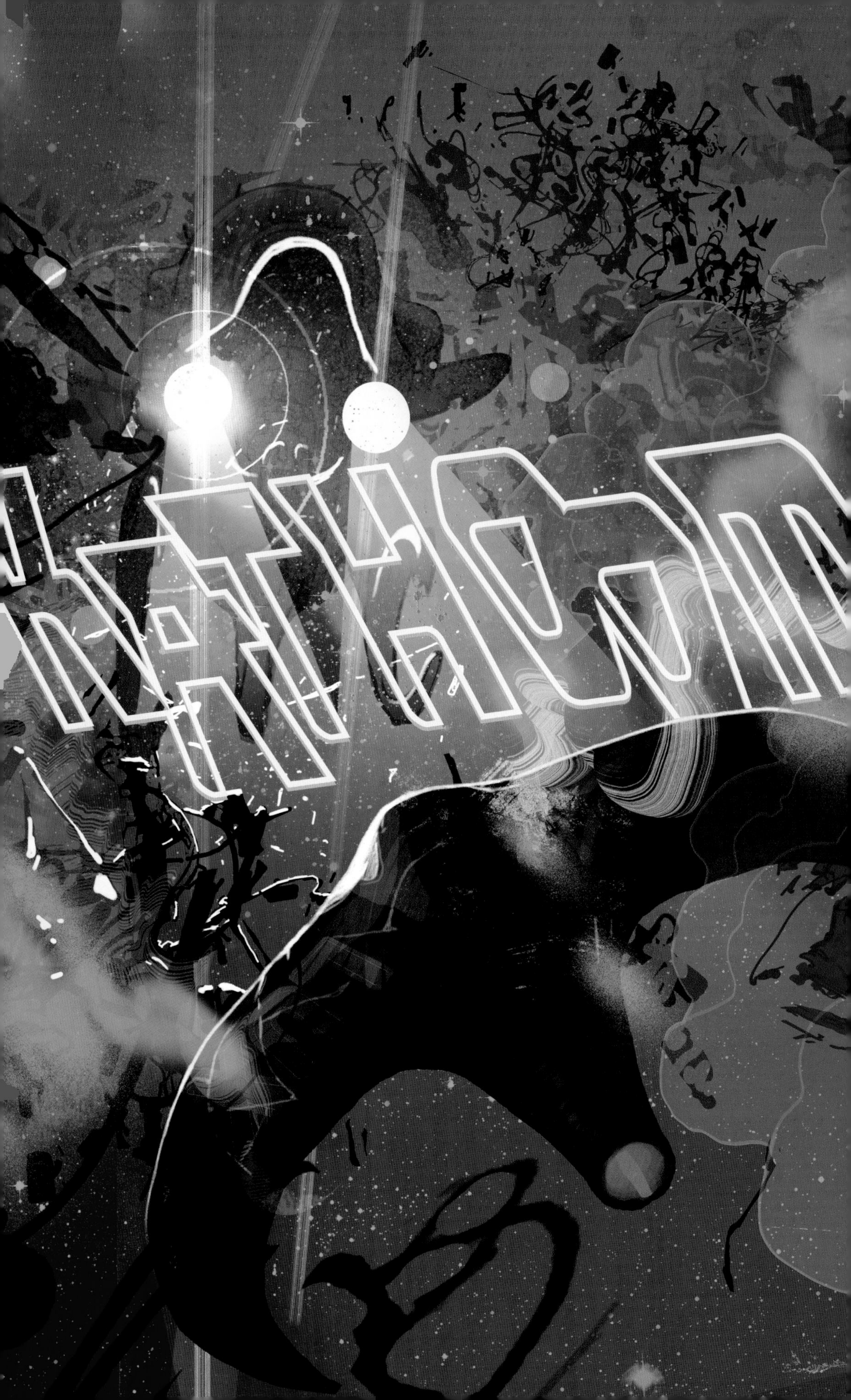

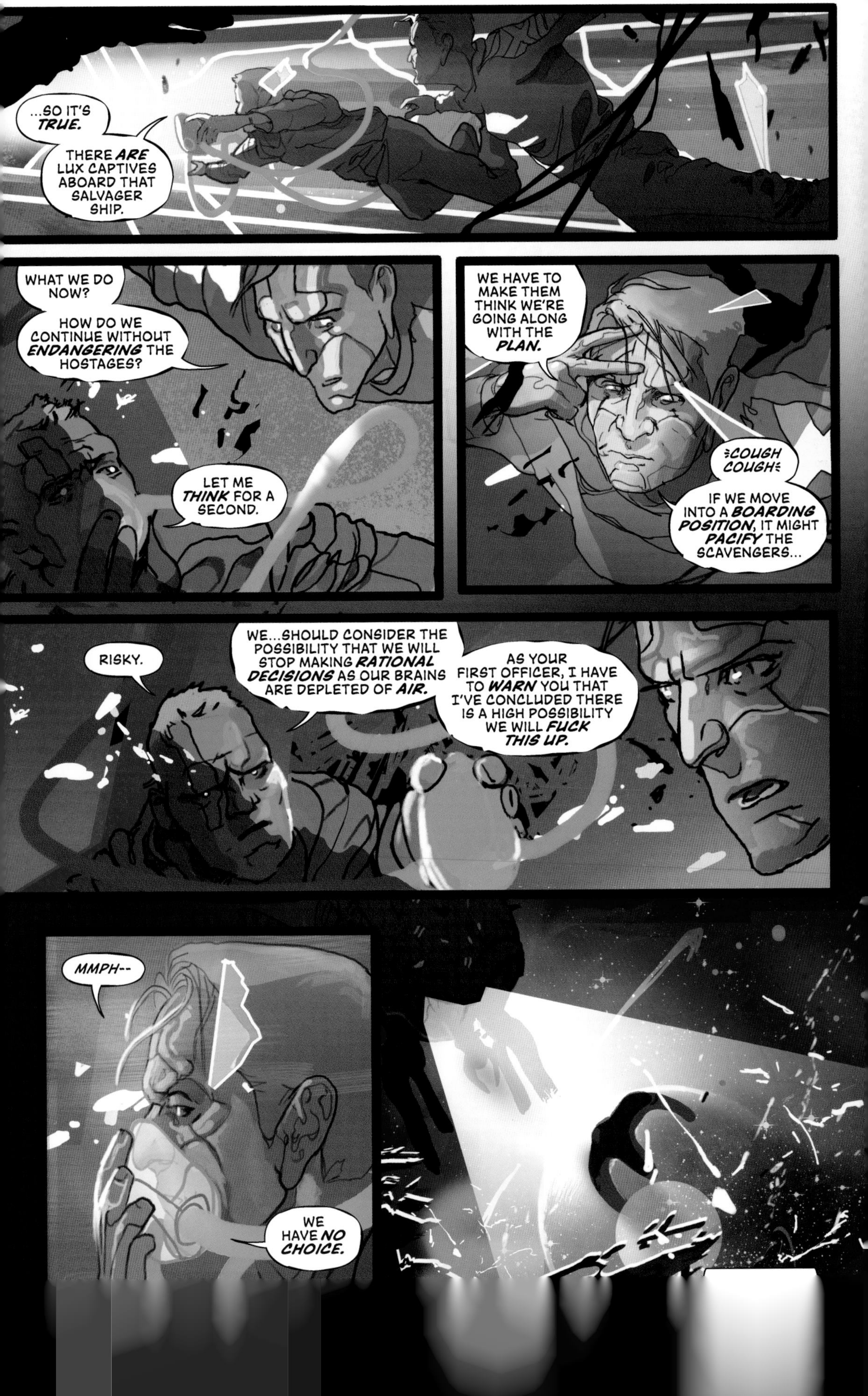
...SO IT'S TRUE.
THERE ARE LUX CAPTIVES ABOARD THAT SALVAGER SHIP.
WHAT WE DO NOW?
HOW DO WE CONTINUE WITHOUT ENDANGERING THE HOSTAGES?
LET ME THINK FOR A SECOND.
WE HAVE TO MAKE THEM THINK WE'RE GOING ALONG WITH THE PLAN.
COUGH COUGH
IF WE MOVE INTO A BOARDING POSITION, IT MIGHT PACIFY THE SCAVENGERS...
RISKY.
WE...SHOULD CONSIDER THE POSSIBILITY THAT WE WILL STOP MAKING RATIONAL DECISIONS AS OUR BRAINS ARE DEPLETED OF AIR.
AS YOUR FIRST OFFICER, I HAVE TO WARN YOU THAT I'VE CONCLUDED THERE IS A HIGH POSSIBILITY WE WILL FUCK THIS UP.
MMPH--
WE HAVE NO CHOICE.

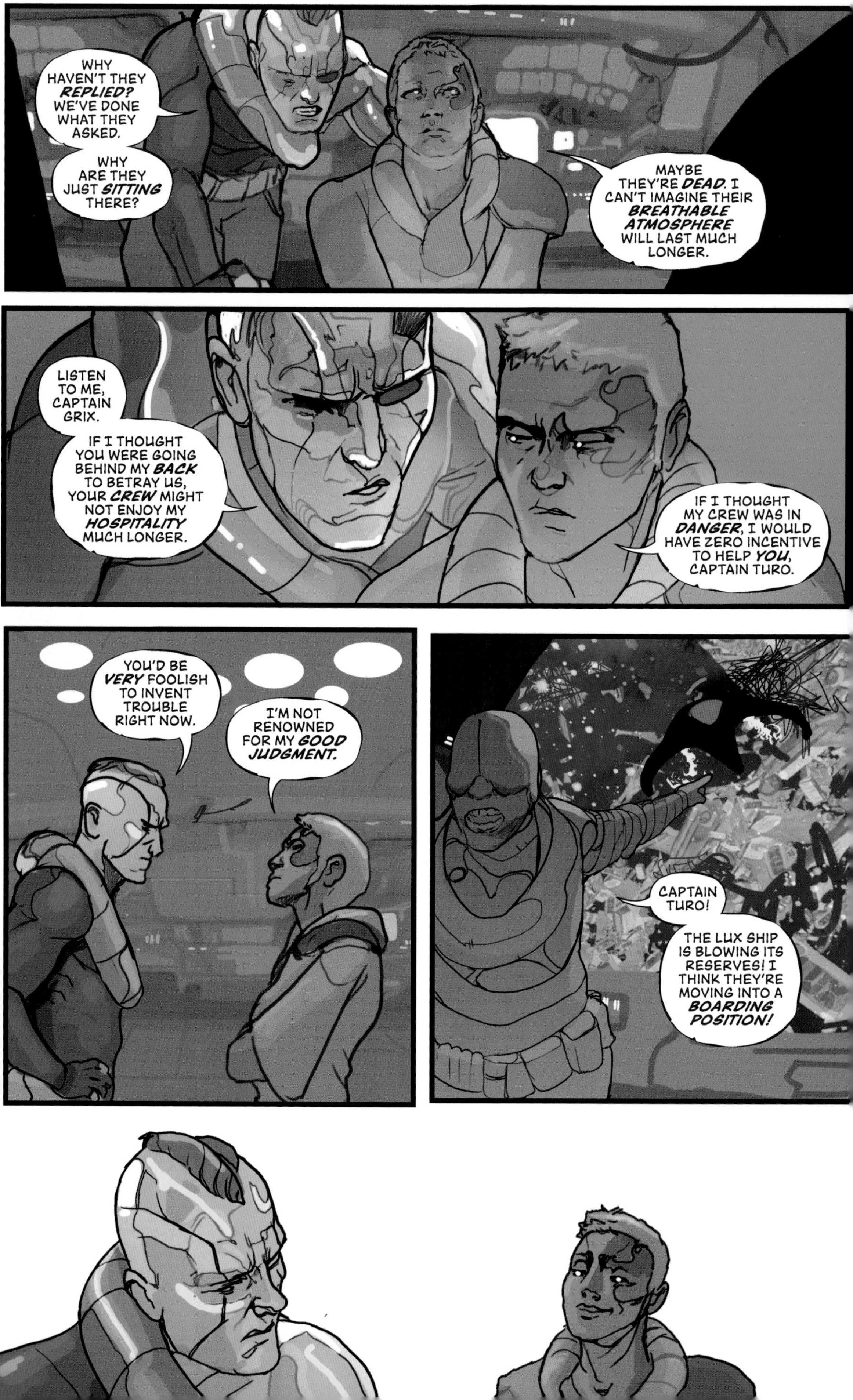
WHY HAVEN'T THEY REPLIED? WE'VE DONE WHAT THEY ASKED.
WHY ARE THEY JUST SITTING THERE?
MAYBE THEY'RE DEAD. I CAN'T IMAGINE THEIR BREATHABLE ATMOSPHERE WILL LAST MUCH LONGER.
LISTEN TO ME, CAPTAIN GRIX.
IF I THOUGHT YOU WERE GOING BEHIND MY BACK TO BETRAY US, YOUR CREW MIGHT NOT ENJOY MY HOSPITALITY MUCH LONGER.
IF I THOUGHT MY CREW WAS IN DANGER, I WOULD HAVE ZERO INCENTIVE TO HELP YOU, CAPTAIN TURO.
YOU'D BE VERY FOOLISH TO INVENT TROUBLE RIGHT NOW.
I'M NOT RENOWNED FOR MY GOOD JUDGMENT.
CAPTAIN TURO!
THE LUX SHIP IS BLOWING ITS RESERVES! I THINK THEY'RE MOVING INTO A BOARDING POSITION!

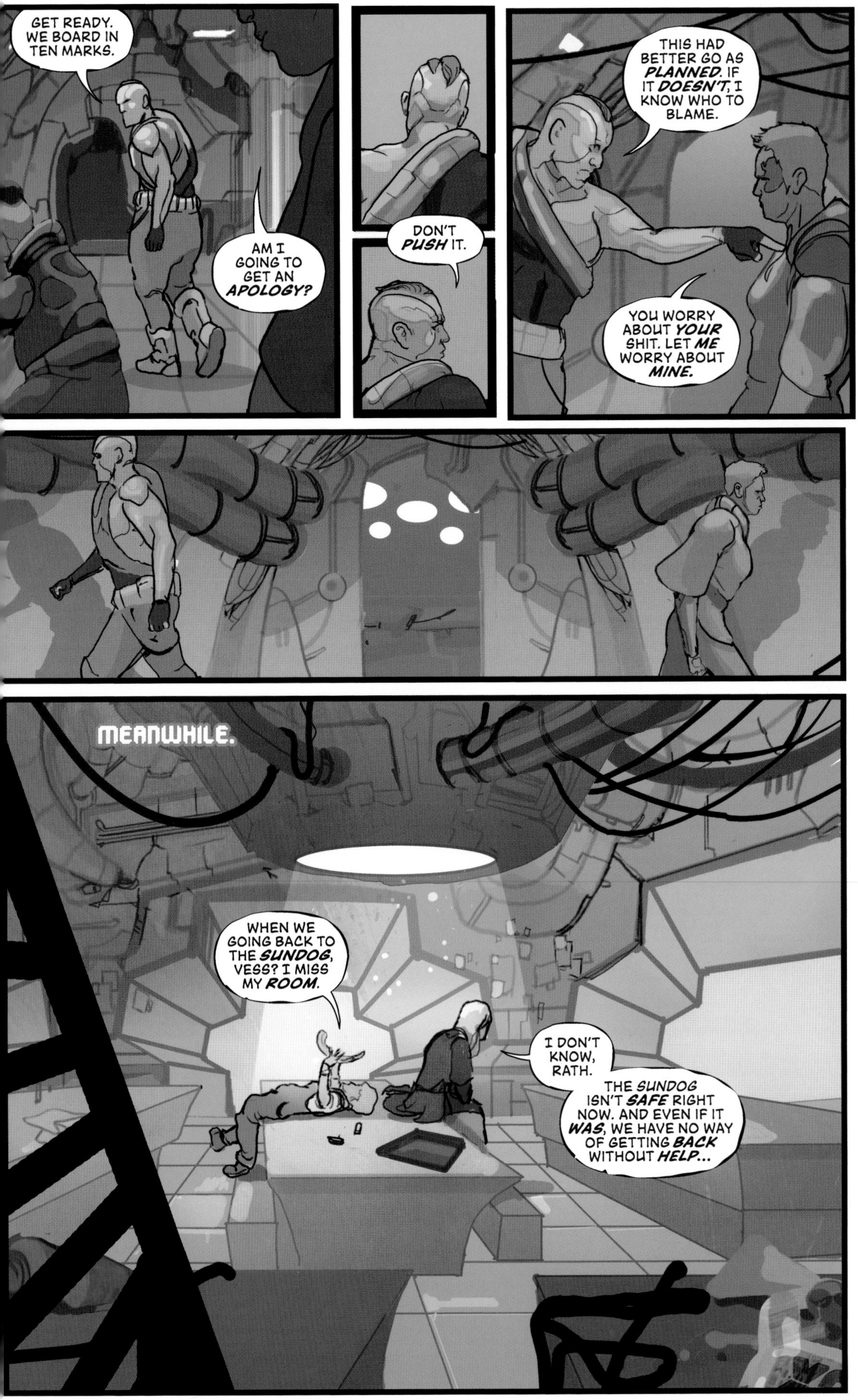

GET READY. WE BOARD IN TEN MARKS.
AM I GOING TO GET AN APOLOGY?
DON'T PUSH IT.
THIS HAD BETTER GO AS PLANNED. IF IT DOESN'T, I KNOW WHO TO BLAME.
YOU WORRY ABOUT YOUR SHIT. LET ME WORRY ABOUT MINE.
MEANWHILE.
WHEN WE GOING BACK TO THE SUNDOG, VESS? I MISS MY ROOM.
I DON'T KNOW, RATH.
THE SUNDOG ISN'T SAFE RIGHT NOW. AND EVEN IF IT WAS, WE HAVE NO WAY OF GETTING BACK WITHOUT HELP...

VESS... ARE WE GONNA *DIE* HERE?

OF COURSE NOT, MY LOVE. WHY WOULD YOU ASK SUCH A THING? YOUR *SISTER* WILL TAKE GOOD CARE OF US. SHE *ALWAYS* DOES.

PROMISE?

I--

VESS! GATHER THE OTHERS, WE HAVE TO BE READY TO MOVE IF WE HAVE TO.

WHAT'S WRONG? WHAT'S *HAPPENED?*

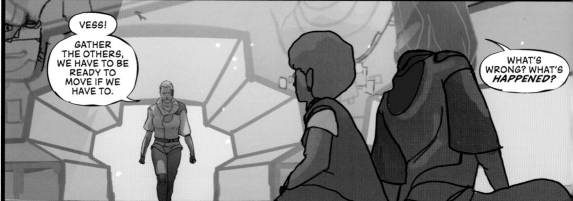

I SENT A *CODED MESSAGE* TO THE LUX SHIP.

TOLD THEM *WE'RE* BEING HELD HOSTAGE AND *THEY'RE* IN DANGER OF ENDING UP THE *SAME WAY* IF THEY LET *TURO* AND HIS *MORONS* BOARD THEIR *SHIP.*

OH *GRIX!* WHAT IF THE RIVETEERS *FIND OUT?*

THEN WE'RE ALL *DEAD.*

WHAT ARE WE GOING TO DO?! *RATH* IS ALREADY *SCARED*--

HEY. WE'VE GOTTEN *THIS* FAR, RIGHT? I MAY NOT BE SMART OR WELL-READ OR EVEN VERY *NICE,* BUT I'M *LUCKY.* AND I *DON'T* GET *SCARED.*

DON'T--

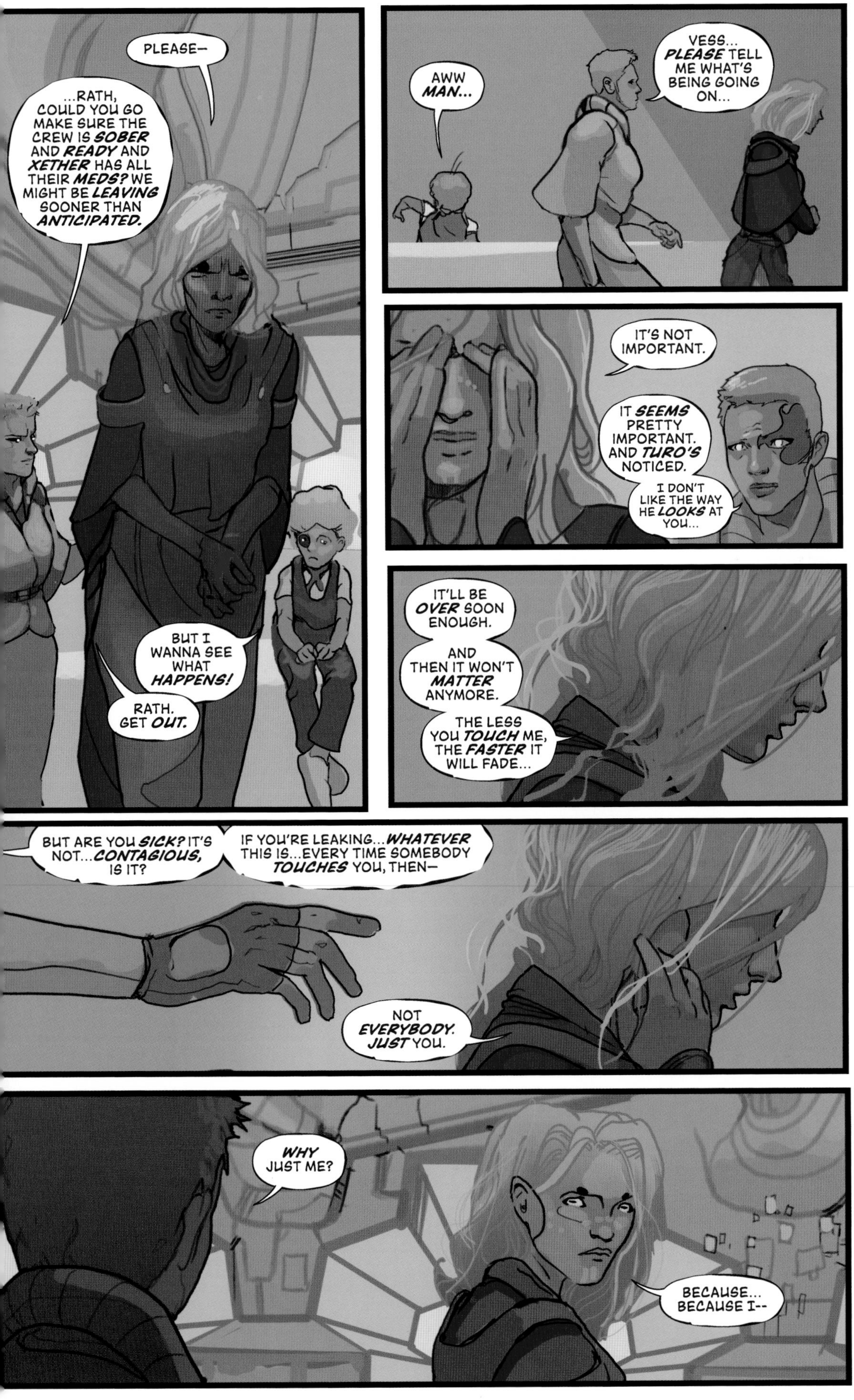
PLEASE—
...RATH, COULD YOU GO MAKE SURE THE CREW IS SOBER AND READY AND XETHER HAS ALL THEIR MEDS? WE MIGHT BE LEAVING SOONER THAN ANTICIPATED.
BUT I WANNA SEE WHAT HAPPENS!
RATH. GET OUT.
AWW MAN...
VESS... PLEASE TELL ME WHAT'S BEING GOING ON...
IT'S NOT IMPORTANT.
IT SEEMS PRETTY IMPORTANT. AND TURO'S NOTICED.
I DON'T LIKE THE WAY HE LOOKS AT YOU...
IT'LL BE OVER SOON ENOUGH.
AND THEN IT WON'T MATTER ANYMORE.
THE LESS YOU TOUCH ME, THE FASTER IT WILL FADE...
BUT ARE YOU SICK? IT'S NOT...CONTAGIOUS, IS IT?
IF YOU'RE LEAKING...WHATEVER THIS IS...EVERY TIME SOMEBODY TOUCHES YOU, THEN—
NOT EVERYBODY. JUST YOU.
WHY JUST ME?
BECAUSE... BECAUSE I--

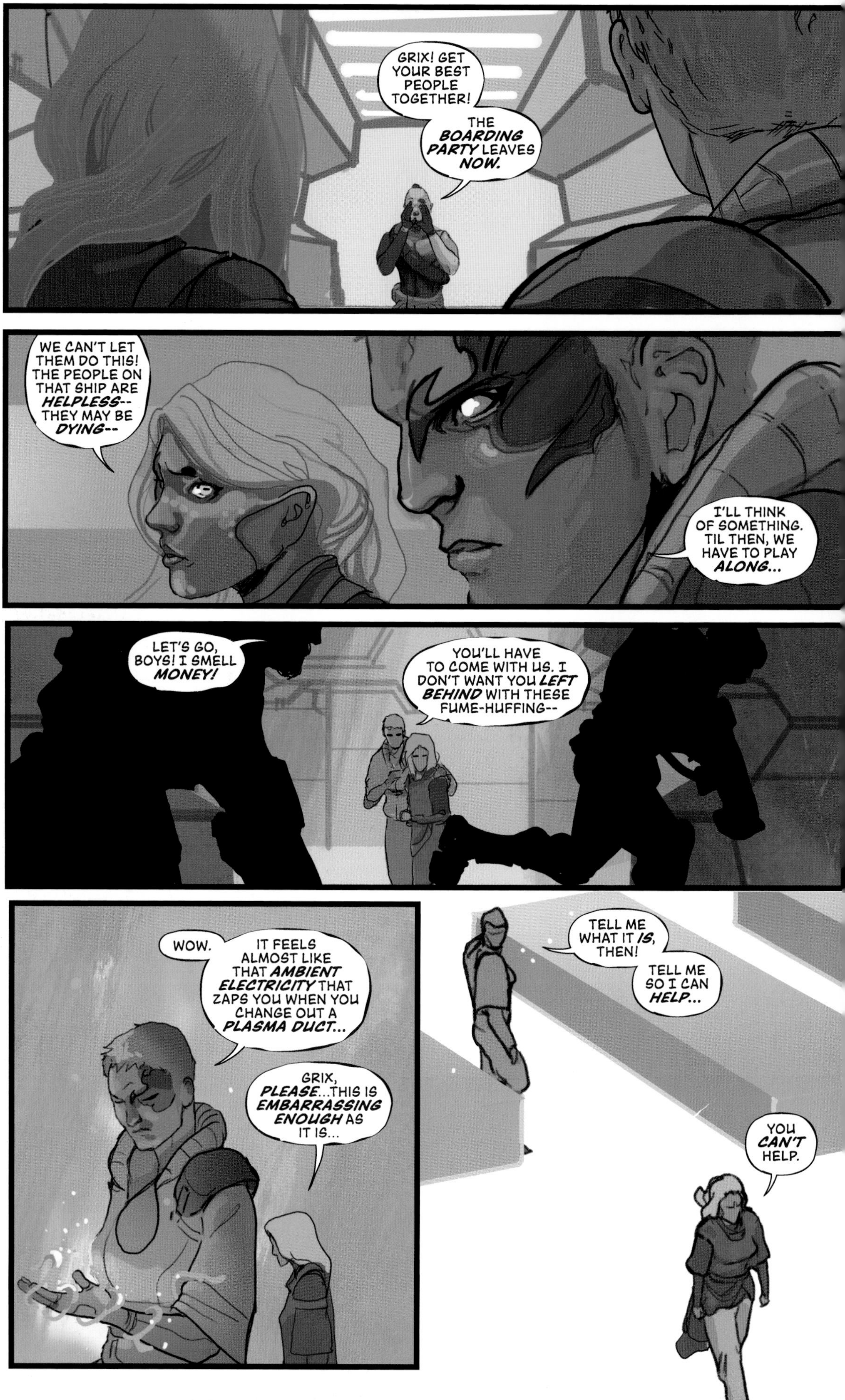
GRIX! GET YOUR BEST PEOPLE TOGETHER!
THE BOARDING PARTY LEAVES NOW.
WE CAN'T LET THEM DO THIS! THE PEOPLE ON THAT SHIP ARE HELPLESS-- THEY MAY BE DYING--
I'LL THINK OF SOMETHING. TIL THEN, WE HAVE TO PLAY ALONG...
LET'S GO, BOYS! I SMELL MONEY!
YOU'LL HAVE TO COME WITH US. I DON'T WANT YOU LEFT BEHIND WITH THESE FUME-HUFFING--
WOW.
IT FEELS ALMOST LIKE THAT AMBIENT ELECTRICITY THAT ZAPS YOU WHEN YOU CHANGE OUT A PLASMA DUCT...
GRIX, PLEASE...THIS IS EMBARRASSING ENOUGH AS IT IS...
TELL ME WHAT IT IS, THEN!
TELL ME SO I CAN HELP...
YOU CAN'T HELP.

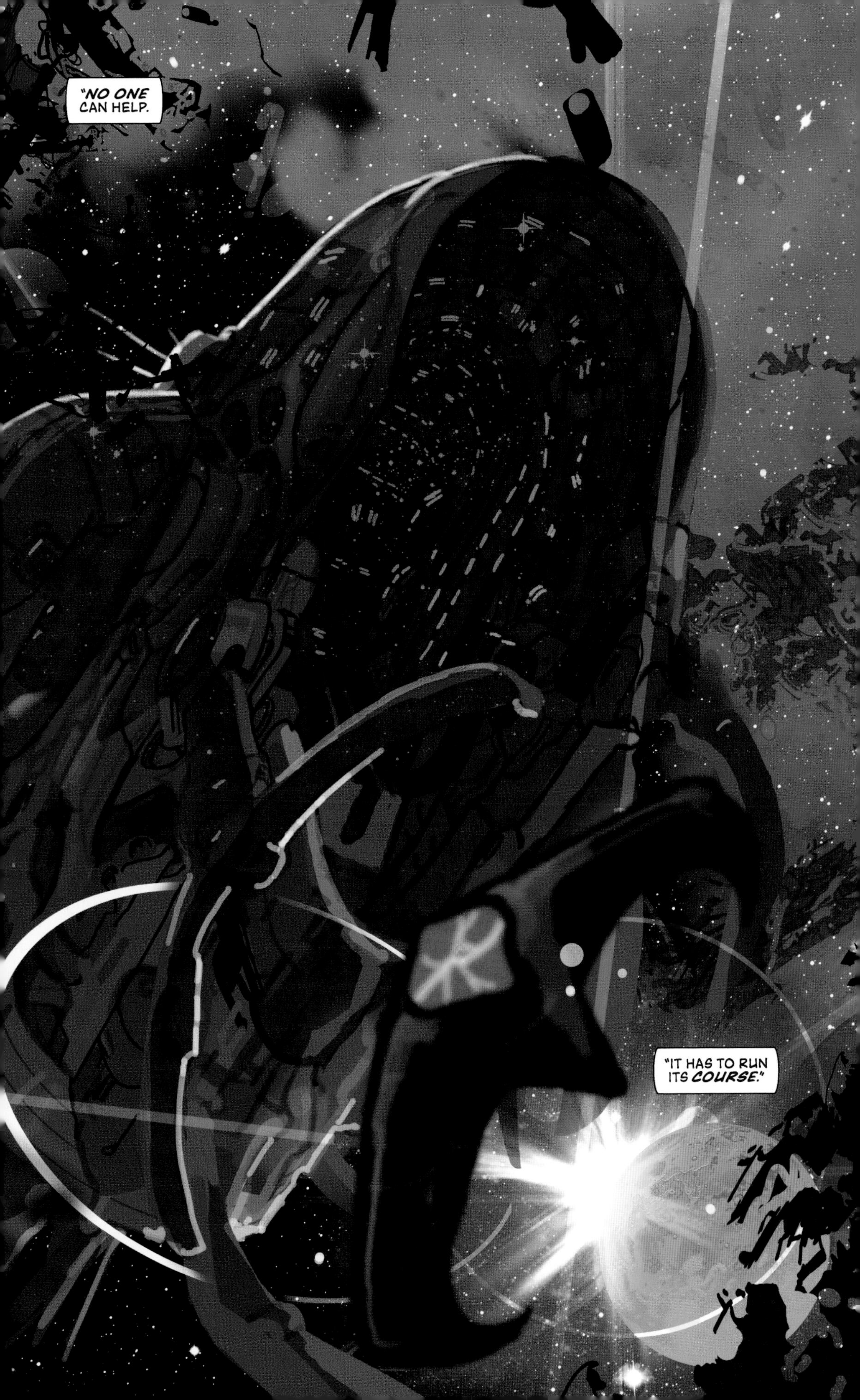
"NO ONE CAN HELP.
"IT HAS TO RUN ITS COURSE."

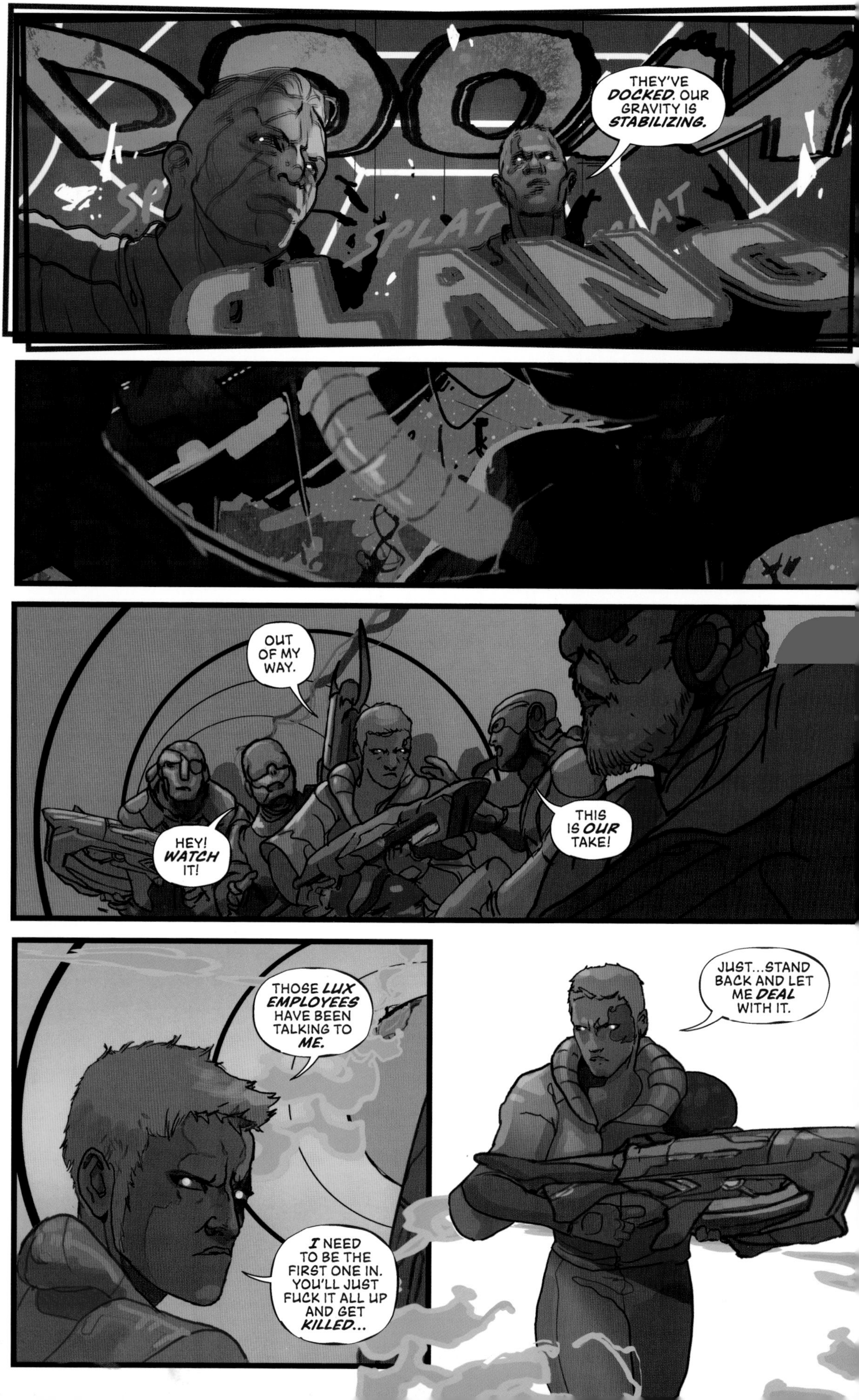
DOOM
THEY'VE DOCKED. OUR GRAVITY IS STABILIZING.
SPLAT
SPLAT
CLANG
OUT OF MY WAY.
HEY! WATCH IT!
THIS IS OUR TAKE!
THOSE LUX EMPLOYEES HAVE BEEN TALKING TO ME.
I NEED TO BE THE FIRST ONE IN. YOU'LL JUST FUCK IT ALL UP AND GET KILLED...
JUST...STAND BACK AND LET ME DEAL WITH IT.

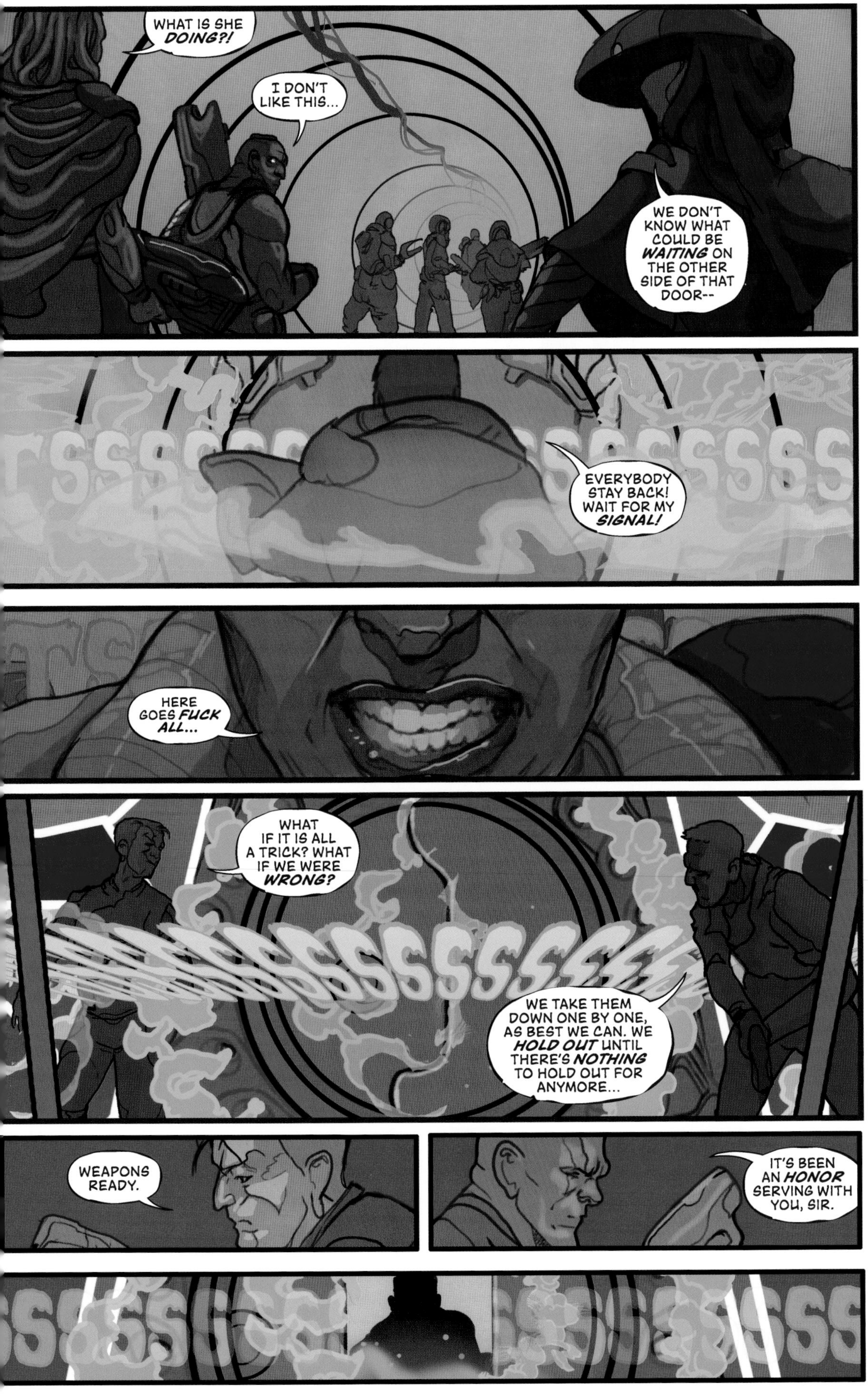
WHAT IS SHE DOING?!
I DON'T LIKE THIS...
WE DON'T KNOW WHAT COULD BE WAITING ON THE OTHER SIDE OF THAT DOOR--
TSSSSSSSSSSSSSS
EVERYBODY STAY BACK! WAIT FOR MY SIGNAL!
HERE GOES FUCK ALL...
WHAT IF IT IS ALL A TRICK? WHAT IF WE WERE WRONG?
WE TAKE THEM DOWN ONE BY ONE, AS BEST WE CAN. WE HOLD OUT UNTIL THERE'S NOTHING TO HOLD OUT FOR ANYMORE...
WEAPONS READY.
IT'S BEEN AN HONOR SERVING WITH YOU, SIR.

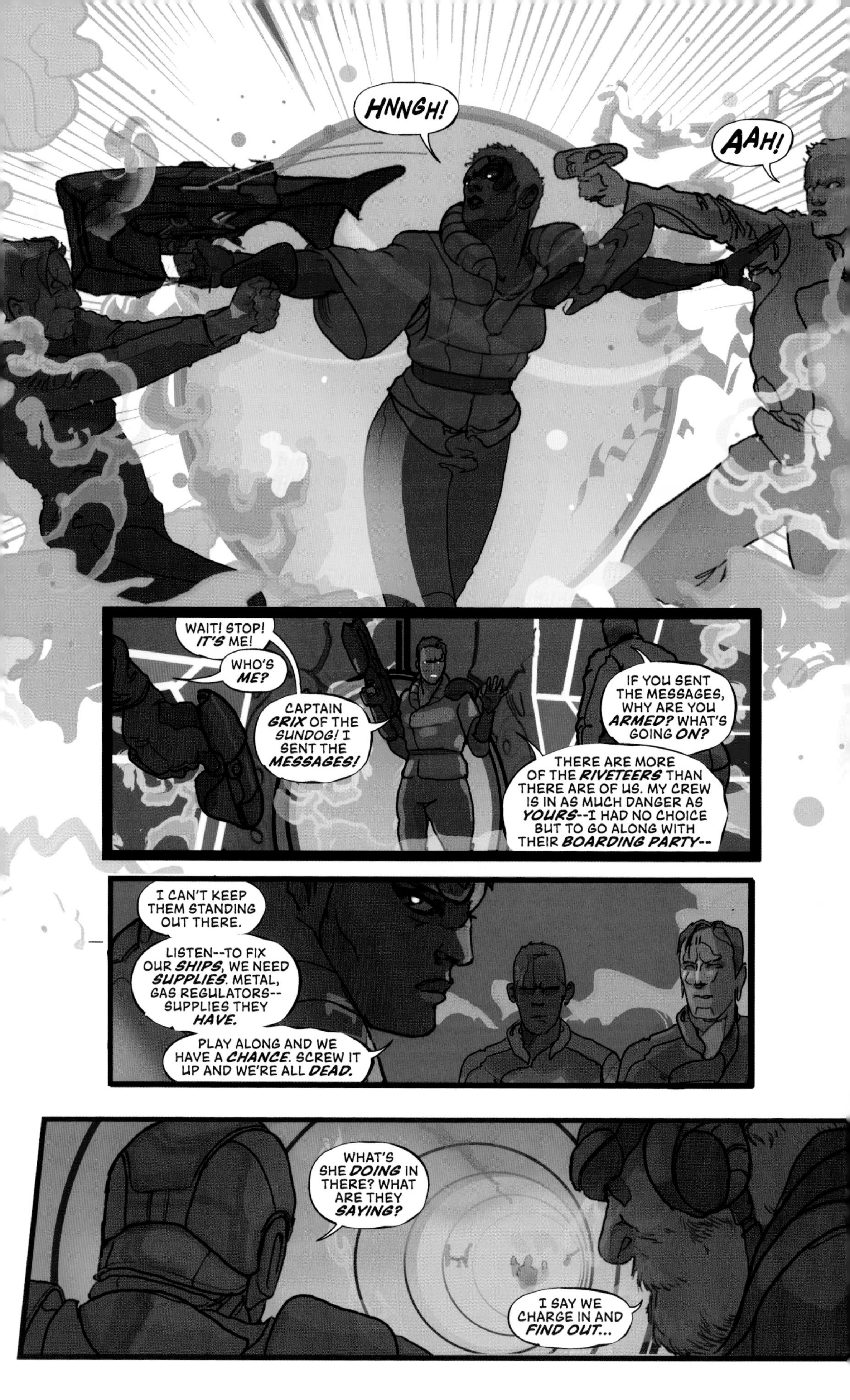
HNNGH!
AAH!
WAIT! STOP! IT'S ME!
WHO'S ME?
CAPTAIN GRIX OF THE SUNDOG! I SENT THE MESSAGES!
IF YOU SENT THE MESSAGES, WHY ARE YOU ARMED? WHAT'S GOING ON?
THERE ARE MORE OF THE RIVETEERS THAN THERE ARE OF US. MY CREW IS IN AS MUCH DANGER AS YOURS--I HAD NO CHOICE BUT TO GO ALONG WITH THEIR BOARDING PARTY--
I CAN'T KEEP THEM STANDING OUT THERE.
LISTEN--TO FIX OUR SHIPS, WE NEED SUPPLIES. METAL, GAS REGULATORS--SUPPLIES THEY HAVE.
PLAY ALONG AND WE HAVE A CHANCE. SCREW IT UP AND WE'RE ALL DEAD.
WHAT'S SHE DOING IN THERE? WHAT ARE THEY SAYING?
I SAY WE CHARGE IN AND FIND OUT...

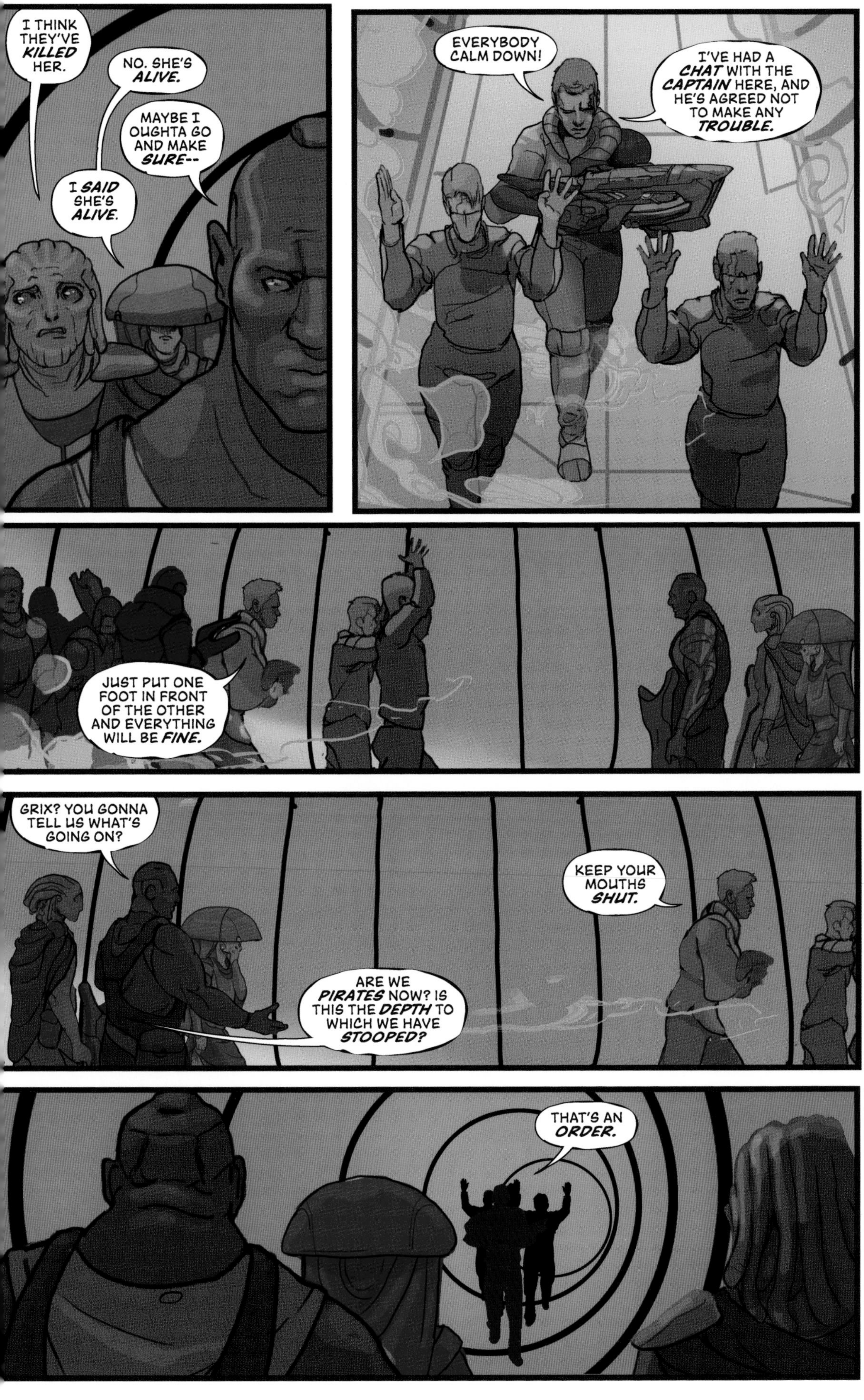
I THINK THEY'VE KILLED HER.
NO. SHE'S ALIVE.
MAYBE I OUGHTA GO AND MAKE SURE--
I SAID SHE'S ALIVE.
EVERYBODY CALM DOWN!
I'VE HAD A CHAT WITH THE CAPTAIN HERE, AND HE'S AGREED NOT TO MAKE ANY TROUBLE.
JUST PUT ONE FOOT IN FRONT OF THE OTHER AND EVERYTHING WILL BE FINE.
GRIX? YOU GONNA TELL US WHAT'S GOING ON?
KEEP YOUR MOUTHS SHUT.
ARE WE PIRATES NOW? IS THIS THE DEPTH TO WHICH WE HAVE STOOPED?
THAT'S AN ORDER.

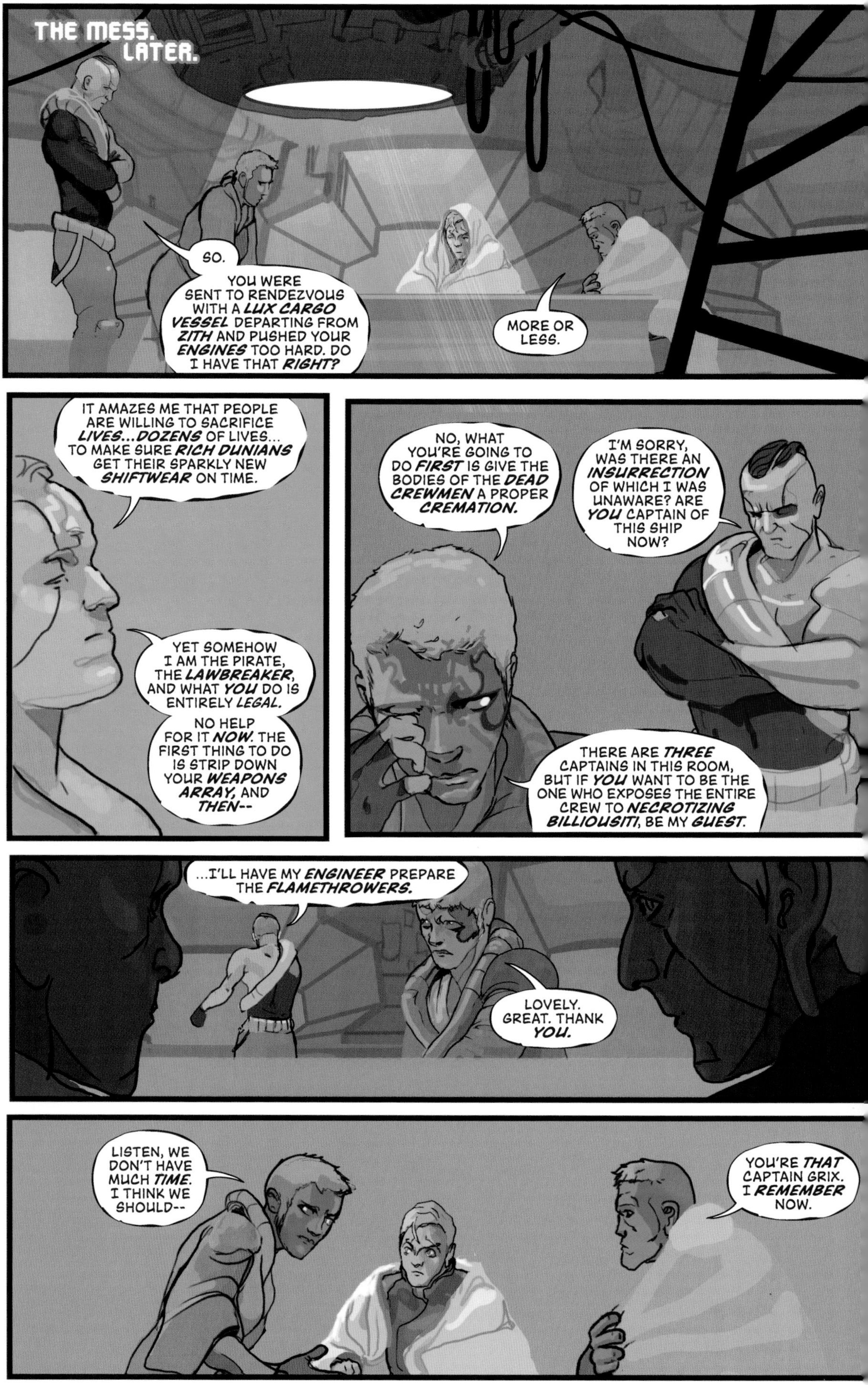
THE MESS. LATER.
SO.
YOU WERE SENT TO RENDEZVOUS WITH A LUX CARGO VESSEL DEPARTING FROM ZITH AND PUSHED YOUR ENGINES TOO HARD. DO I HAVE THAT RIGHT?
MORE OR LESS.
IT AMAZES ME THAT PEOPLE ARE WILLING TO SACRIFICE LIVES...DOZENS OF LIVES... TO MAKE SURE RICH DUNIANS GET THEIR SPARKLY NEW SHIFTWEAR ON TIME.
YET SOMEHOW I AM THE PIRATE, THE LAWBREAKER, AND WHAT YOU DO IS ENTIRELY LEGAL.
NO HELP FOR IT NOW. THE FIRST THING TO DO IS STRIP DOWN YOUR WEAPONS ARRAY, AND THEN--
NO, WHAT YOU'RE GOING TO DO FIRST IS GIVE THE BODIES OF THE DEAD CREWMEN A PROPER CREMATION.
I'M SORRY, WAS THERE AN INSURRECTION OF WHICH I WAS UNAWARE? ARE YOU CAPTAIN OF THIS SHIP NOW?
THERE ARE THREE CAPTAINS IN THIS ROOM, BUT IF YOU WANT TO BE THE ONE WHO EXPOSES THE ENTIRE CREW TO NECROTIZING BILLIOUSITI, BE MY GUEST.
...I'LL HAVE MY ENGINEER PREPARE THE FLAMETHROWERS.
LOVELY. GREAT. THANK YOU.
LISTEN, WE DON'T HAVE MUCH TIME. I THINK WE SHOULD--
YOU'RE THAT CAPTAIN GRIX. I REMEMBER NOW.

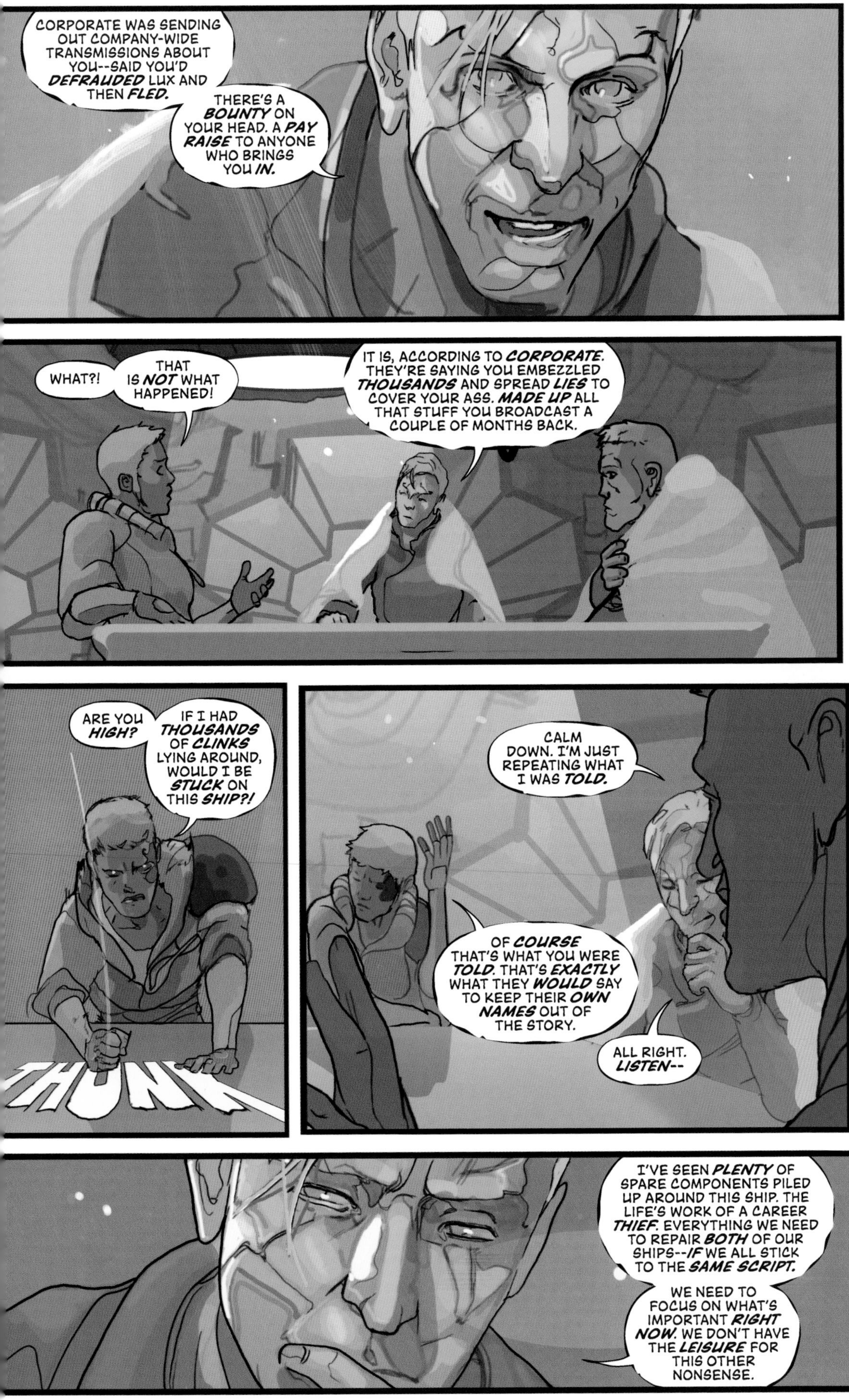

CORPORATE WAS SENDING OUT COMPANY-WIDE TRANSMISSIONS ABOUT YOU--SAID YOU'D DEFRAUDED LUX AND THEN FLED.
THERE'S A BOUNTY ON YOUR HEAD. A PAY RAISE TO ANYONE WHO BRINGS YOU IN.
WHAT?!
THAT IS NOT WHAT HAPPENED!
IT IS, ACCORDING TO CORPORATE. THEY'RE SAYING YOU EMBEZZLED THOUSANDS AND SPREAD LIES TO COVER YOUR ASS. MADE UP ALL THAT STUFF YOU BROADCAST A COUPLE OF MONTHS BACK.
ARE YOU HIGH?
IF I HAD THOUSANDS OF CLINKS LYING AROUND, WOULD I BE STUCK ON THIS SHIP?!
THUNK
CALM DOWN. I'M JUST REPEATING WHAT I WAS TOLD.
OF COURSE THAT'S WHAT YOU WERE TOLD. THAT'S EXACTLY WHAT THEY WOULD SAY TO KEEP THEIR OWN NAMES OUT OF THE STORY.
ALL RIGHT. LISTEN--
I'VE SEEN PLENTY OF SPARE COMPONENTS PILED UP AROUND THIS SHIP. THE LIFE'S WORK OF A CAREER THIEF. EVERYTHING WE NEED TO REPAIR BOTH OF OUR SHIPS--IF WE ALL STICK TO THE SAME SCRIPT.
WE NEED TO FOCUS ON WHAT'S IMPORTANT RIGHT NOW. WE DON'T HAVE THE LEISURE FOR THIS OTHER NONSENSE.

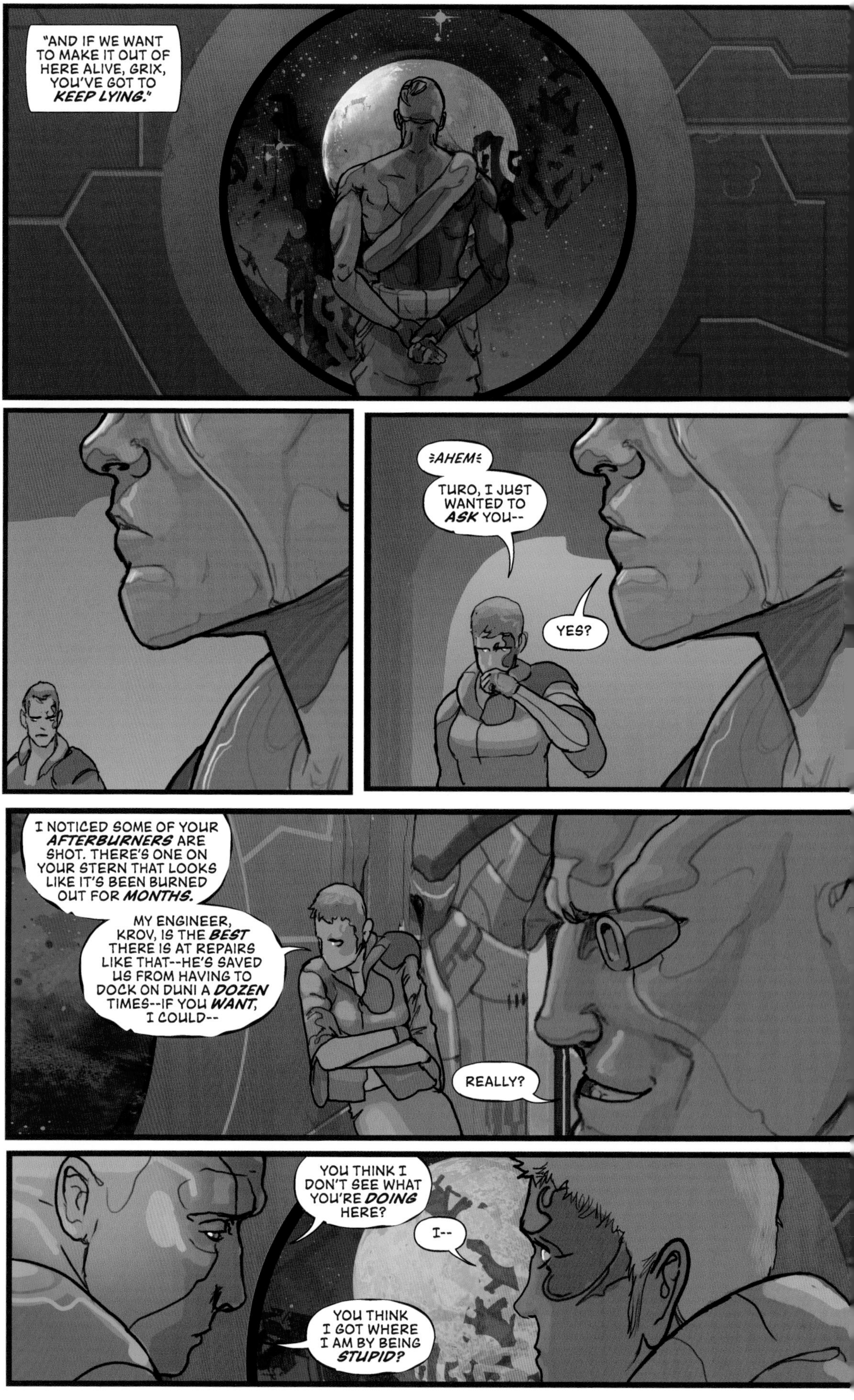
"AND IF WE WANT TO MAKE IT OUT OF HERE ALIVE, GRIX, YOU'VE GOT TO KEEP LYING."
AHEM
TURO, I JUST WANTED TO ASK YOU--
YES?
I NOTICED SOME OF YOUR AFTERBURNERS ARE SHOT. THERE'S ONE ON YOUR STERN THAT LOOKS LIKE IT'S BEEN BURNED OUT FOR MONTHS.
MY ENGINEER, KROV, IS THE BEST THERE IS AT REPAIRS LIKE THAT--HE'S SAVED US FROM HAVING TO DOCK ON DUNI A DOZEN TIMES--IF YOU WANT, I COULD--
REALLY?
YOU THINK I DON'T SEE WHAT YOU'RE DOING HERE?
I--
YOU THINK I GOT WHERE I AM BY BEING STUPID?

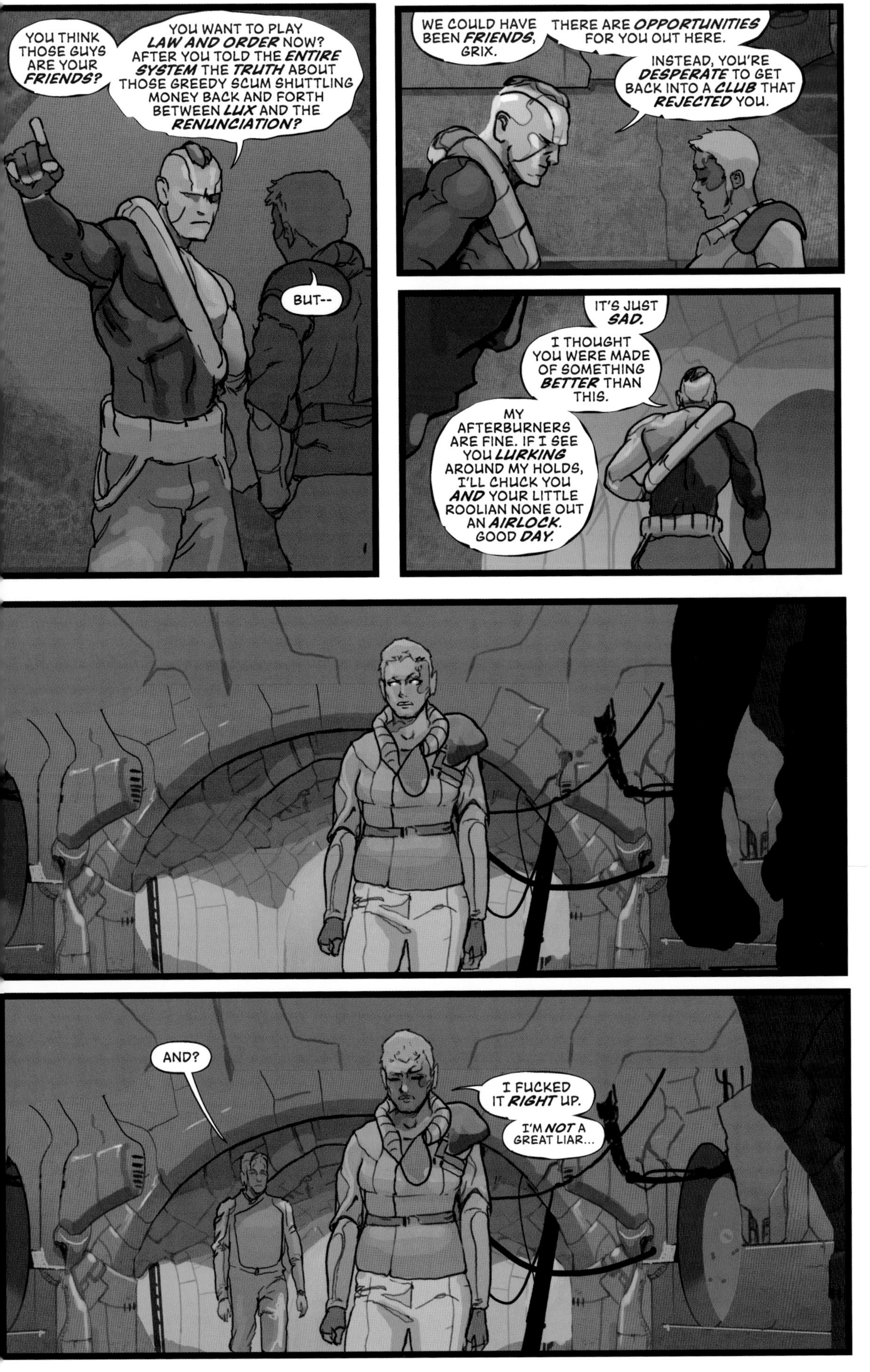

YOU THINK THOSE GUYS ARE YOUR FRIENDS?
YOU WANT TO PLAY LAW AND ORDER NOW? AFTER YOU TOLD THE ENTIRE SYSTEM THE TRUTH ABOUT THOSE GREEDY SCUM SHUTTLING MONEY BACK AND FORTH BETWEEN LUX AND THE RENUNCIATION?
BUT--
WE COULD HAVE BEEN FRIENDS, GRIX.
THERE ARE OPPORTUNITIES FOR YOU OUT HERE.
INSTEAD, YOU'RE DESPERATE TO GET BACK INTO A CLUB THAT REJECTED YOU.
IT'S JUST SAD.
I THOUGHT YOU WERE MADE OF SOMETHING BETTER THAN THIS.
MY AFTERBURNERS ARE FINE. IF I SEE YOU LURKING AROUND MY HOLDS, I'LL CHUCK YOU AND YOUR LITTLE ROOLIAN NONE OUT AN AIRLOCK. GOOD DAY.
AND?
I FUCKED IT RIGHT UP.
I'M NOT A GREAT LIAR...

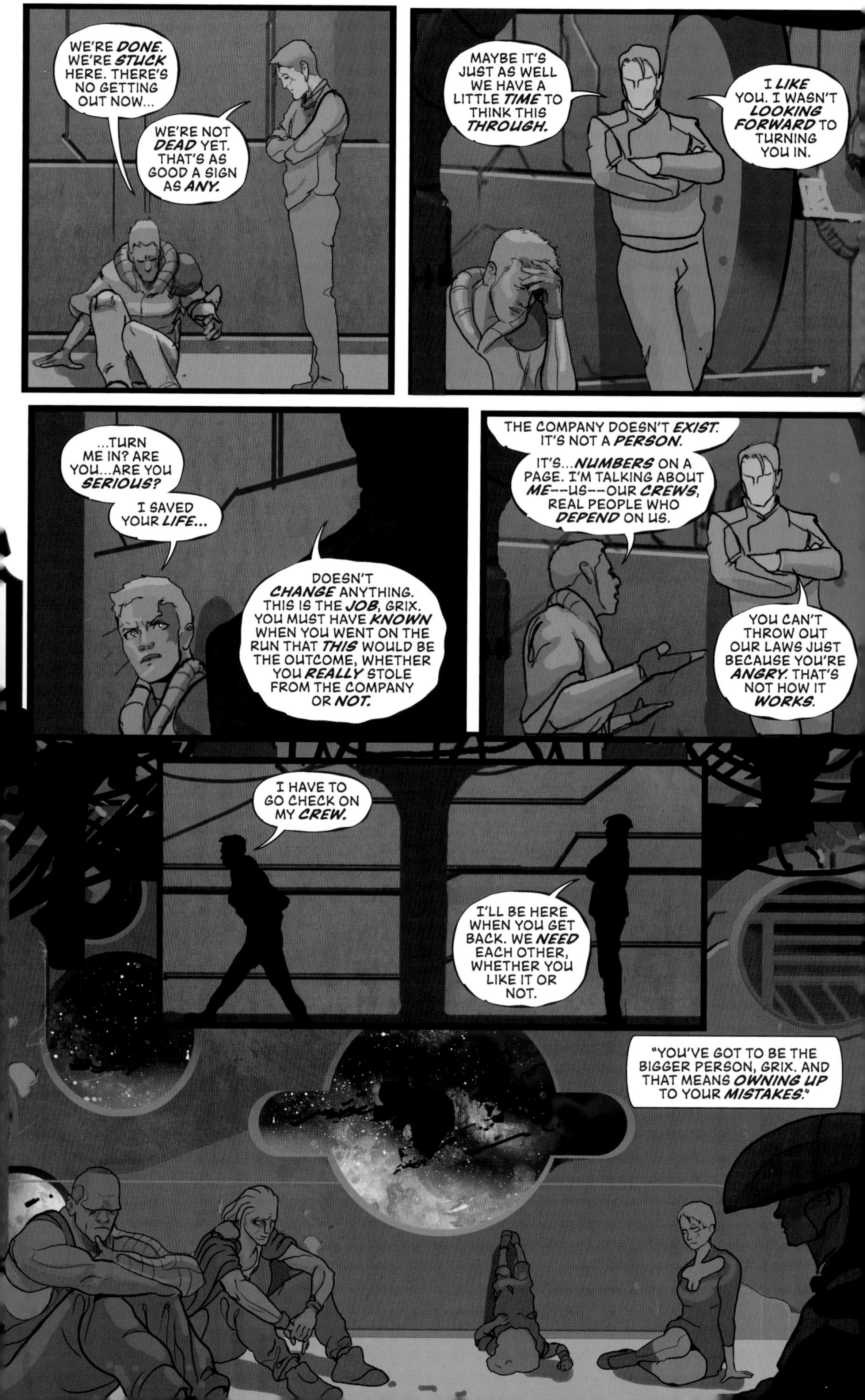
WE'RE DONE. WE'RE STUCK HERE. THERE'S NO GETTING OUT NOW...
WE'RE NOT DEAD YET. THAT'S AS GOOD A SIGN AS ANY.
MAYBE IT'S JUST AS WELL WE HAVE A LITTLE TIME TO THINK THIS THROUGH.
I LIKE YOU. I WASN'T LOOKING FORWARD TO TURNING YOU IN.
...TURN ME IN? ARE YOU...ARE YOU SERIOUS?
I SAVED YOUR LIFE...
DOESN'T CHANGE ANYTHING. THIS IS THE JOB, GRIX. YOU MUST HAVE KNOWN WHEN YOU WENT ON THE RUN THAT THIS WOULD BE THE OUTCOME, WHETHER YOU REALLY STOLE FROM THE COMPANY OR NOT.
THE COMPANY DOESN'T EXIST. IT'S NOT A PERSON.
IT'S...NUMBERS ON A PAGE. I'M TALKING ABOUT ME--US--OUR CREWS, REAL PEOPLE WHO DEPEND ON US.
YOU CAN'T THROW OUT OUR LAWS JUST BECAUSE YOU'RE ANGRY. THAT'S NOT HOW IT WORKS.
I HAVE TO GO CHECK ON MY CREW.
I'LL BE HERE WHEN YOU GET BACK. WE NEED EACH OTHER, WHETHER YOU LIKE IT OR NOT.
"YOU'VE GOT TO BE THE BIGGER PERSON, GRIX. AND THAT MEANS OWNING UP TO YOUR MISTAKES."

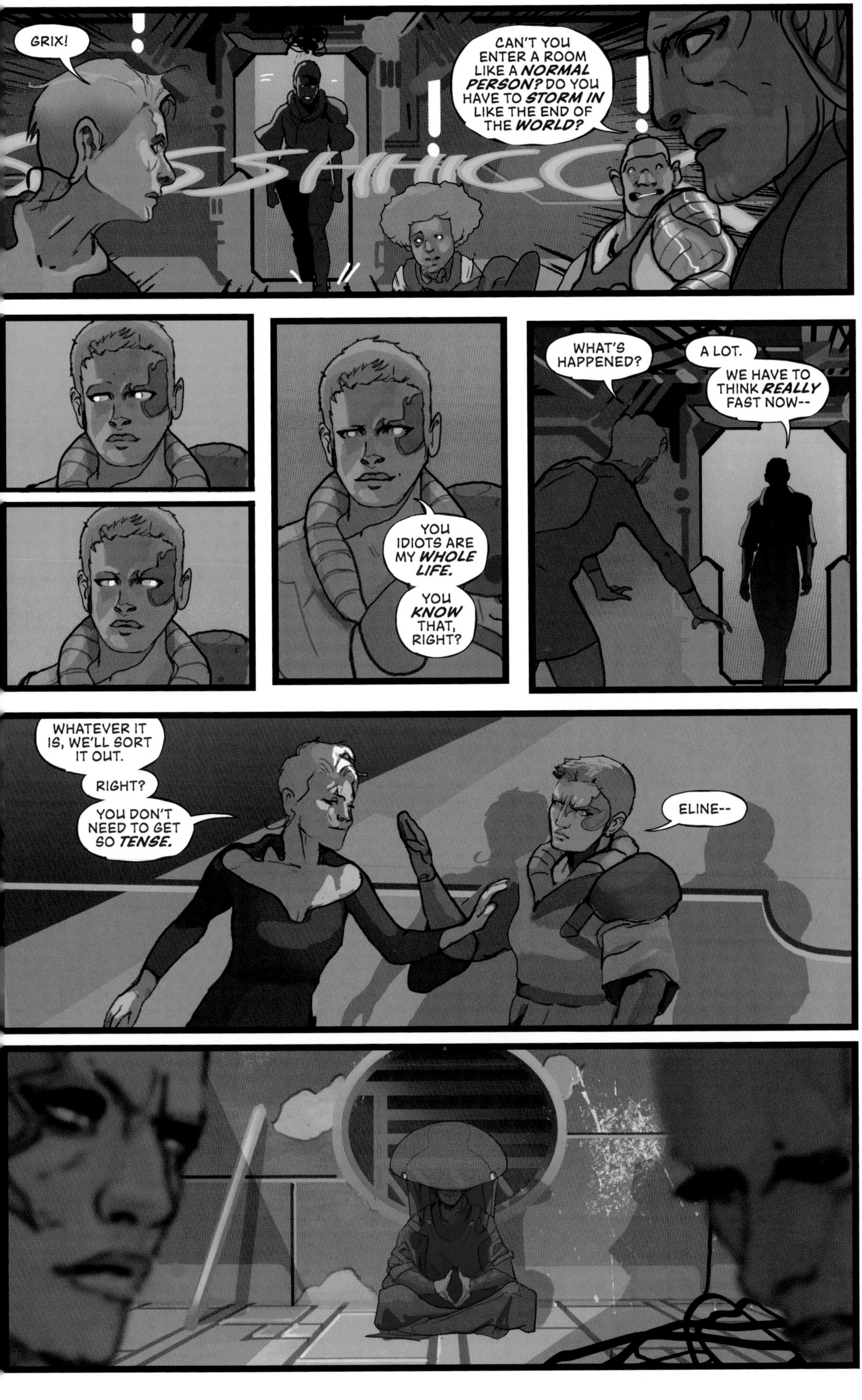
GRIX!
SSHHKK
CAN'T YOU ENTER A ROOM LIKE A NORMAL PERSON? DO YOU HAVE TO STORM IN LIKE THE END OF THE WORLD?
YOU IDIOTS ARE MY WHOLE LIFE.
YOU KNOW THAT, RIGHT?
WHAT'S HAPPENED?
A LOT.
WE HAVE TO THINK REALLY FAST NOW--
WHATEVER IT IS, WE'LL SORT IT OUT.
RIGHT?
YOU DON'T NEED TO GET SO TENSE.
ELINE--

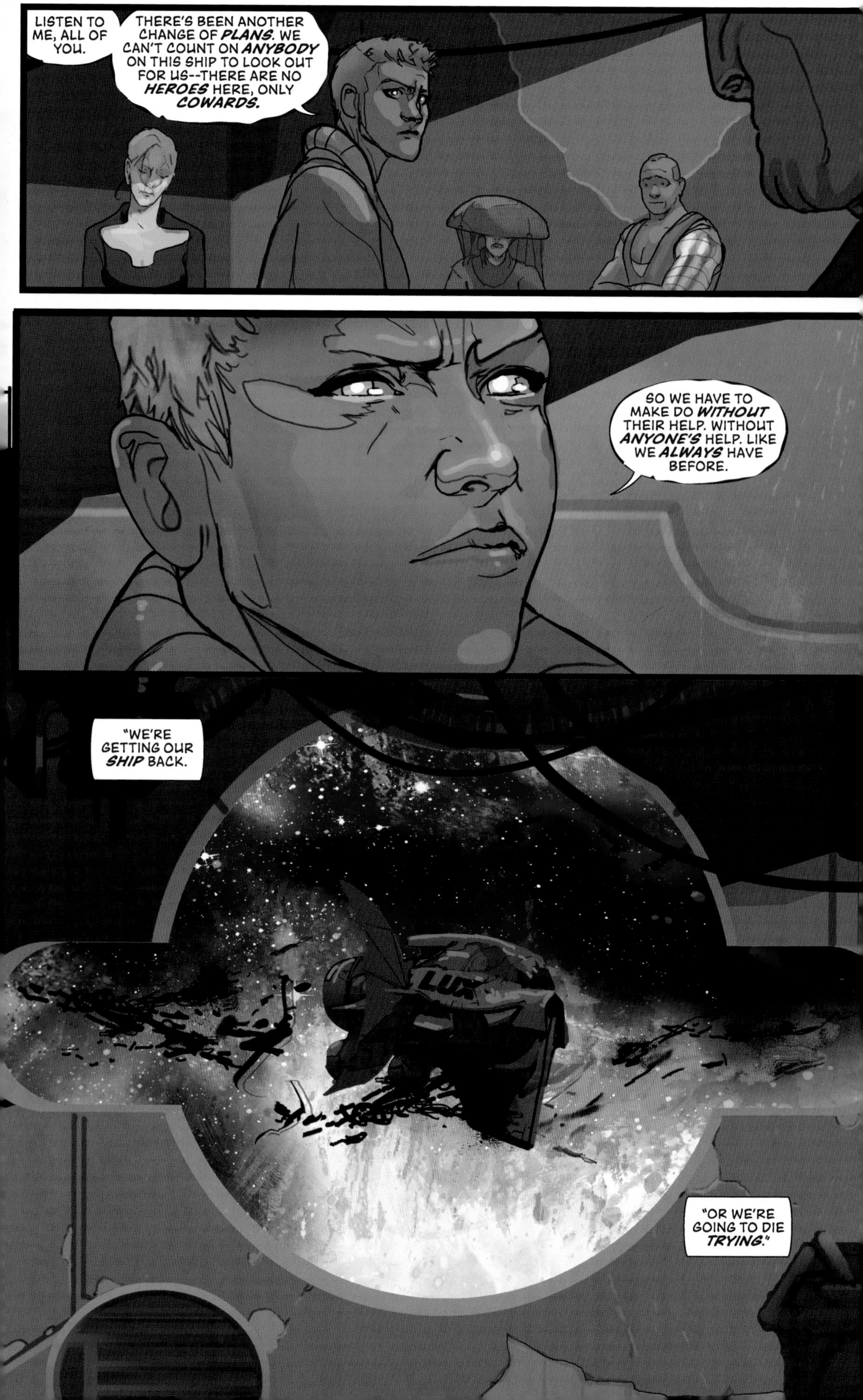
LISTEN TO ME, ALL OF YOU.
THERE'S BEEN ANOTHER CHANGE OF PLANS. WE CAN'T COUNT ON ANYBODY ON THIS SHIP TO LOOK OUT FOR US--THERE ARE NO HEROES HERE, ONLY COWARDS.
SO WE HAVE TO MAKE DO WITHOUT THEIR HELP. WITHOUT ANYONE'S HELP. LIKE WE ALWAYS HAVE BEFORE.
"WE'RE GETTING OUR SHIP BACK.
LUX
"OR WE'RE GOING TO DIE TRYING."

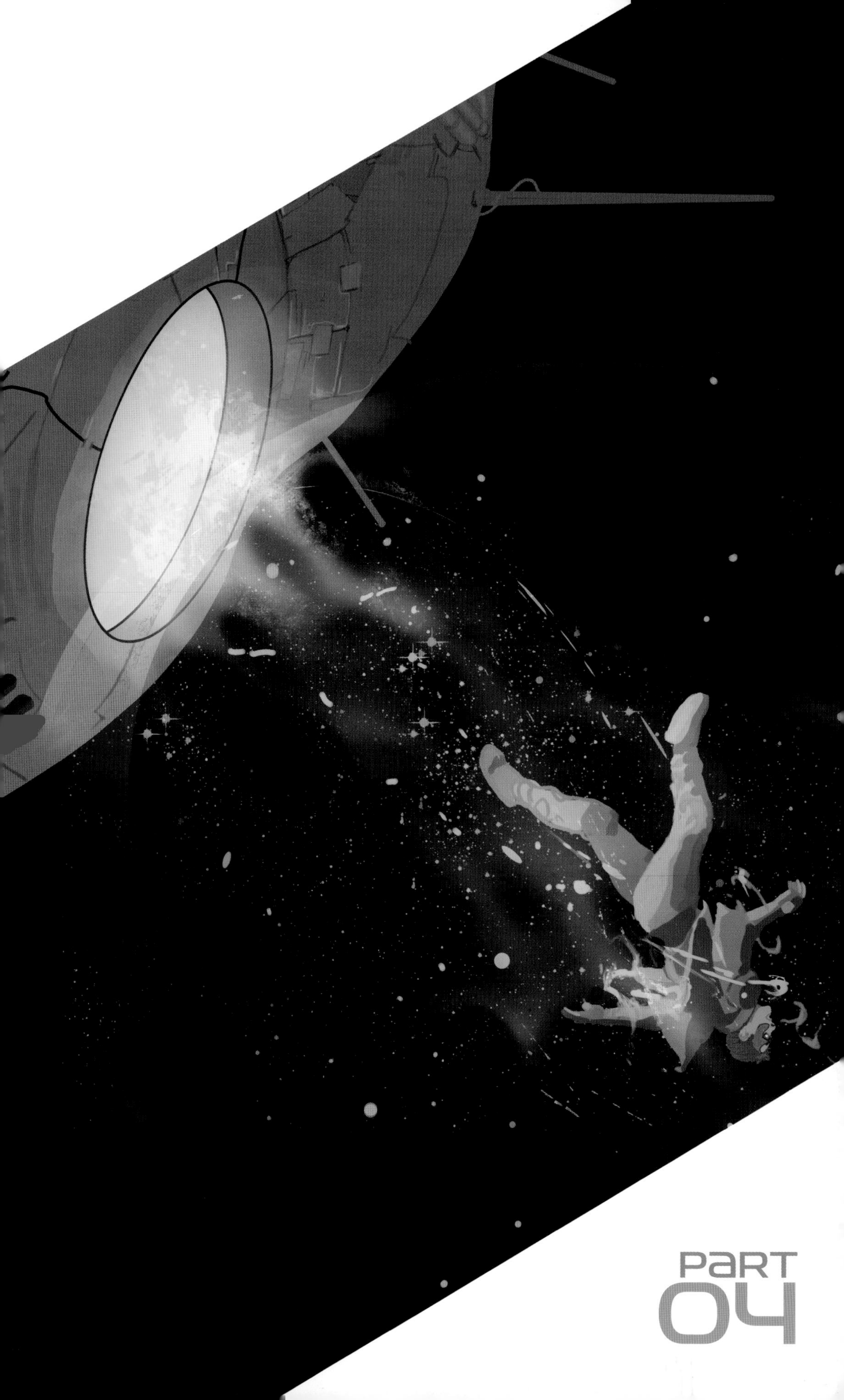

PART 04

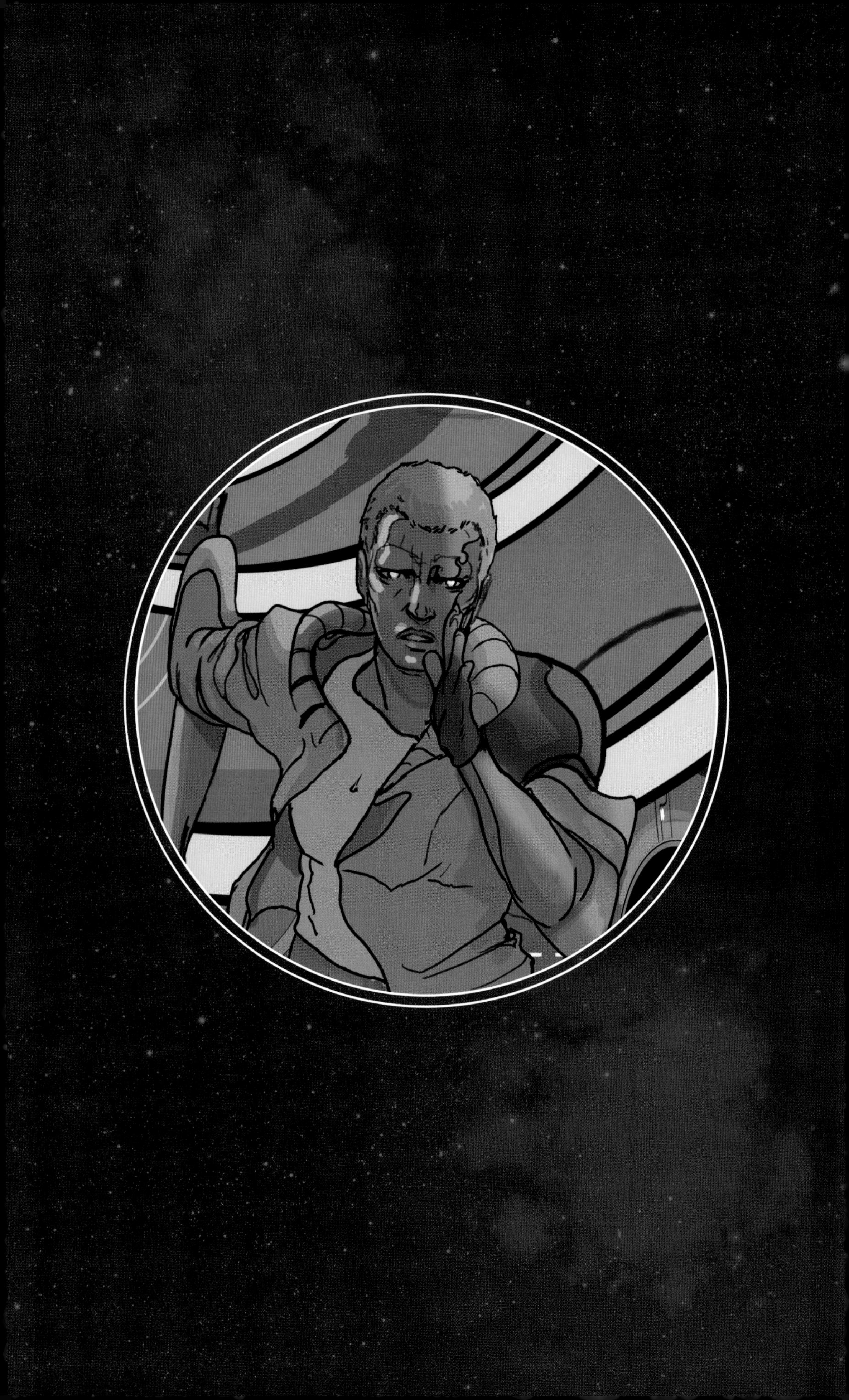

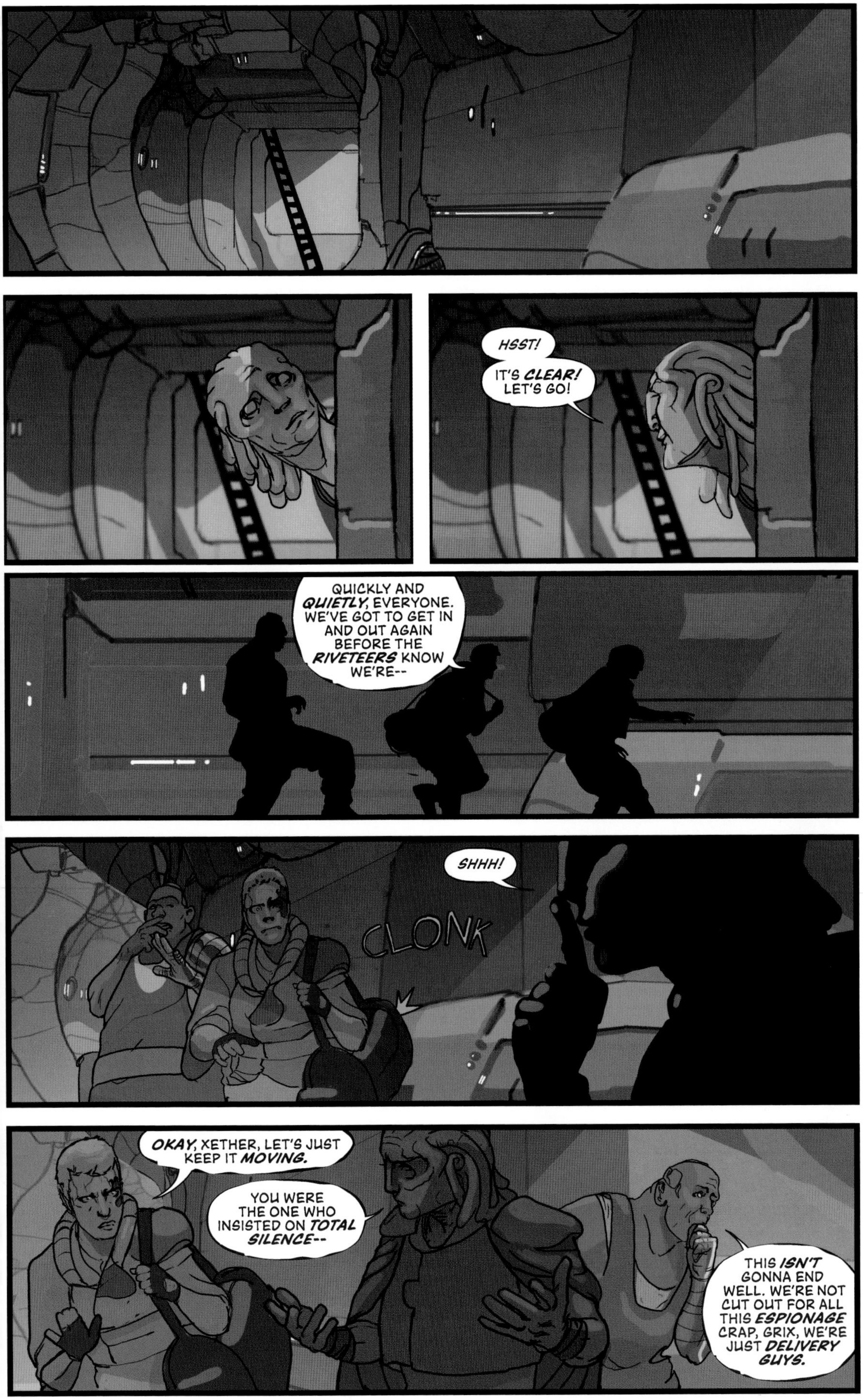
HSST!
IT'S CLEAR! LET'S GO!
QUICKLY AND QUIETLY, EVERYONE. WE'VE GOT TO GET IN AND OUT AGAIN BEFORE THE RIVETEERS KNOW WE'RE--
SHHH!
CLONK
OKAY, XETHER, LET'S JUST KEEP IT MOVING.
YOU WERE THE ONE WHO INSISTED ON TOTAL SILENCE--
THIS ISN'T GONNA END WELL. WE'RE NOT CUT OUT FOR ALL THIS ESPIONAGE CRAP, GRIX, WE'RE JUST DELIVERY GUYS.

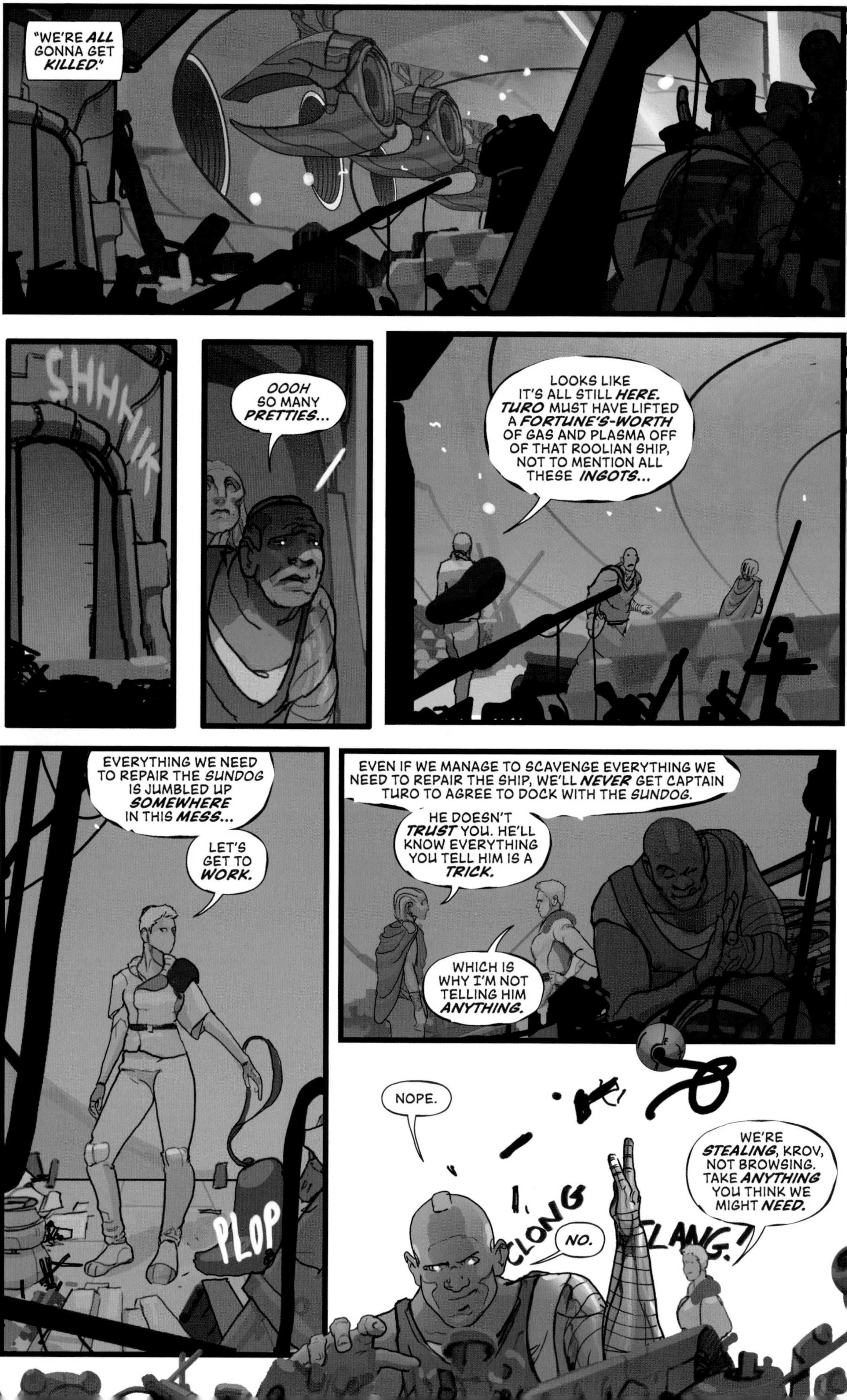
"WE'RE ALL GONNA GET KILLED."
SHHHIK
OOOH SO MANY PRETTIES...
LOOKS LIKE IT'S ALL STILL HERE. TURO MUST HAVE LIFTED A FORTUNE'S-WORTH OF GAS AND PLASMA OFF OF THAT ROOLIAN SHIP, NOT TO MENTION ALL THESE INGOTS...
EVERYTHING WE NEED TO REPAIR THE SUNDOG IS JUMBLED UP SOMEWHERE IN THIS MESS...
LET'S GET TO WORK.
PLOP
EVEN IF WE MANAGE TO SCAVENGE EVERYTHING WE NEED TO REPAIR THE SHIP, WE'LL NEVER GET CAPTAIN TURO TO AGREE TO DOCK WITH THE SUNDOG.
HE DOESN'T TRUST YOU. HE'LL KNOW EVERYTHING YOU TELL HIM IS A TRICK.
WHICH IS WHY I'M NOT TELLING HIM ANYTHING.
NOPE.
WE'RE STEALING, KROV, NOT BROWSING. TAKE ANYTHING YOU THINK WE MIGHT NEED.
CLONG
NO.
CLANG!

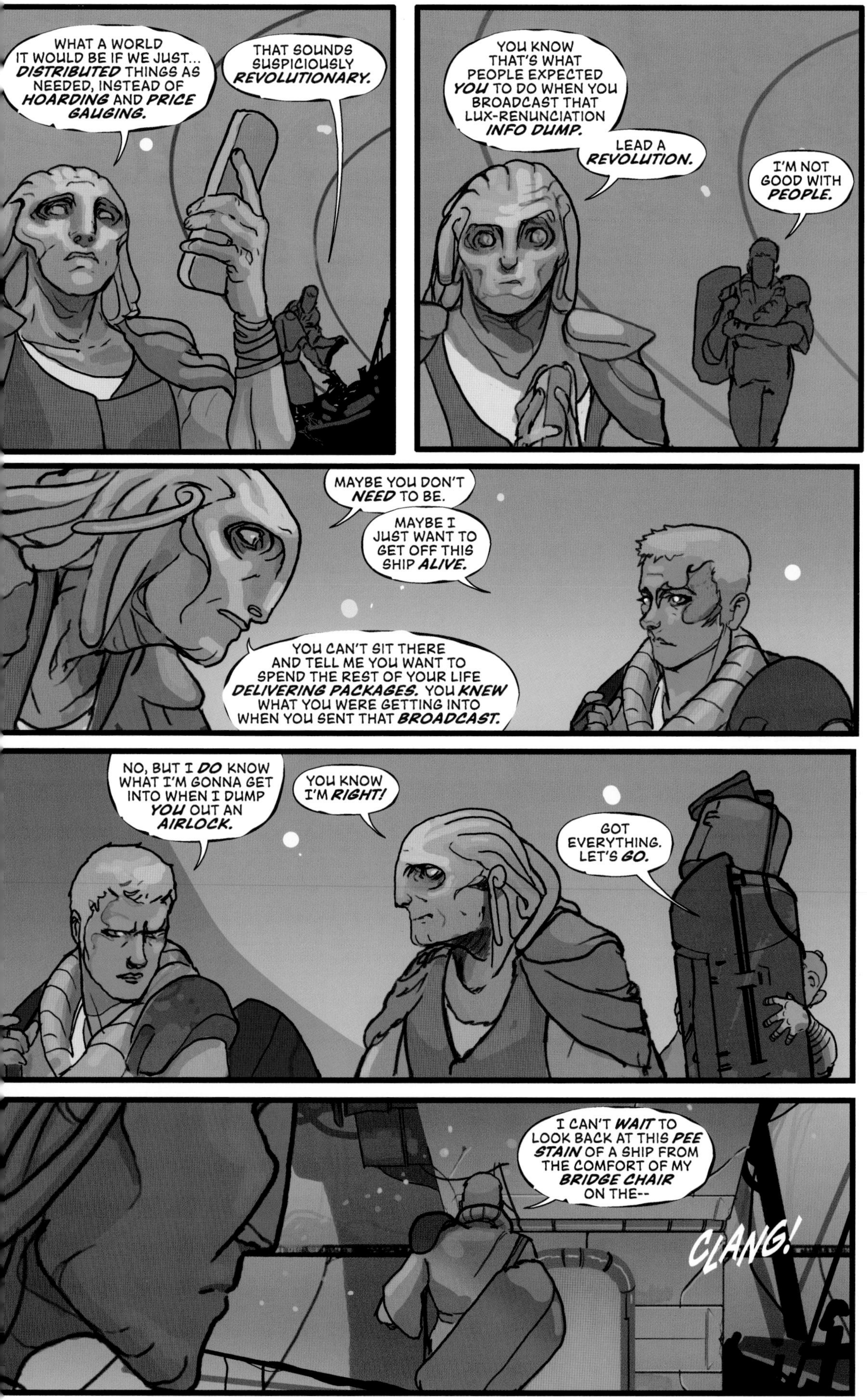
WHAT A WORLD IT WOULD BE IF WE JUST... DISTRIBUTED THINGS AS NEEDED, INSTEAD OF HOARDING AND PRICE GAUGING.
THAT SOUNDS SUSPICIOUSLY REVOLUTIONARY.
YOU KNOW THAT'S WHAT PEOPLE EXPECTED YOU TO DO WHEN YOU BROADCAST THAT LUX-RENUNCIATION INFO DUMP.
LEAD A REVOLUTION.
I'M NOT GOOD WITH PEOPLE.
MAYBE YOU DON'T NEED TO BE.
MAYBE I JUST WANT TO GET OFF THIS SHIP ALIVE.
YOU CAN'T SIT THERE AND TELL ME YOU WANT TO SPEND THE REST OF YOUR LIFE DELIVERING PACKAGES. YOU KNEW WHAT YOU WERE GETTING INTO WHEN YOU SENT THAT BROADCAST.
NO, BUT I DO KNOW WHAT I'M GONNA GET INTO WHEN I DUMP YOU OUT AN AIRLOCK.
YOU KNOW I'M RIGHT!
GOT EVERYTHING. LET'S GO.
I CAN'T WAIT TO LOOK BACK AT THIS PEE STAIN OF A SHIP FROM THE COMFORT OF MY BRIDGE CHAIR ON THE--
CLANG!

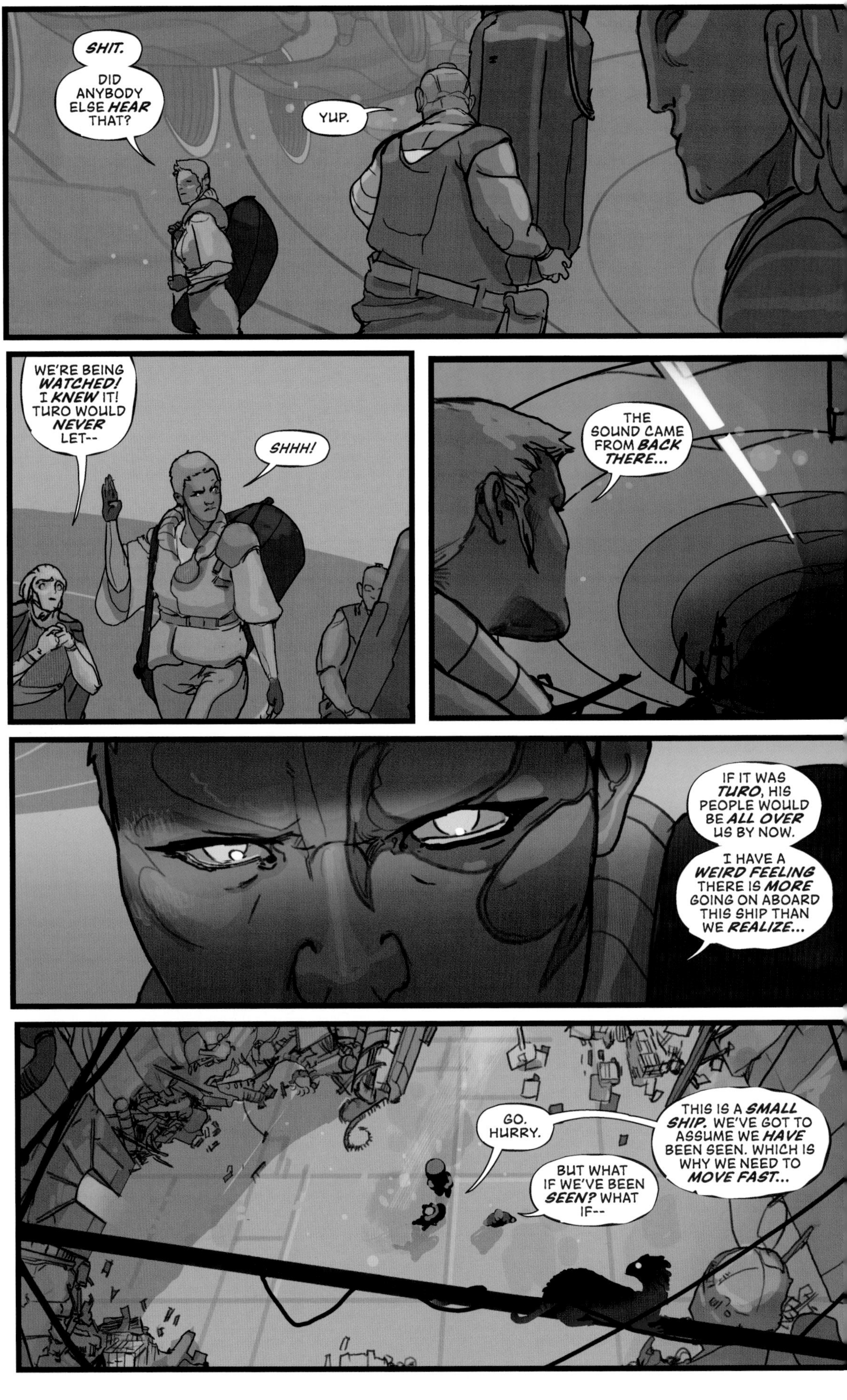

SHIT.
DID ANYBODY ELSE HEAR THAT?
YUP.
WE'RE BEING WATCHED! I KNEW IT! TURO WOULD NEVER LET--
SHHH!
THE SOUND CAME FROM BACK THERE...
IF IT WAS TURO, HIS PEOPLE WOULD BE ALL OVER US BY NOW.
I HAVE A WEIRD FEELING THERE IS MORE GOING ON ABOARD THIS SHIP THAN WE REALIZE...
GO. HURRY.
BUT WHAT IF WE'VE BEEN SEEN? WHAT IF--
THIS IS A SMALL SHIP. WE'VE GOT TO ASSUME WE HAVE BEEN SEEN. WHICH IS WHY WE NEED TO MOVE FAST...

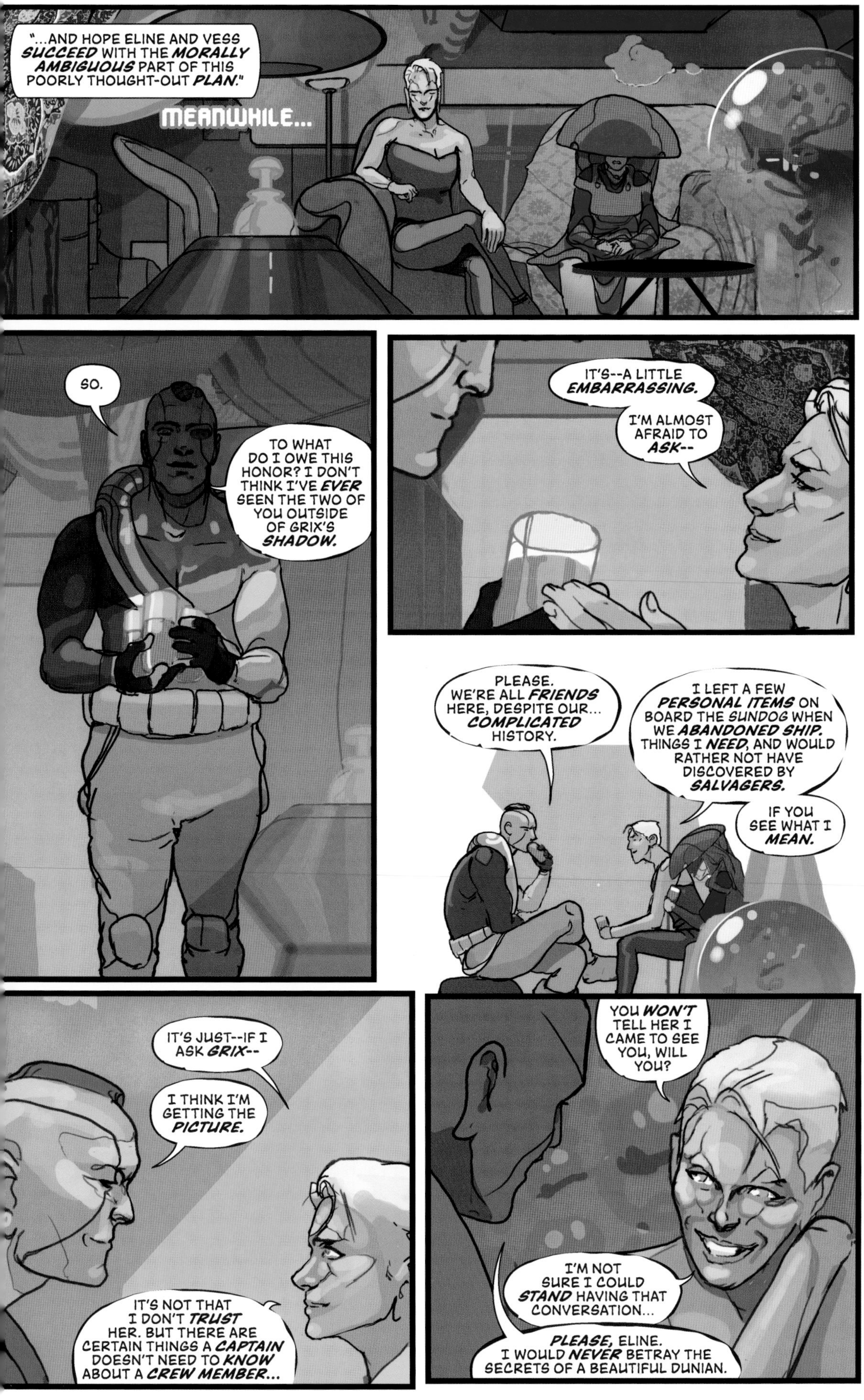
"...AND HOPE ELINE AND VESS SUCCEED WITH THE MORALLY AMBIGUOUS PART OF THIS POORLY THOUGHT-OUT PLAN."
MEANWHILE...
SO.
TO WHAT DO I OWE THIS HONOR? I DON'T THINK I'VE EVER SEEN THE TWO OF YOU OUTSIDE OF GRIX'S SHADOW.
IT'S--A LITTLE EMBARRASSING.
I'M ALMOST AFRAID TO ASK--
PLEASE. WE'RE ALL FRIENDS HERE, DESPITE OUR... COMPLICATED HISTORY.
I LEFT A FEW PERSONAL ITEMS ON BOARD THE SUNDOG WHEN WE ABANDONED SHIP. THINGS I NEED, AND WOULD RATHER NOT HAVE DISCOVERED BY SALVAGERS.
IF YOU SEE WHAT I MEAN.
IT'S JUST--IF I ASK GRIX--
I THINK I'M GETTING THE PICTURE.
IT'S NOT THAT I DON'T TRUST HER. BUT THERE ARE CERTAIN THINGS A CAPTAIN DOESN'T NEED TO KNOW ABOUT A CREW MEMBER...
YOU WON'T TELL HER I CAME TO SEE YOU, WILL YOU?
I'M NOT SURE I COULD STAND HAVING THAT CONVERSATION...
PLEASE, ELINE. I WOULD NEVER BETRAY THE SECRETS OF A BEAUTIFUL DUNIAN.

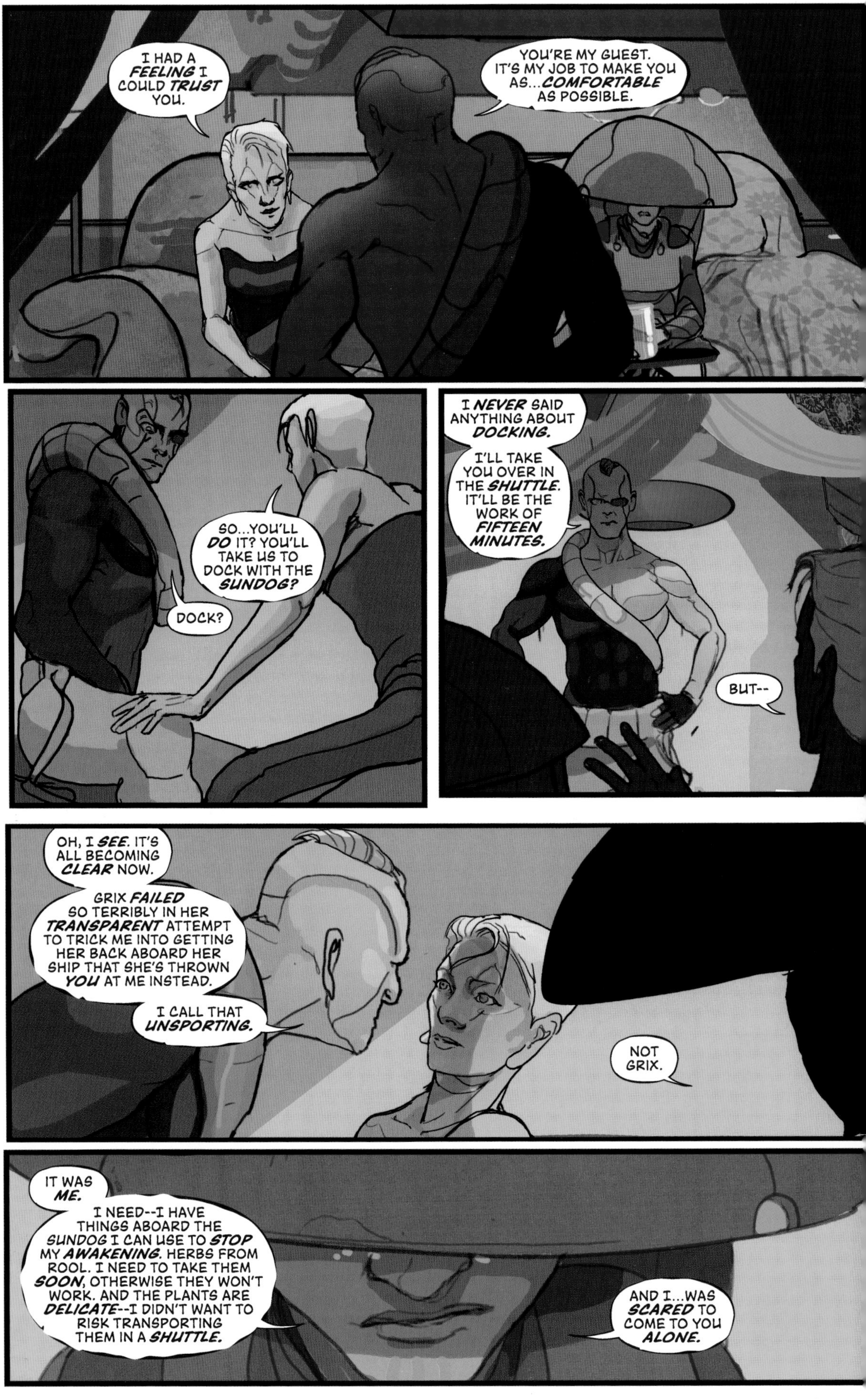

I HAD A FEELING I COULD TRUST YOU.
YOU'RE MY GUEST. IT'S MY JOB TO MAKE YOU AS...COMFORTABLE AS POSSIBLE.
SO...YOU'LL DO IT? YOU'LL TAKE US TO DOCK WITH THE SUNDOG?
DOCK?
I NEVER SAID ANYTHING ABOUT DOCKING.
I'LL TAKE YOU OVER IN THE SHUTTLE. IT'LL BE THE WORK OF FIFTEEN MINUTES.
BUT--
OH, I SEE. IT'S ALL BECOMING CLEAR NOW.
GRIX FAILED SO TERRIBLY IN HER TRANSPARENT ATTEMPT TO TRICK ME INTO GETTING HER BACK ABOARD HER SHIP THAT SHE'S THROWN YOU AT ME INSTEAD.
I CALL THAT UNSPORTING.
NOT GRIX.
IT WAS ME.
I NEED--I HAVE THINGS ABOARD THE SUNDOG I CAN USE TO STOP MY AWAKENING. HERBS FROM ROOL. I NEED TO TAKE THEM SOON, OTHERWISE THEY WON'T WORK. AND THE PLANTS ARE DELICATE--I DIDN'T WANT TO RISK TRANSPORTING THEM IN A SHUTTLE.
AND I...WAS SCARED TO COME TO YOU ALONE.

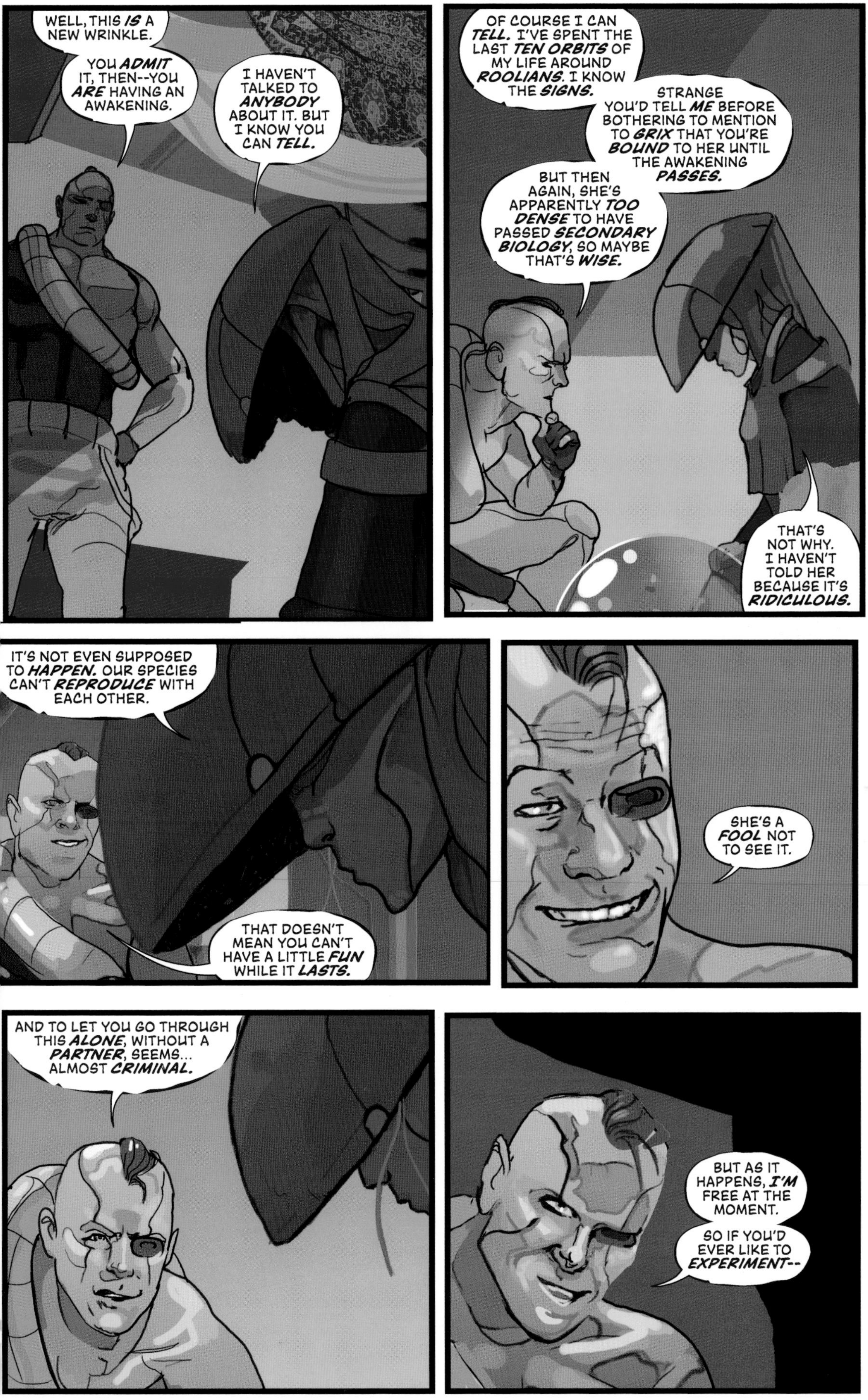
WELL, THIS *IS* A NEW WRINKLE.
YOU *ADMIT* IT, THEN--YOU *ARE* HAVING AN AWAKENING.
I HAVEN'T TALKED TO *ANYBODY* ABOUT IT. BUT I KNOW YOU CAN *TELL*.
OF COURSE I CAN *TELL*. I'VE SPENT THE LAST *TEN ORBITS* OF MY LIFE AROUND *ROOLIANS*. I KNOW THE *SIGNS*.
STRANGE YOU'D TELL *ME* BEFORE BOTHERING TO MENTION TO *GRIX* THAT YOU'RE *BOUND* TO HER UNTIL THE AWAKENING *PASSES*.
BUT THEN AGAIN, SHE'S APPARENTLY *TOO DENSE* TO HAVE PASSED *SECONDARY BIOLOGY*, SO MAYBE THAT'S *WISE*.
THAT'S NOT WHY. I HAVEN'T TOLD HER BECAUSE IT'S *RIDICULOUS*.
IT'S NOT EVEN SUPPOSED TO *HAPPEN*. OUR SPECIES CAN'T *REPRODUCE* WITH EACH OTHER.
THAT DOESN'T MEAN YOU CAN'T HAVE A LITTLE *FUN* WHILE IT *LASTS*.
SHE'S A *FOOL* NOT TO SEE IT.
AND TO LET YOU GO THROUGH THIS *ALONE*, WITHOUT A *PARTNER*, SEEMS... ALMOST *CRIMINAL*.
BUT AS IT HAPPENS, *I'M* FREE AT THE MOMENT.
SO IF YOU'D EVER LIKE TO *EXPERIMENT*--

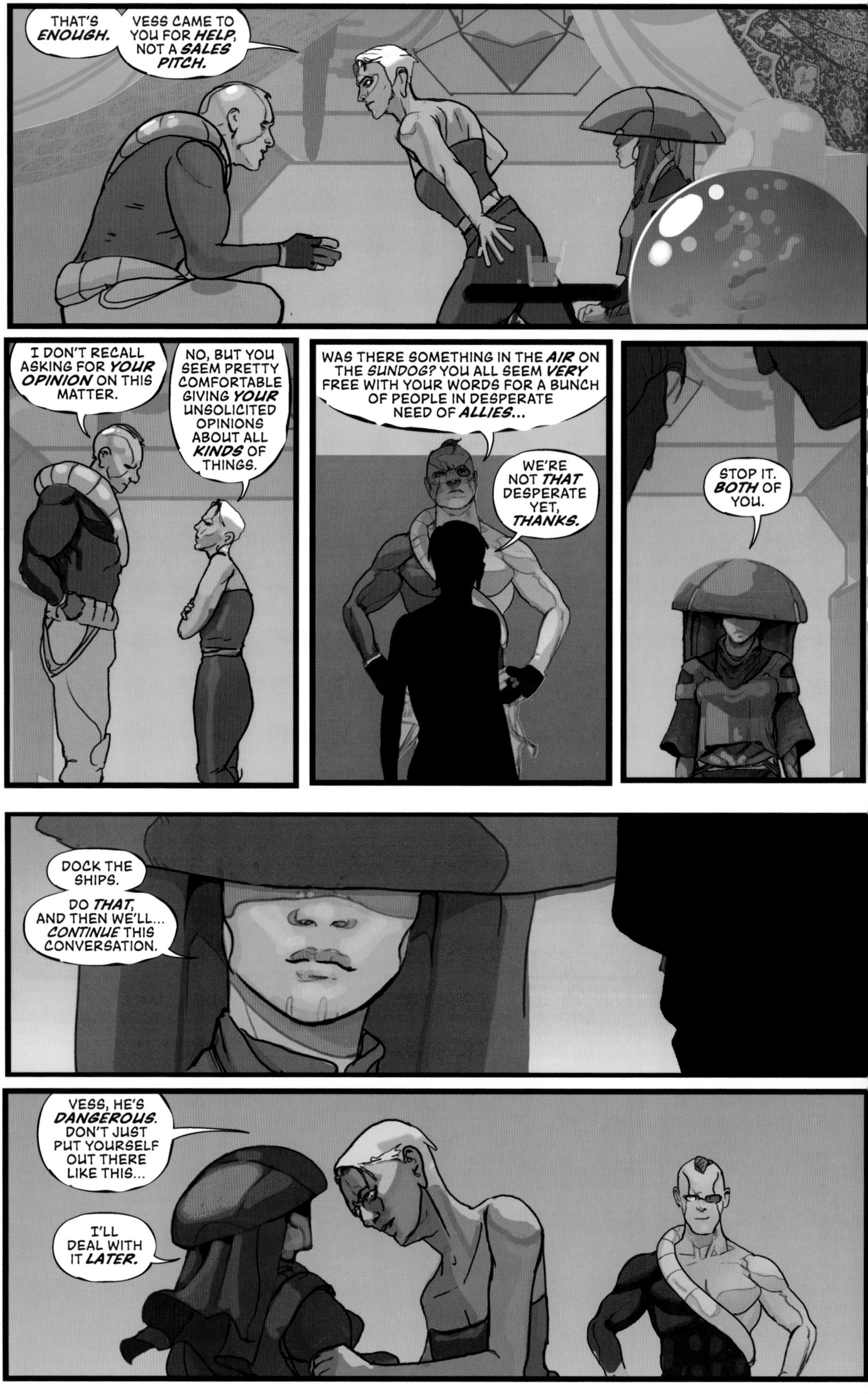

THAT'S ENOUGH.
VESS CAME TO YOU FOR HELP, NOT A SALES PITCH.
I DON'T RECALL ASKING FOR YOUR OPINION ON THIS MATTER.
NO, BUT YOU SEEM PRETTY COMFORTABLE GIVING YOUR UNSOLICITED OPINIONS ABOUT ALL KINDS OF THINGS.
WAS THERE SOMETHING IN THE AIR ON THE SUNDOG? YOU ALL SEEM VERY FREE WITH YOUR WORDS FOR A BUNCH OF PEOPLE IN DESPERATE NEED OF ALLIES...
WE'RE NOT THAT DESPERATE YET, THANKS.
STOP IT. BOTH OF YOU.
DOCK THE SHIPS.
DO THAT, AND THEN WE'LL... CONTINUE THIS CONVERSATION.
VESS, HE'S DANGEROUS. DON'T JUST PUT YOURSELF OUT THERE LIKE THIS...
I'LL DEAL WITH IT LATER.

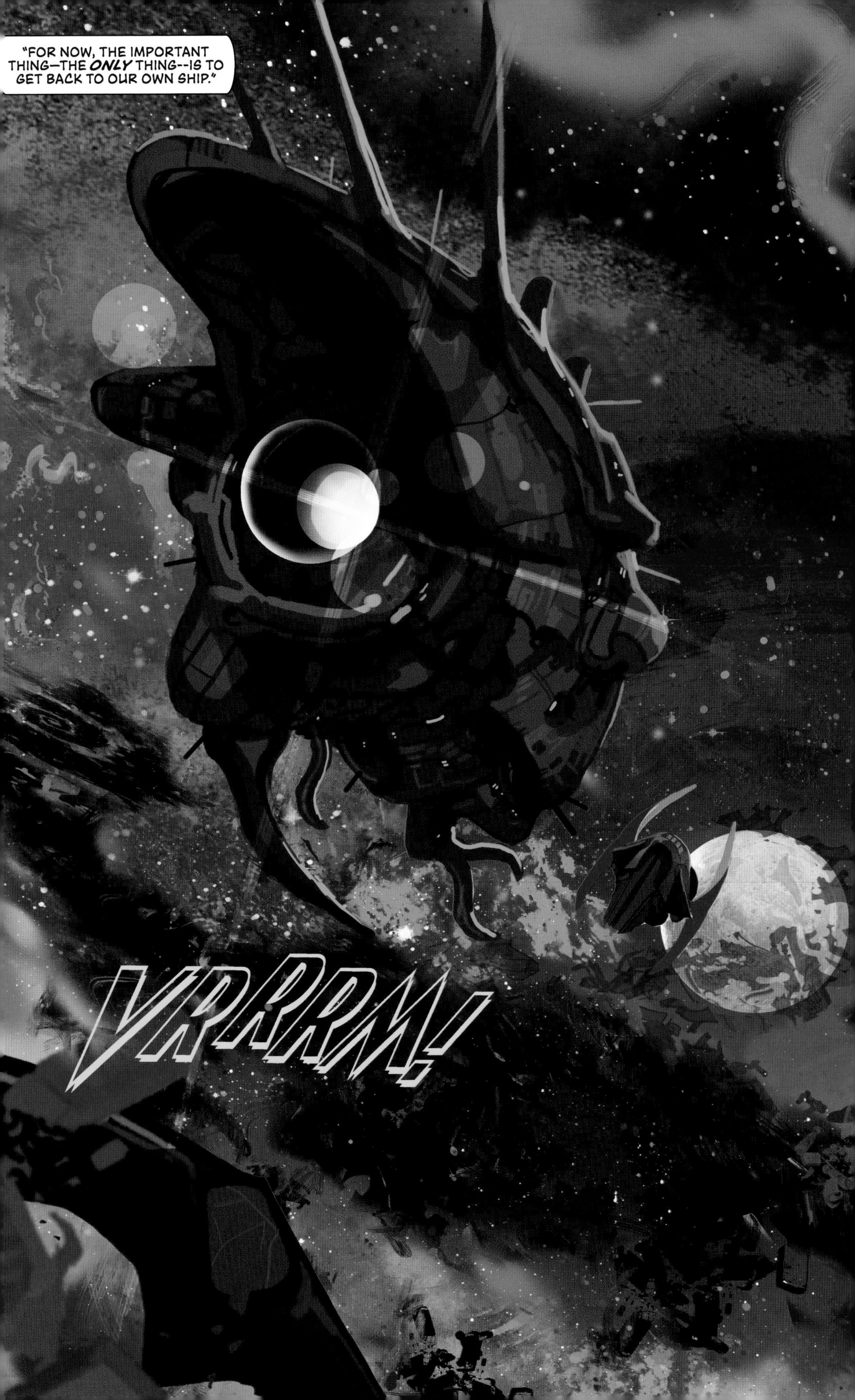
"FOR NOW, THE IMPORTANT THING—THE ONLY THING--IS TO GET BACK TO OUR OWN SHIP."
VRRRM!

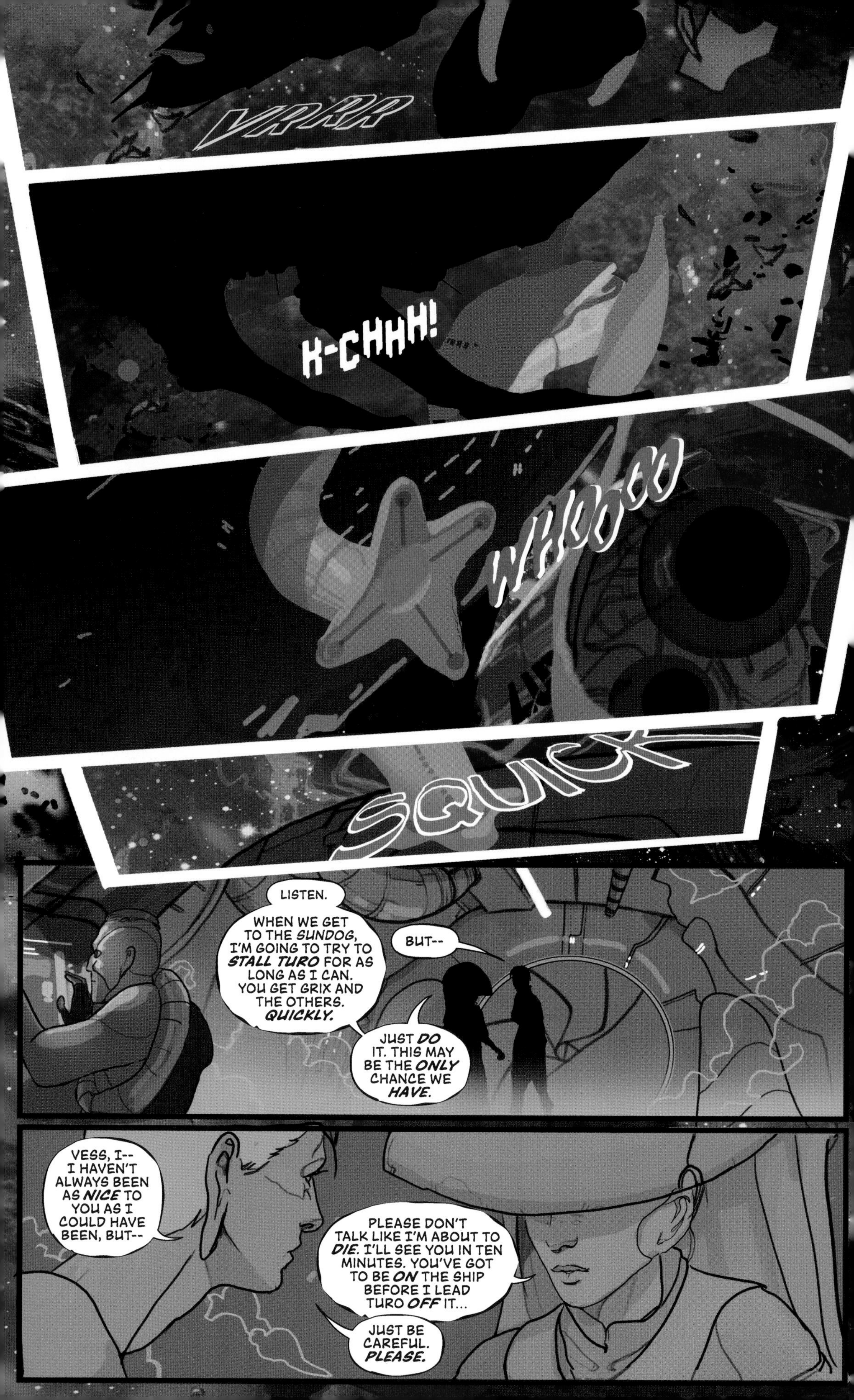
VRRR
K-CHHH!
WHOOOO
SQUICK
LISTEN.
WHEN WE GET TO THE SUNDOG, I'M GOING TO TRY TO STALL TURO FOR AS LONG AS I CAN. YOU GET GRIX AND THE OTHERS. QUICKLY.
BUT--
JUST DO IT. THIS MAY BE THE ONLY CHANCE WE HAVE.
VESS, I-- I HAVEN'T ALWAYS BEEN AS NICE TO YOU AS I COULD HAVE BEEN, BUT--
PLEASE DON'T TALK LIKE I'M ABOUT TO DIE. I'LL SEE YOU IN TEN MINUTES. YOU'VE GOT TO BE ON THE SHIP BEFORE I LEAD TURO OFF IT...
JUST BE CAREFUL. PLEASE.

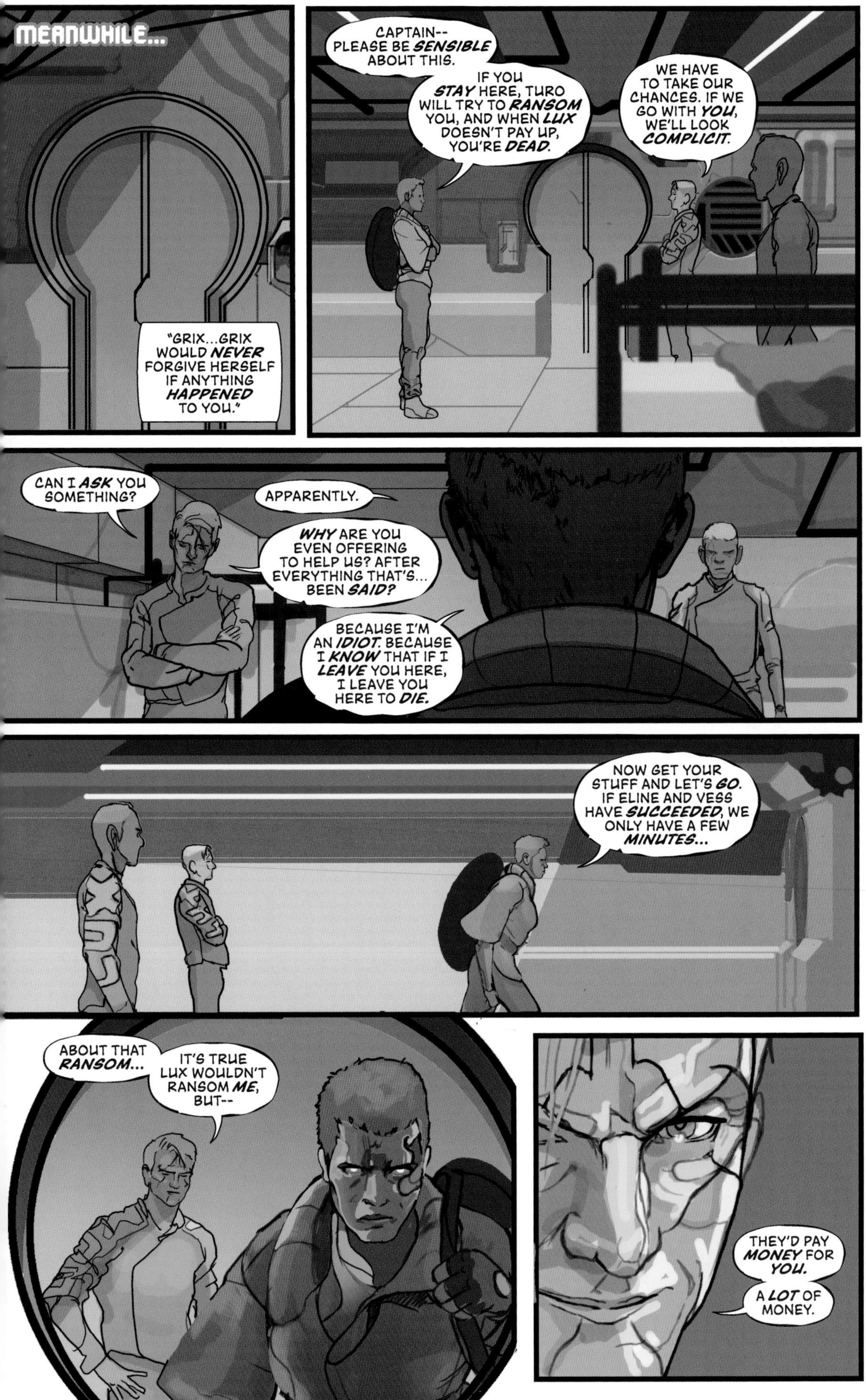
MEANWHILE...
"GRIX...GRIX WOULD NEVER FORGIVE HERSELF IF ANYTHING HAPPENED TO YOU."
CAPTAIN-- PLEASE BE SENSIBLE ABOUT THIS.
IF YOU STAY HERE, TURO WILL TRY TO RANSOM YOU, AND WHEN LUX DOESN'T PAY UP, YOU'RE DEAD.
WE HAVE TO TAKE OUR CHANCES. IF WE GO WITH YOU, WE'LL LOOK COMPLICIT.
CAN I ASK YOU SOMETHING?
APPARENTLY.
WHY ARE YOU EVEN OFFERING TO HELP US? AFTER EVERYTHING THAT'S... BEEN SAID?
BECAUSE I'M AN IDIOT. BECAUSE I KNOW THAT IF I LEAVE YOU HERE, I LEAVE YOU HERE TO DIE.
NOW GET YOUR STUFF AND LET'S GO. IF ELINE AND VESS HAVE SUCCEEDED, WE ONLY HAVE A FEW MINUTES...
ABOUT THAT RANSOM...
IT'S TRUE LUX WOULDN'T RANSOM ME, BUT--
THEY'D PAY MONEY FOR YOU.
A LOT OF MONEY.

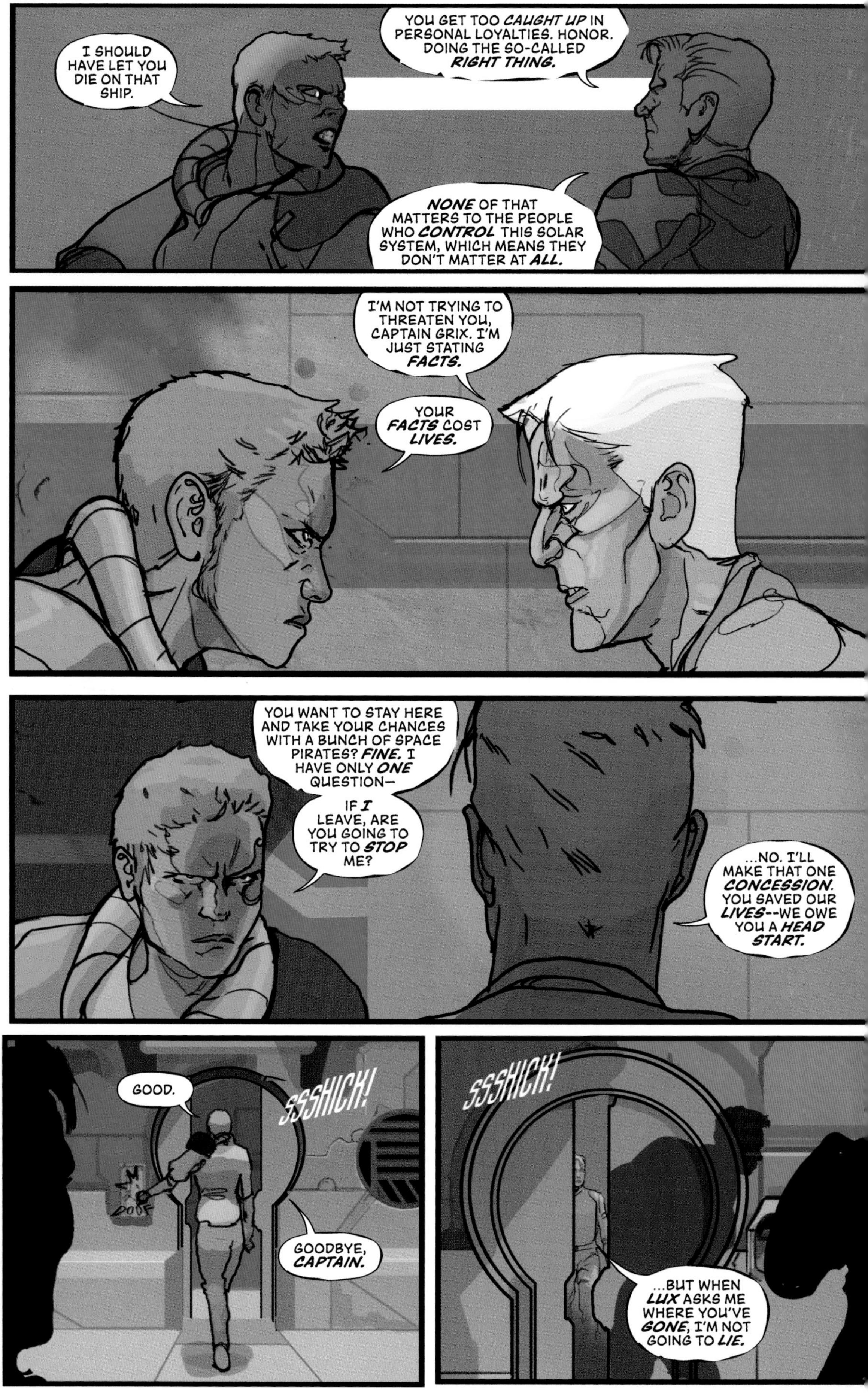
I SHOULD HAVE LET YOU DIE ON THAT SHIP.
YOU GET TOO CAUGHT UP IN PERSONAL LOYALTIES. HONOR. DOING THE SO-CALLED RIGHT THING.
NONE OF THAT MATTERS TO THE PEOPLE WHO CONTROL THIS SOLAR SYSTEM, WHICH MEANS THEY DON'T MATTER AT ALL.
I'M NOT TRYING TO THREATEN YOU, CAPTAIN GRIX. I'M JUST STATING FACTS.
YOUR FACTS COST LIVES.
YOU WANT TO STAY HERE AND TAKE YOUR CHANCES WITH A BUNCH OF SPACE PIRATES? FINE. I HAVE ONLY ONE QUESTION—
IF I LEAVE, ARE YOU GOING TO TRY TO STOP ME?
...NO. I'LL MAKE THAT ONE CONCESSION. YOU SAVED OUR LIVES--WE OWE YOU A HEAD START.
GOOD.
SSSHICK!
DOOF
GOODBYE, CAPTAIN.
SSSHICK!
...BUT WHEN LUX ASKS ME WHERE YOU'VE GONE, I'M NOT GOING TO LIE.

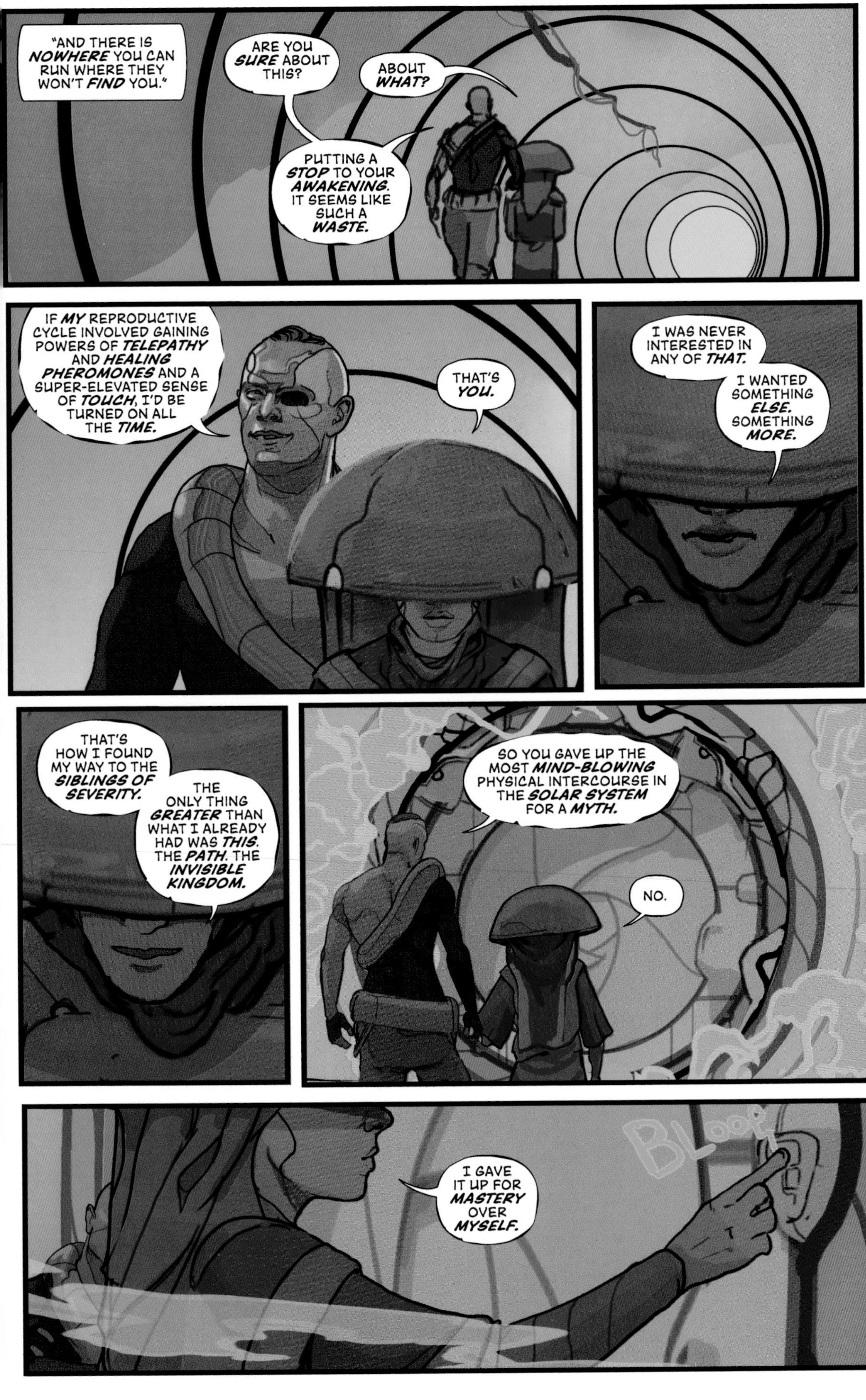
"AND THERE IS NOWHERE YOU CAN RUN WHERE THEY WON'T FIND YOU."
ARE YOU SURE ABOUT THIS?
ABOUT WHAT?
PUTTING A STOP TO YOUR AWAKENING. IT SEEMS LIKE SUCH A WASTE.
IF MY REPRODUCTIVE CYCLE INVOLVED GAINING POWERS OF TELEPATHY AND HEALING PHEROMONES AND A SUPER-ELEVATED SENSE OF TOUCH, I'D BE TURNED ON ALL THE TIME.
THAT'S YOU.
I WAS NEVER INTERESTED IN ANY OF THAT.
I WANTED SOMETHING ELSE. SOMETHING MORE.
THAT'S HOW I FOUND MY WAY TO THE SIBLINGS OF SEVERITY.
THE ONLY THING GREATER THAN WHAT I ALREADY HAD WAS THIS. THE PATH. THE INVISIBLE KINGDOM.
SO YOU GAVE UP THE MOST MIND-BLOWING PHYSICAL INTERCOURSE IN THE SOLAR SYSTEM FOR A MYTH.
NO.
BLOOP
I GAVE IT UP FOR MASTERY OVER MYSELF.

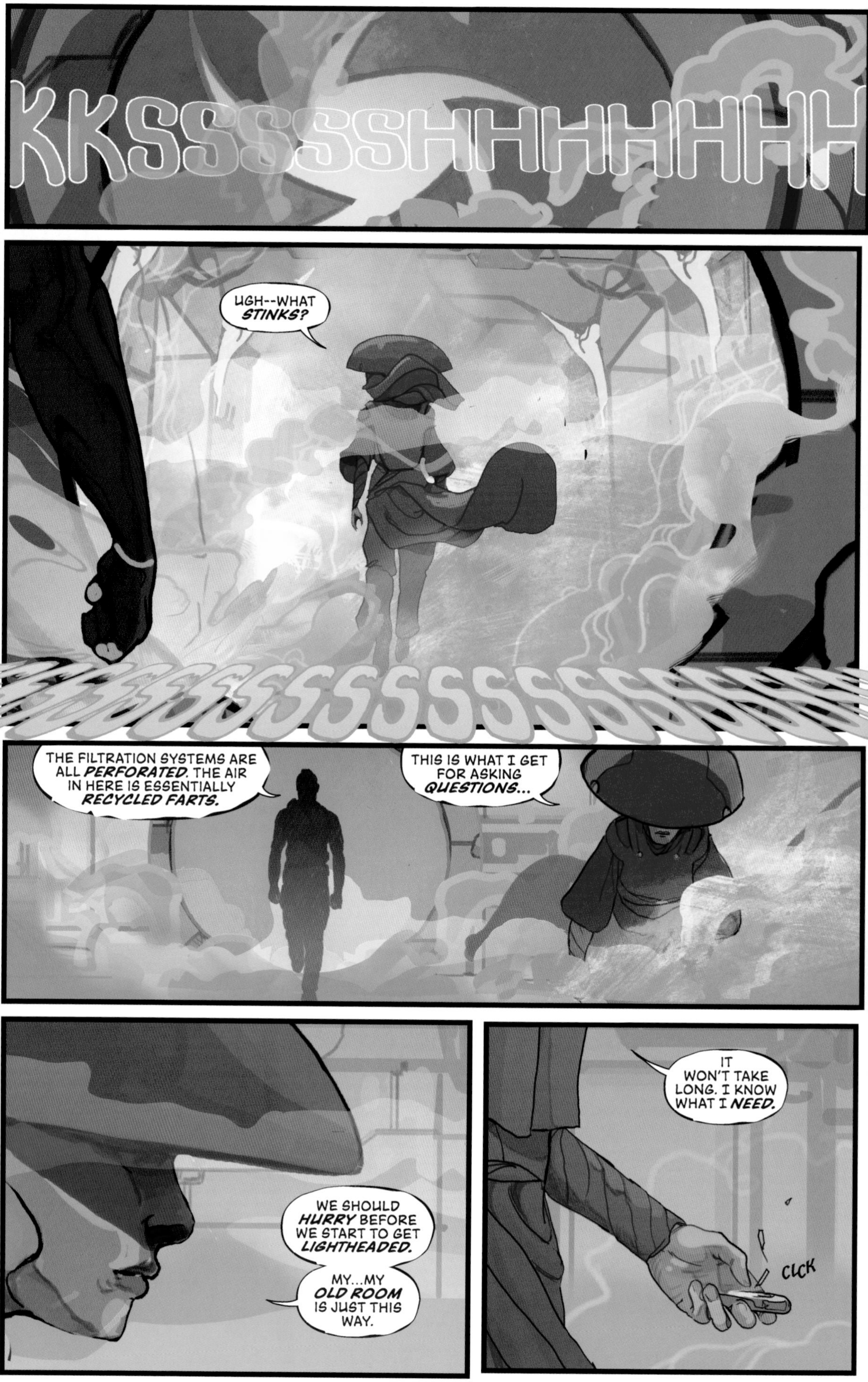
KKSSSSSSHHHHHHH
UGH--WHAT STINKS?
SSSSSSSSSSSSSSSSSS
THE FILTRATION SYSTEMS ARE ALL PERFORATED. THE AIR IN HERE IS ESSENTIALLY RECYCLED FARTS.
THIS IS WHAT I GET FOR ASKING QUESTIONS...
WE SHOULD HURRY BEFORE WE START TO GET LIGHTHEADED.
MY...MY OLD ROOM IS JUST THIS WAY.
IT WON'T TAKE LONG. I KNOW WHAT I NEED.
CLCK

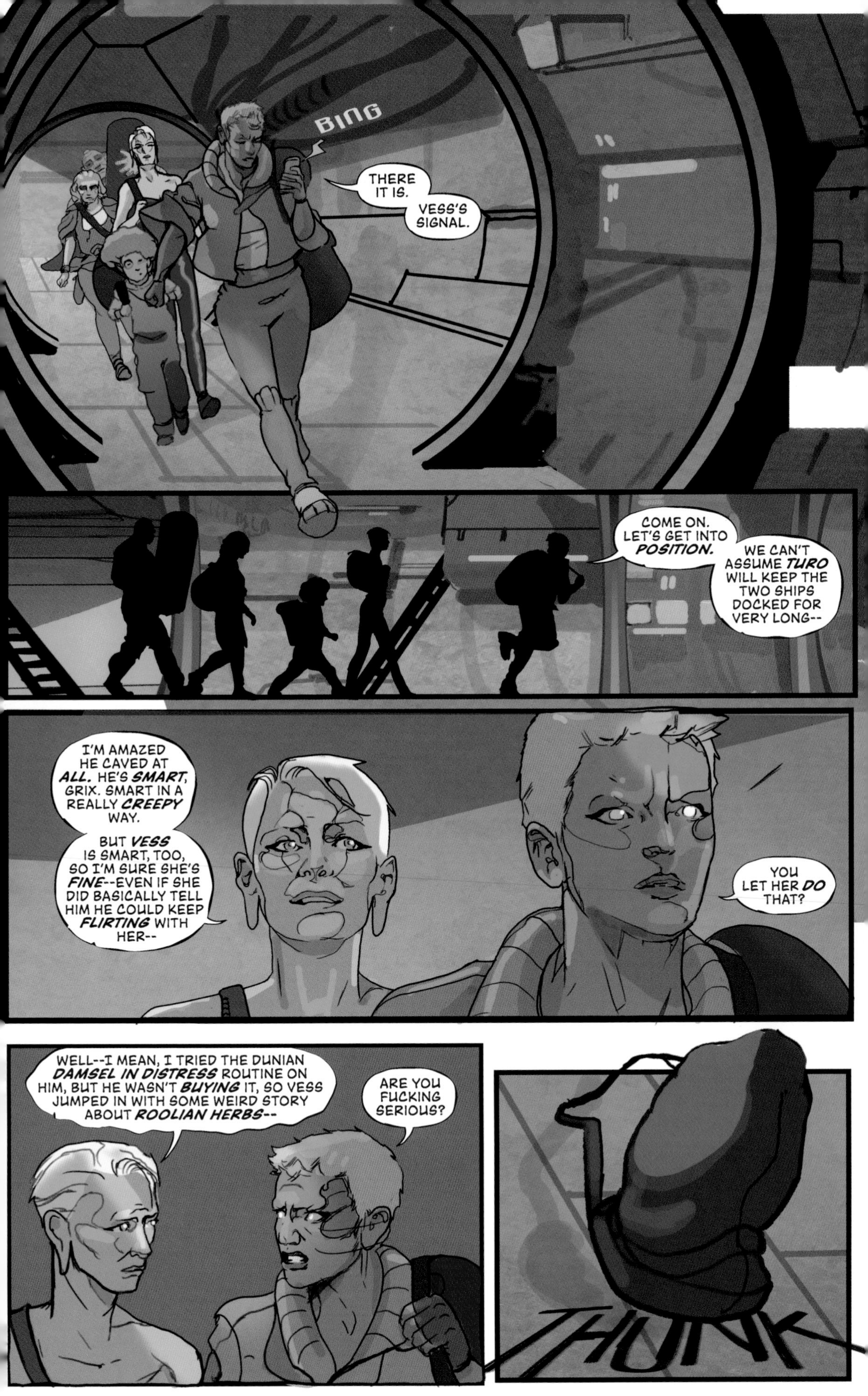

BING
THERE IT IS.
VESS'S SIGNAL.
COME ON. LET'S GET INTO POSITION.
WE CAN'T ASSUME TURO WILL KEEP THE TWO SHIPS DOCKED FOR VERY LONG--
I'M AMAZED HE CAVED AT ALL. HE'S SMART, GRIX. SMART IN A REALLY CREEPY WAY.
BUT VESS IS SMART, TOO, SO I'M SURE SHE'S FINE--EVEN IF SHE DID BASICALLY TELL HIM HE COULD KEEP FLIRTING WITH HER--
YOU LET HER DO THAT?
WELL--I MEAN, I TRIED THE DUNIAN DAMSEL IN DISTRESS ROUTINE ON HIM, BUT HE WASN'T BUYING IT, SO VESS JUMPED IN WITH SOME WEIRD STORY ABOUT ROOLIAN HERBS--
ARE YOU FUCKING SERIOUS?
THUNK

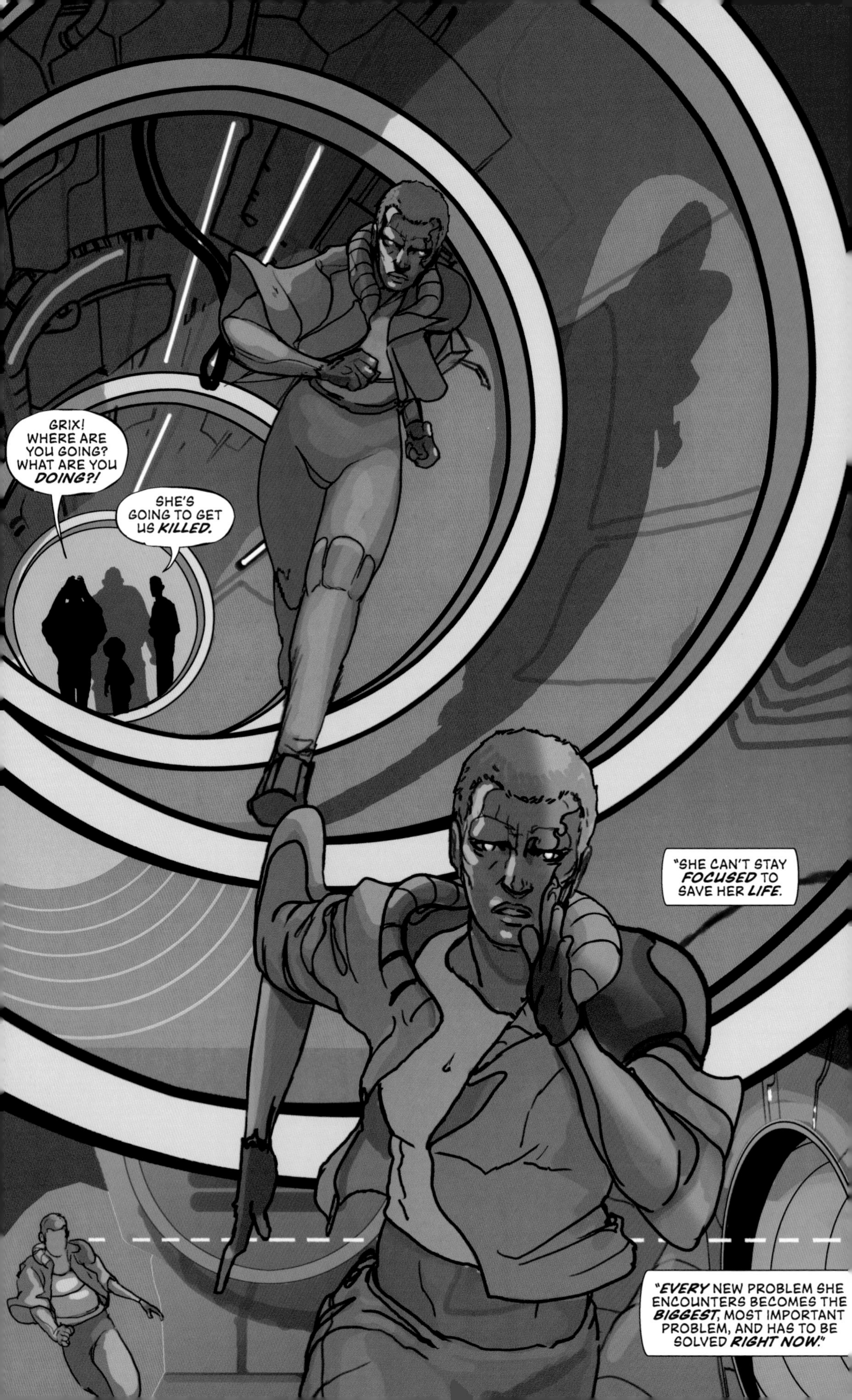
GRIX! WHERE ARE YOU GOING? WHAT ARE YOU DOING?!
SHE'S GOING TO GET US KILLED.
"SHE CAN'T STAY FOCUSED TO SAVE HER LIFE.
"EVERY NEW PROBLEM SHE ENCOUNTERS BECOMES THE BIGGEST, MOST IMPORTANT PROBLEM, AND HAS TO BE SOLVED RIGHT NOW."

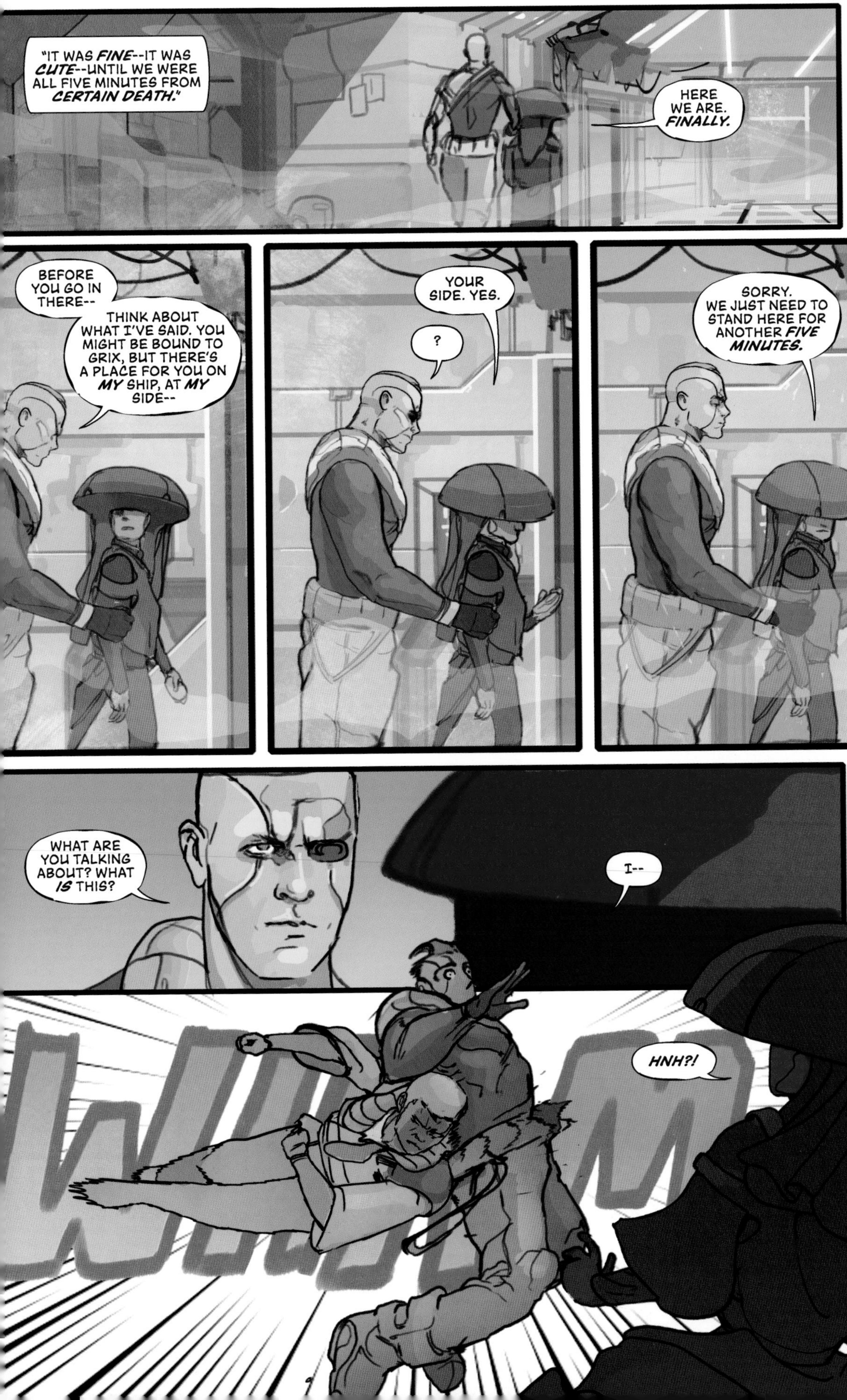
"IT WAS FINE--IT WAS CUTE--UNTIL WE WERE ALL FIVE MINUTES FROM CERTAIN DEATH."
HERE WE ARE. FINALLY.
BEFORE YOU GO IN THERE--
THINK ABOUT WHAT I'VE SAID. YOU MIGHT BE BOUND TO GRIX, BUT THERE'S A PLACE FOR YOU ON MY SHIP, AT MY SIDE--
?
YOUR SIDE. YES.
SORRY. WE JUST NEED TO STAND HERE FOR ANOTHER FIVE MINUTES.
WHAT ARE YOU TALKING ABOUT? WHAT IS THIS?
I--
HNH?!

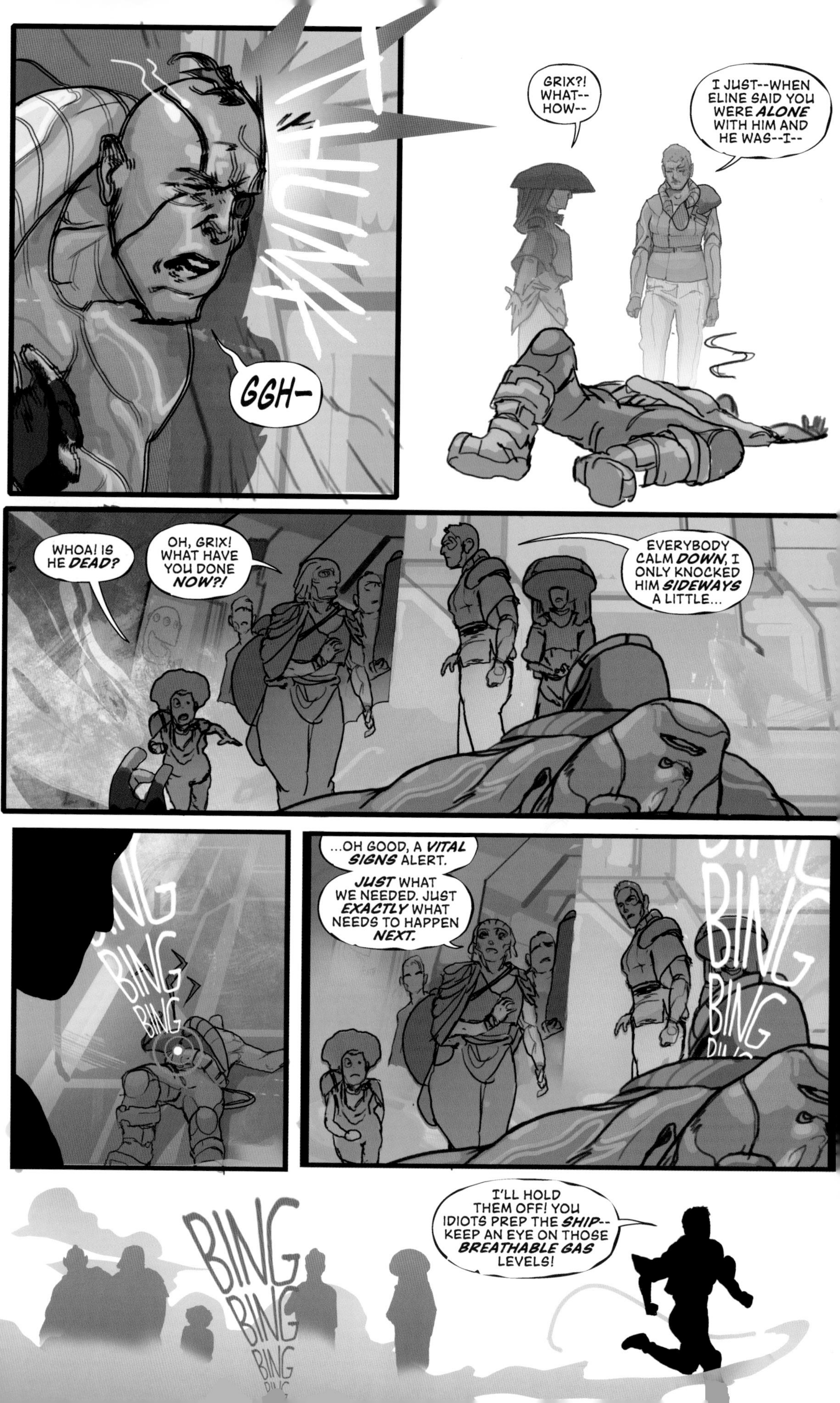
THUNK
GGH-
GRIX?! WHAT-- HOW--
I JUST--WHEN ELINE SAID YOU WERE ALONE WITH HIM AND HE WAS--I--
WHOA! IS HE DEAD?
OH, GRIX! WHAT HAVE YOU DONE NOW?!
EVERYBODY CALM DOWN, I ONLY KNOCKED HIM SIDEWAYS A LITTLE...
BING BING BING
...OH GOOD, A VITAL SIGNS ALERT.
JUST WHAT WE NEEDED. JUST EXACTLY WHAT NEEDS TO HAPPEN NEXT.
BING BING
BING BING BING
I'LL HOLD THEM OFF! YOU IDIOTS PREP THE SHIP-- KEEP AN EYE ON THOSE BREATHABLE GAS LEVELS!

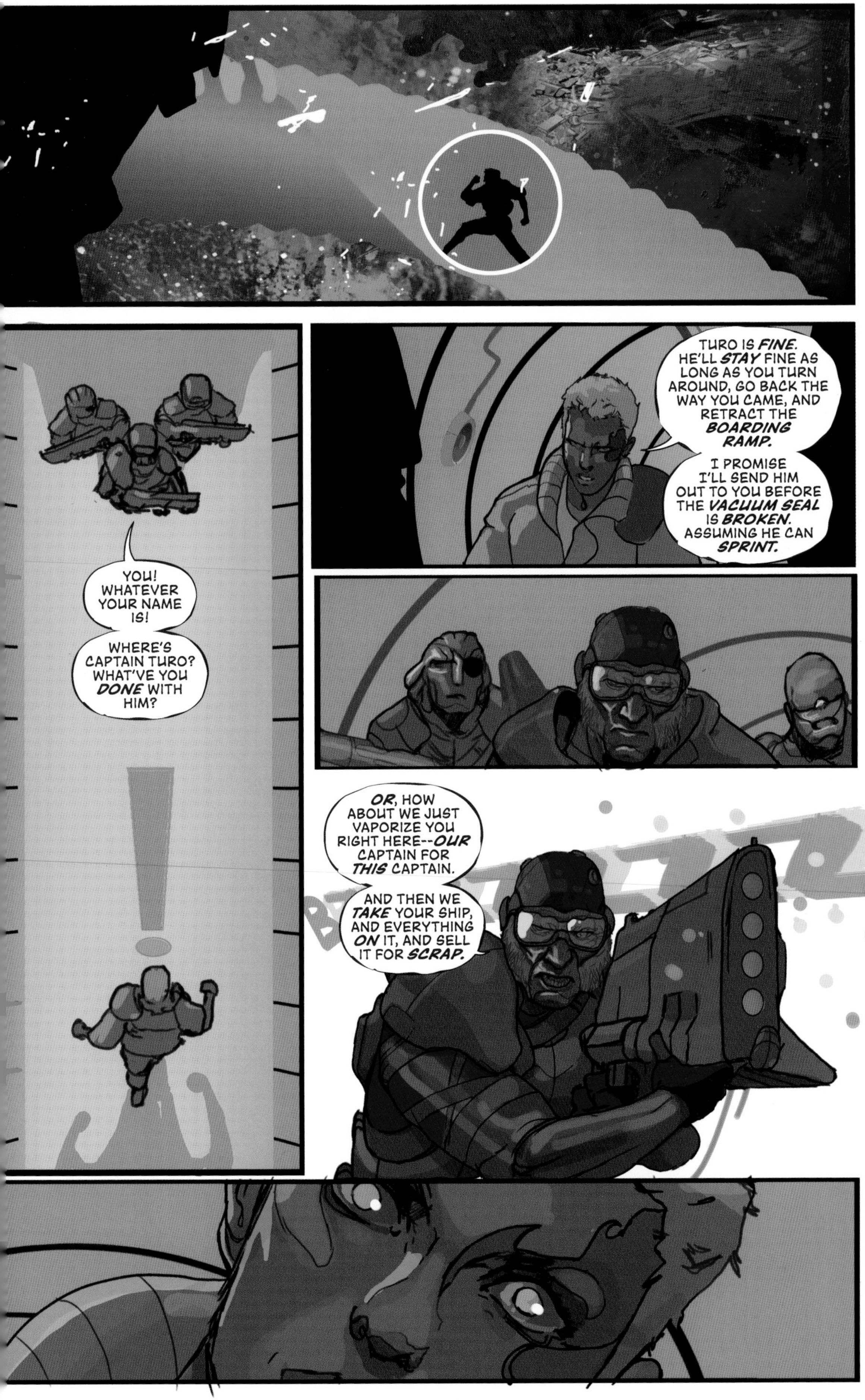
YOU! WHATEVER YOUR NAME IS!
WHERE'S CAPTAIN TURO? WHAT'VE YOU *DONE* WITH HIM?
TURO IS *FINE*. HE'LL *STAY* FINE AS LONG AS YOU TURN AROUND, GO BACK THE WAY YOU CAME, AND RETRACT THE *BOARDING RAMP*.
I PROMISE I'LL SEND HIM OUT TO YOU BEFORE THE *VACUUM SEAL* IS *BROKEN*. ASSUMING HE CAN *SPRINT*.
!
OR, HOW ABOUT WE JUST VAPORIZE YOU RIGHT HERE--*OUR* CAPTAIN FOR *THIS* CAPTAIN.
AND THEN WE *TAKE* YOUR SHIP, AND EVERYTHING *ON* IT, AND SELL IT FOR *SCRAP*.

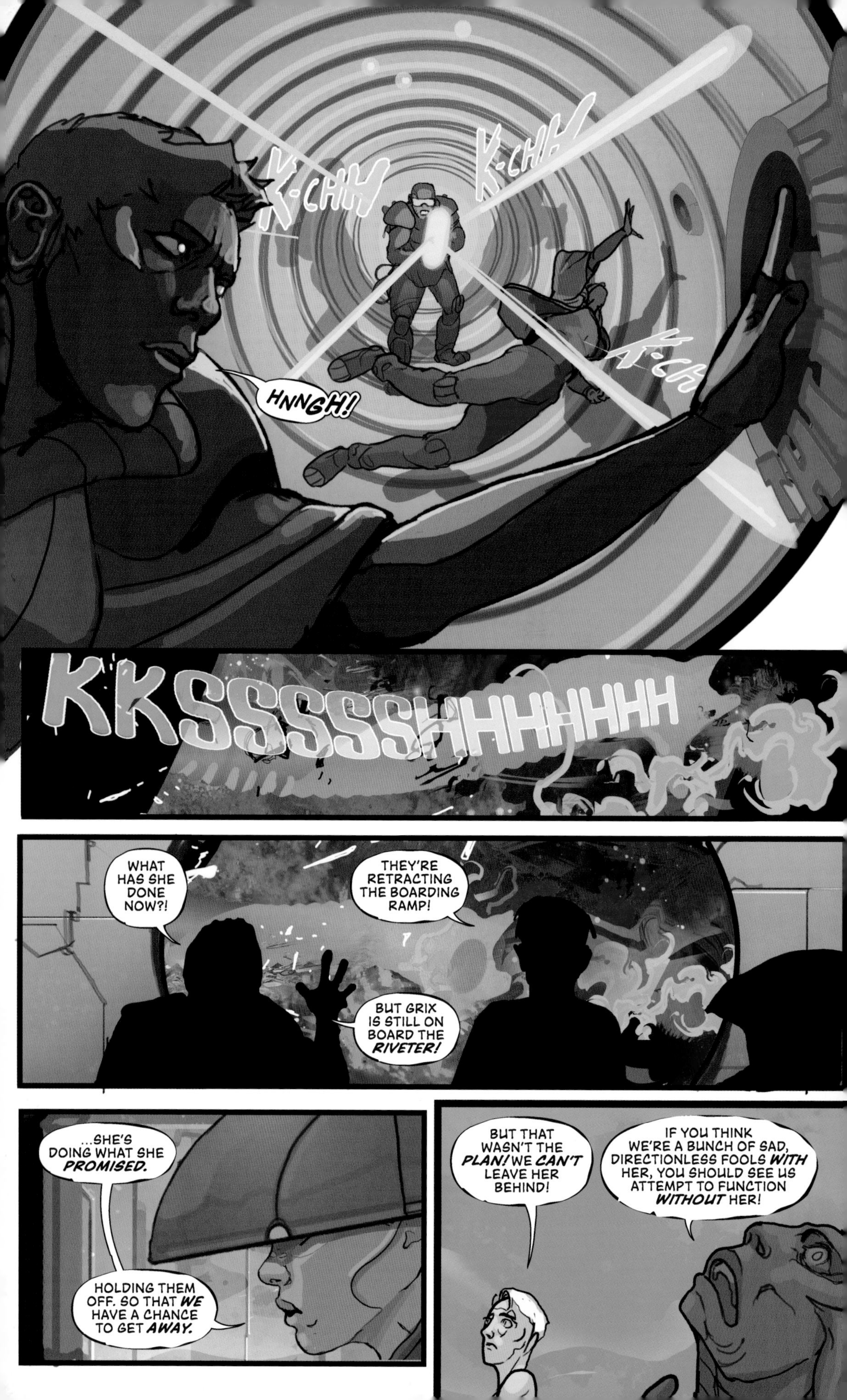
K-CHH
K-CHH
HNNGH!
K-CH
KKSSSSSHHHHHHH
WHAT HAS SHE DONE NOW?!
THEY'RE RETRACTING THE BOARDING RAMP!
BUT GRIX IS STILL ON BOARD THE *RIVETER!*
...SHE'S DOING WHAT SHE *PROMISED.*
HOLDING THEM OFF. SO THAT *WE* HAVE A CHANCE TO GET *AWAY.*
BUT THAT WASN'T THE *PLAN!* WE *CAN'T* LEAVE HER BEHIND!
IF YOU THINK WE'RE A BUNCH OF SAD, DIRECTIONLESS FOOLS *WITH* HER, YOU SHOULD SEE US ATTEMPT TO FUNCTION *WITHOUT* HER!

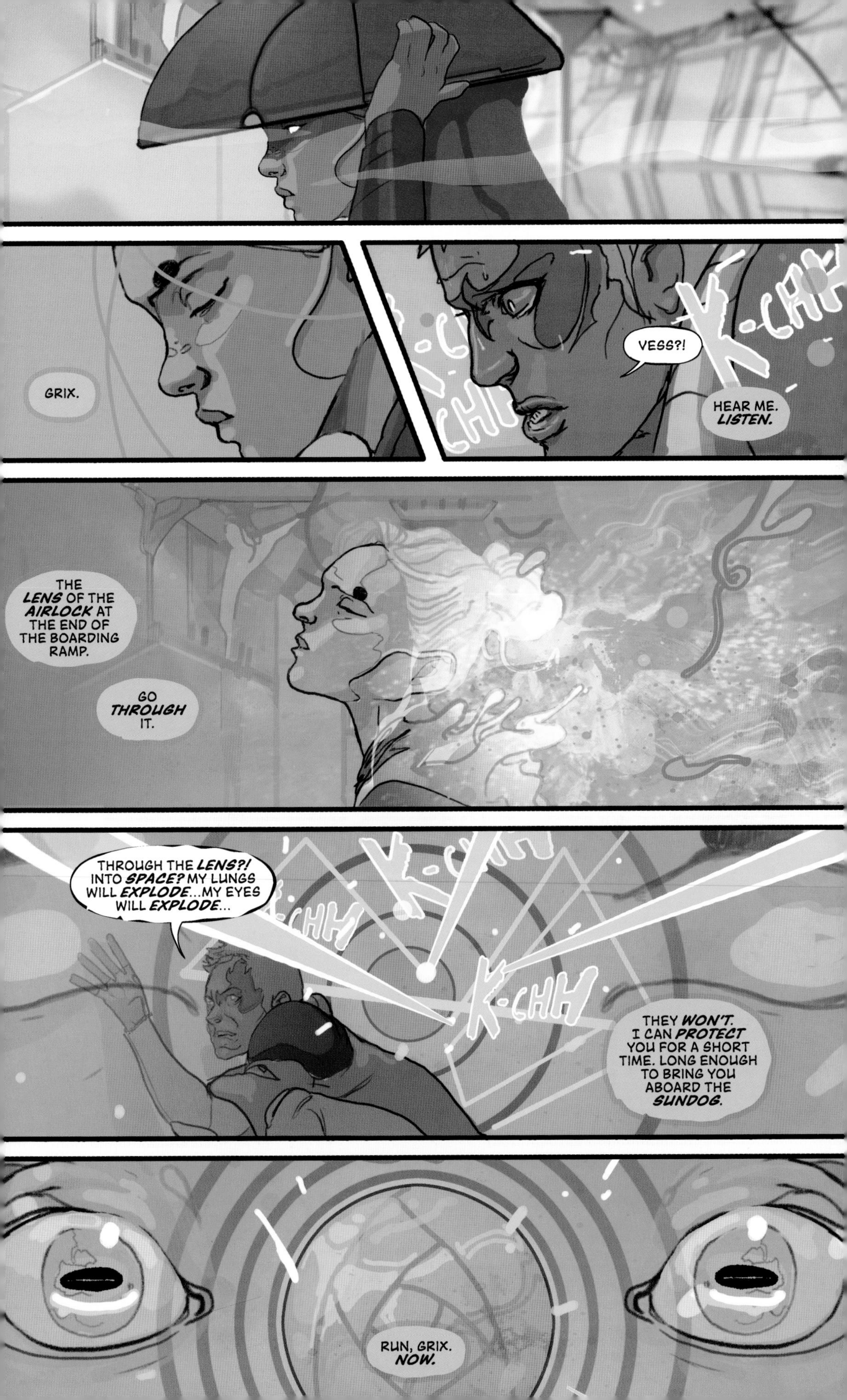
GRIX.
VESS?!
HEAR ME. LISTEN.
K-CHH
THE LENS OF THE AIRLOCK AT THE END OF THE BOARDING RAMP.
GO THROUGH IT.
THROUGH THE LENS?! INTO SPACE? MY LUNGS WILL EXPLODE...MY EYES WILL EXPLODE...
K-CHH
K-CHH
THEY WON'T. I CAN PROTECT YOU FOR A SHORT TIME. LONG ENOUGH TO BRING YOU ABOARD THE SUNDOG.
RUN, GRIX. NOW.

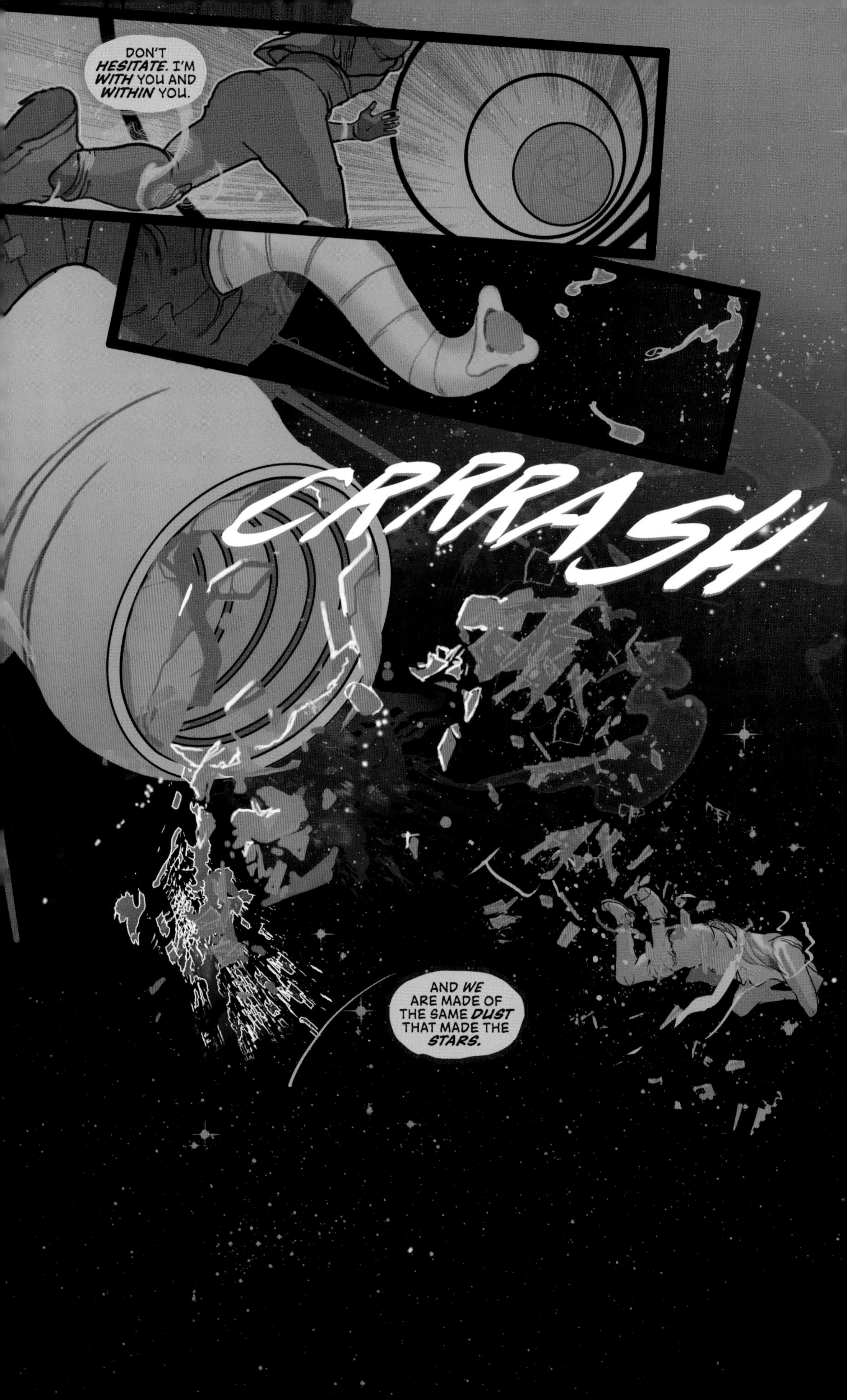

DON'T *HESITATE*. I'M *WITH* YOU AND *WITHIN* YOU.
CRRRASH
AND *WE* ARE MADE OF THE SAME *DUST* THAT MADE THE *STARS.*

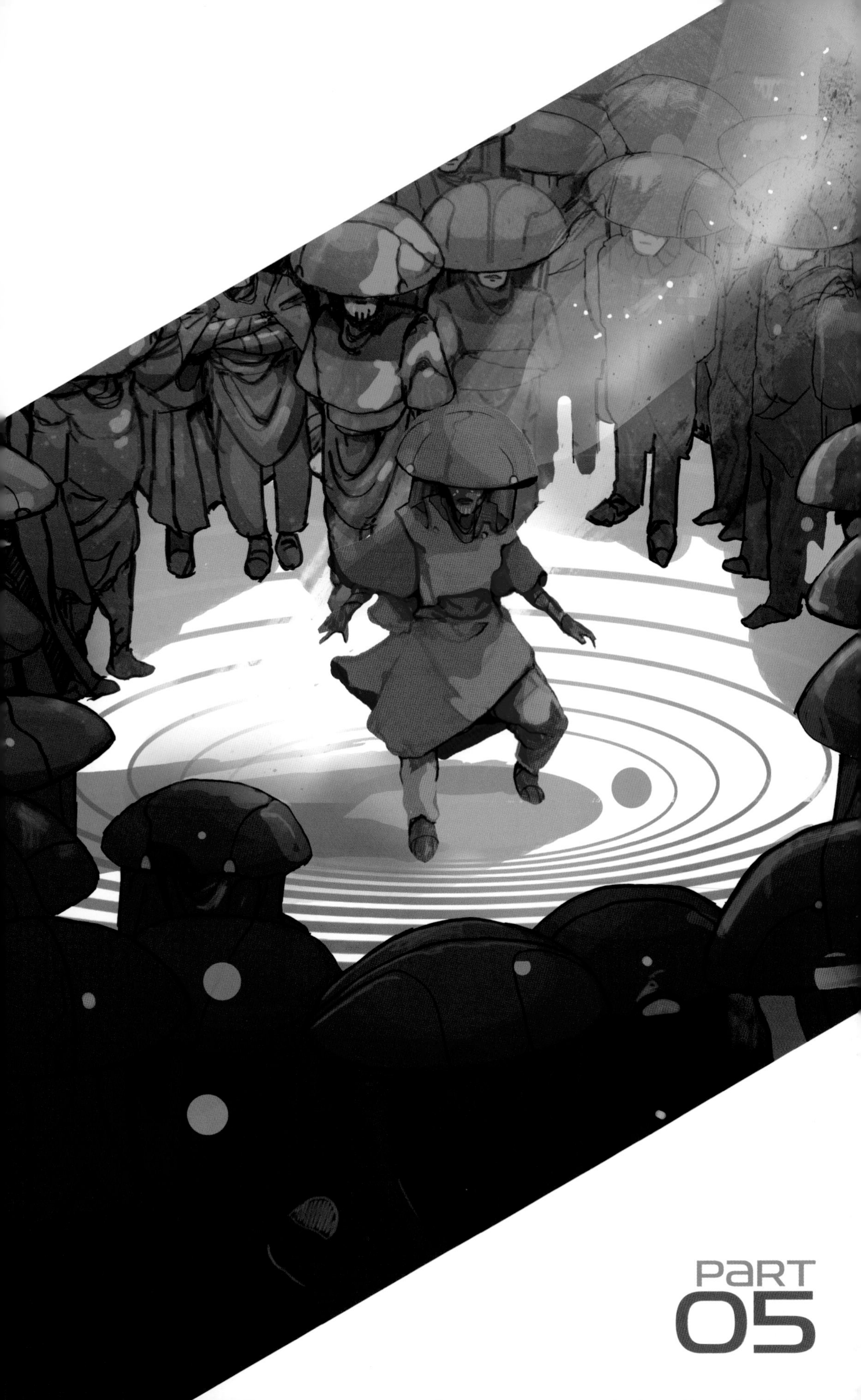

PART 05

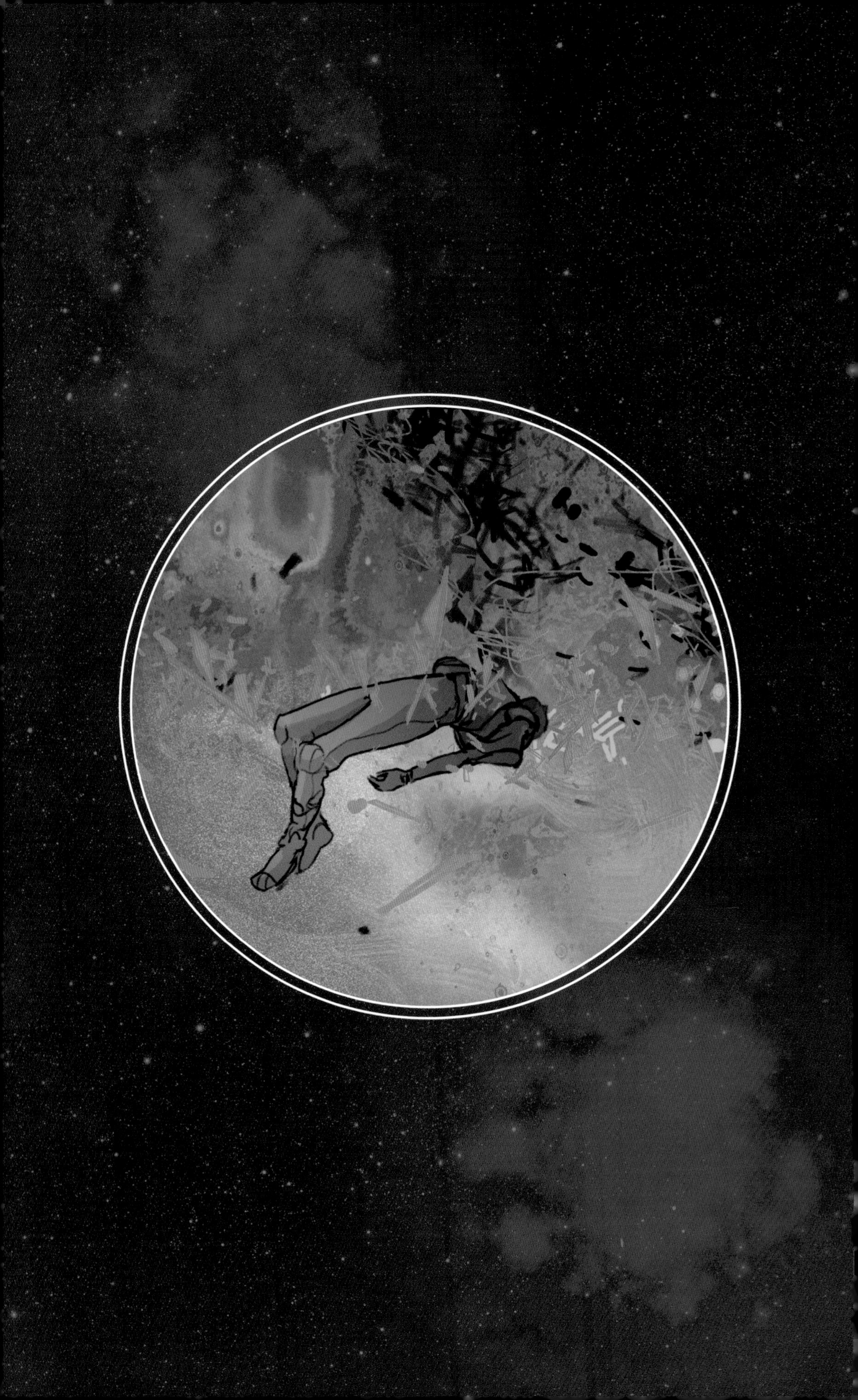

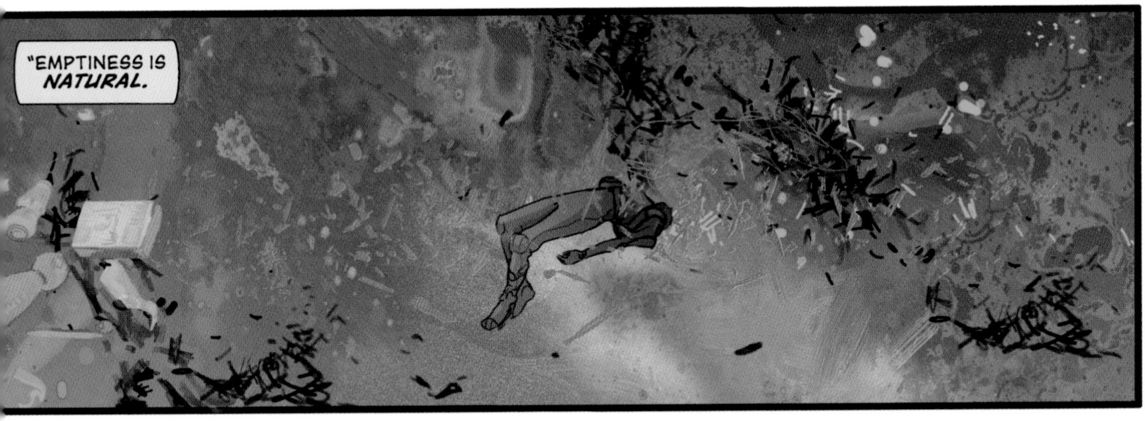
"EMPTINESS IS *NATURAL.*

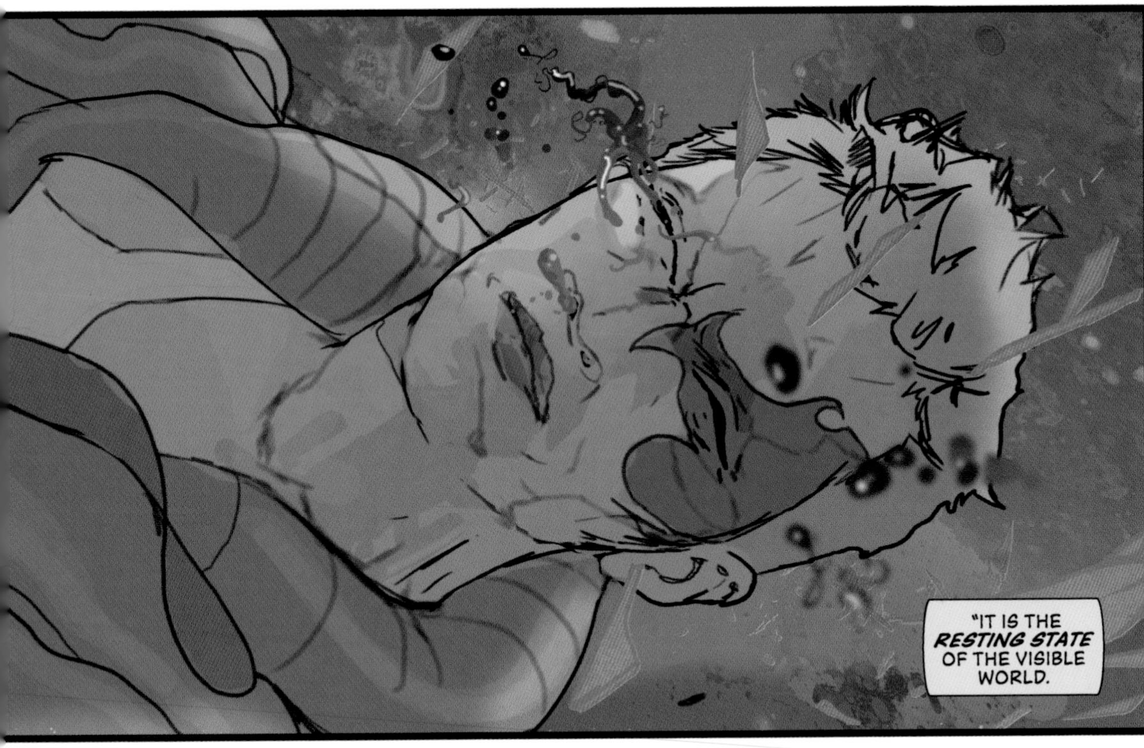
"IT IS THE *RESTING STATE* OF THE VISIBLE WORLD.

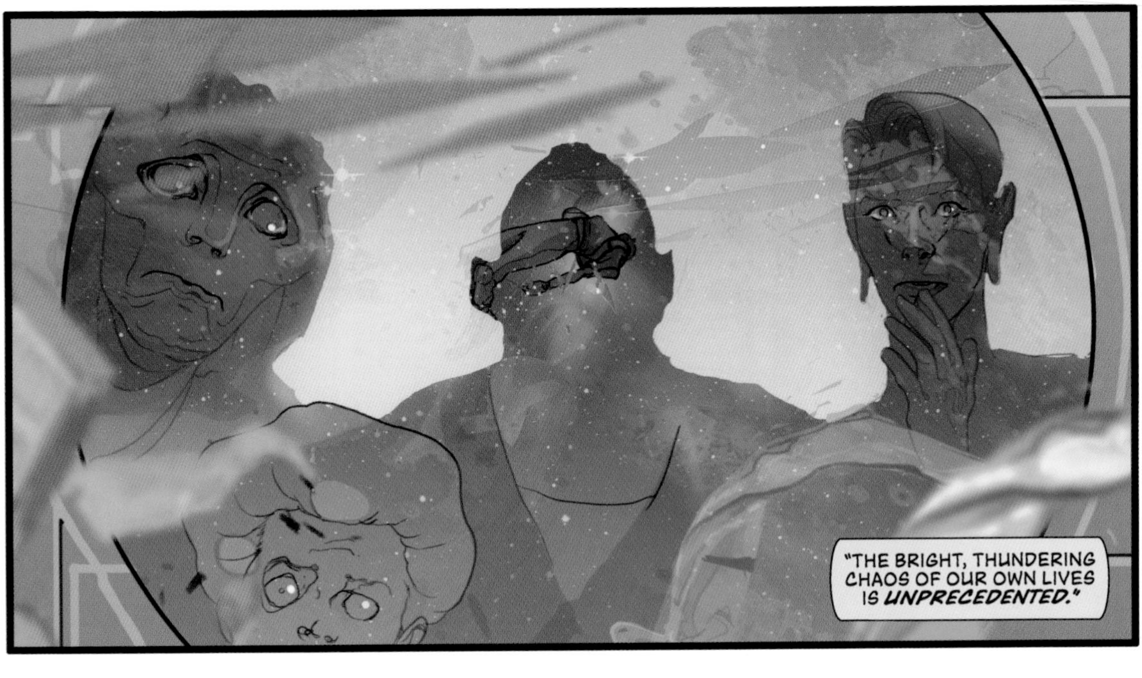
"THE BRIGHT, THUNDERING CHAOS OF OUR OWN LIVES IS *UNPRECEDENTED.*"

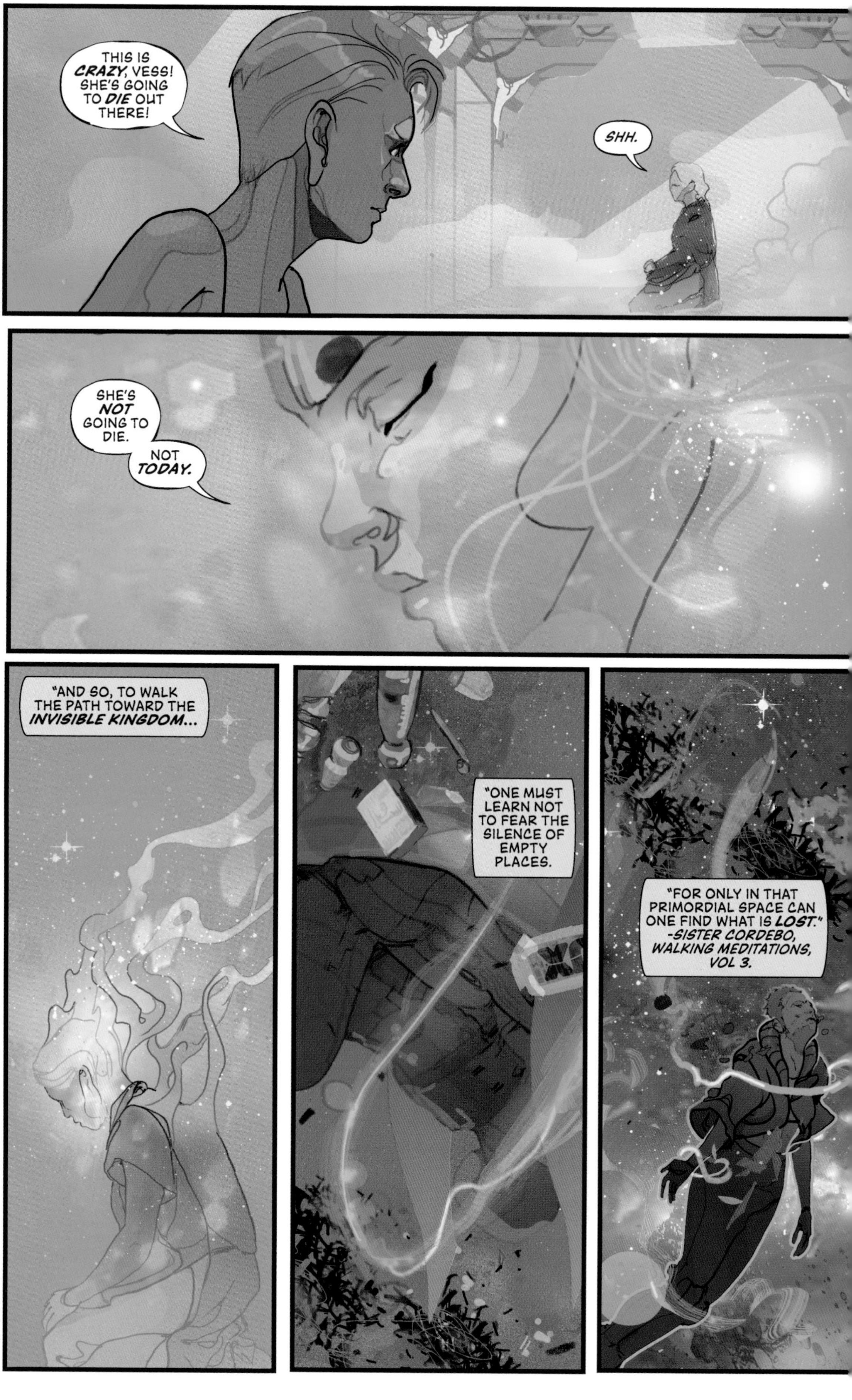
THIS IS CRAZY, VESS! SHE'S GOING TO DIE OUT THERE!
SHH.
SHE'S NOT GOING TO DIE.
NOT TODAY.
"AND SO, TO WALK THE PATH TOWARD THE INVISIBLE KINGDOM...
"ONE MUST LEARN NOT TO FEAR THE SILENCE OF EMPTY PLACES.
"FOR ONLY IN THAT PRIMORDIAL SPACE CAN ONE FIND WHAT IS LOST." -SISTER CORDEBO, WALKING MEDITATIONS, VOL 3.

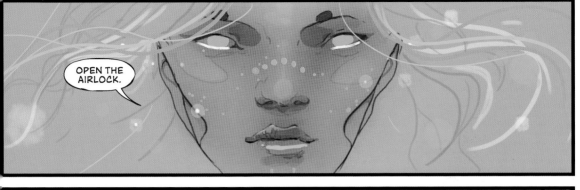

OPEN THE AIRLOCK.

KK-CHHHH!

NNGH--

SPACK

UNNH--

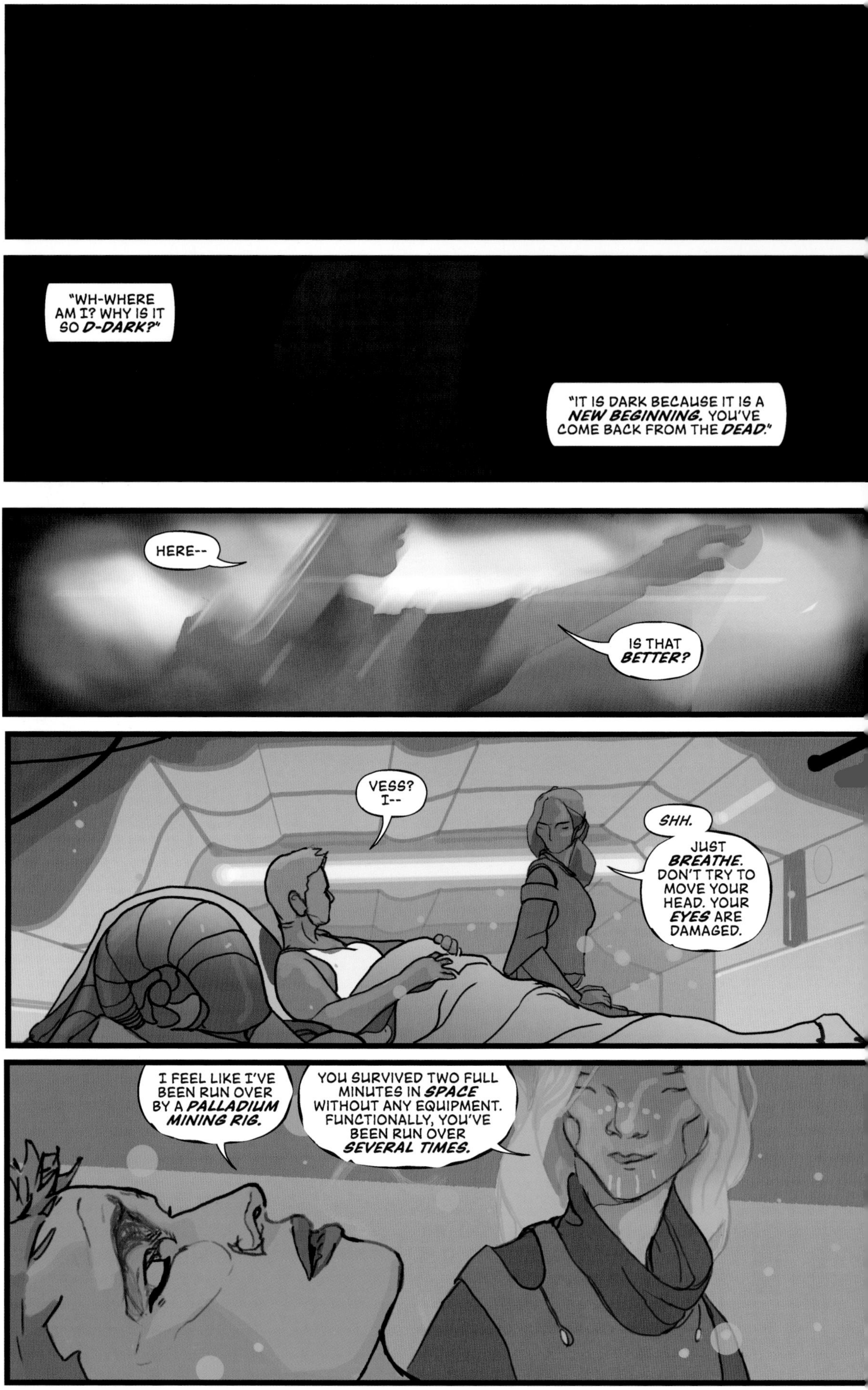
"WH-WHERE AM I? WHY IS IT SO *D-DARK?*"
"IT IS DARK BECAUSE IT IS A *NEW BEGINNING.* YOU'VE COME BACK FROM THE *DEAD.*"
HERE--
IS THAT *BETTER?*
VESS? I--
SHH.
JUST *BREATHE*. DON'T TRY TO MOVE YOUR HEAD. YOUR *EYES* ARE DAMAGED.
I FEEL LIKE I'VE BEEN RUN OVER BY A *PALLADIUM MINING RIG.*
YOU SURVIVED TWO FULL MINUTES IN *SPACE* WITHOUT ANY EQUIPMENT. FUNCTIONALLY, YOU'VE BEEN RUN OVER *SEVERAL TIMES.*

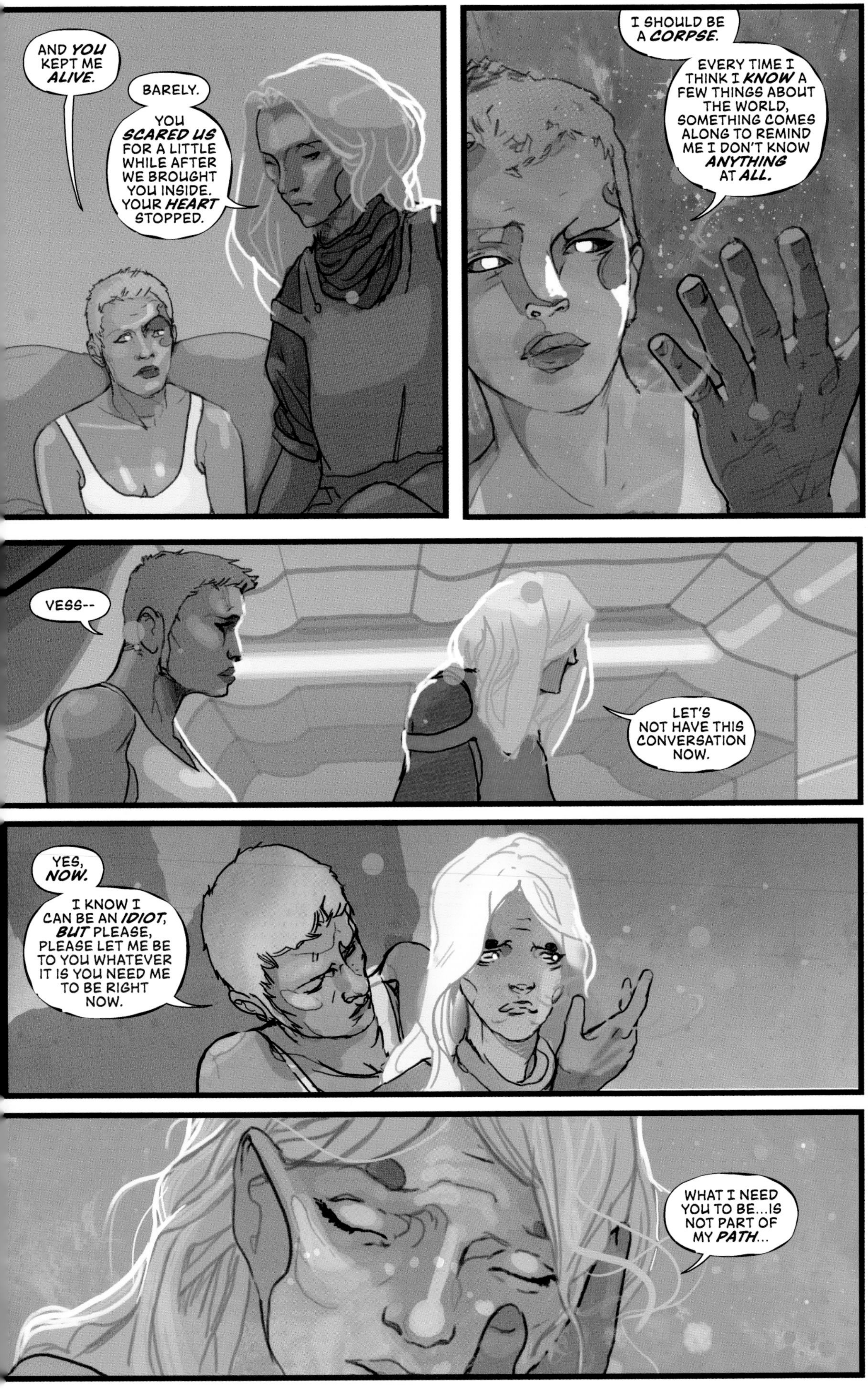
AND YOU KEPT ME ALIVE.
BARELY.
YOU SCARED US FOR A LITTLE WHILE AFTER WE BROUGHT YOU INSIDE. YOUR HEART STOPPED.
I SHOULD BE A CORPSE.
EVERY TIME I THINK I KNOW A FEW THINGS ABOUT THE WORLD, SOMETHING COMES ALONG TO REMIND ME I DON'T KNOW ANYTHING AT ALL.
VESS--
LET'S NOT HAVE THIS CONVERSATION NOW.
YES, NOW.
I KNOW I CAN BE AN IDIOT, BUT PLEASE, PLEASE LET ME BE TO YOU WHATEVER IT IS YOU NEED ME TO BE RIGHT NOW.
WHAT I NEED YOU TO BE...IS NOT PART OF MY PATH...

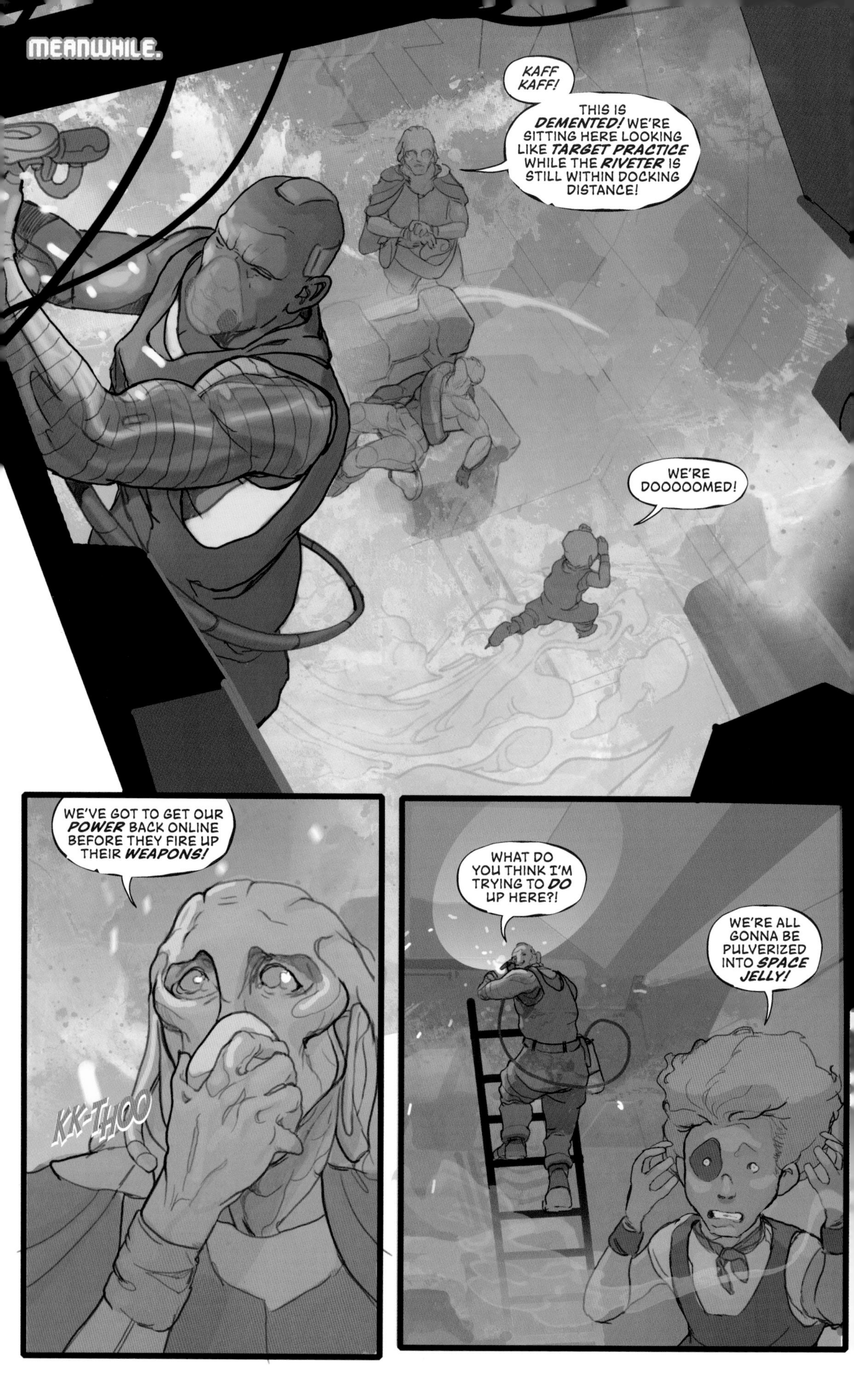
MEANWHILE.
KAFF KAFF!
THIS IS DEMENTED! WE'RE SITTING HERE LOOKING LIKE TARGET PRACTICE WHILE THE RIVETER IS STILL WITHIN DOCKING DISTANCE!
WE'RE DOOOOOMED!
WE'VE GOT TO GET OUR POWER BACK ONLINE BEFORE THEY FIRE UP THEIR WEAPONS!
KK-THOO
WHAT DO YOU THINK I'M TRYING TO DO UP HERE?!
WE'RE ALL GONNA BE PULVERIZED INTO SPACE JELLY!

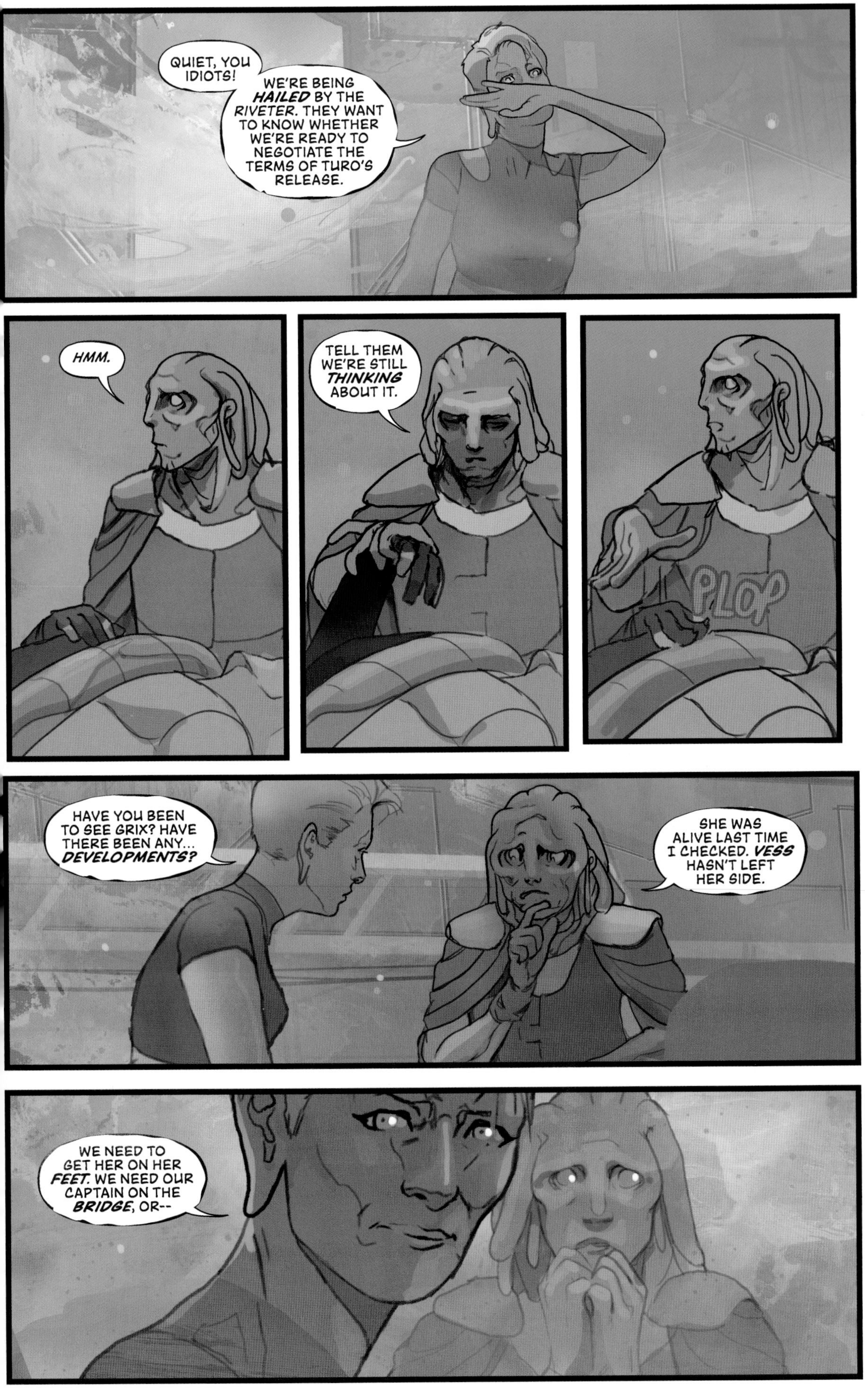

QUIET, YOU IDIOTS!
WE'RE BEING HAILED BY THE RIVETER. THEY WANT TO KNOW WHETHER WE'RE READY TO NEGOTIATE THE TERMS OF TURO'S RELEASE.
HMM.
TELL THEM WE'RE STILL THINKING ABOUT IT.
PLOP
HAVE YOU BEEN TO SEE GRIX? HAVE THERE BEEN ANY... DEVELOPMENTS?
SHE WAS ALIVE LAST TIME I CHECKED. VESS HASN'T LEFT HER SIDE.
WE NEED TO GET HER ON HER FEET. WE NEED OUR CAPTAIN ON THE BRIDGE, OR--

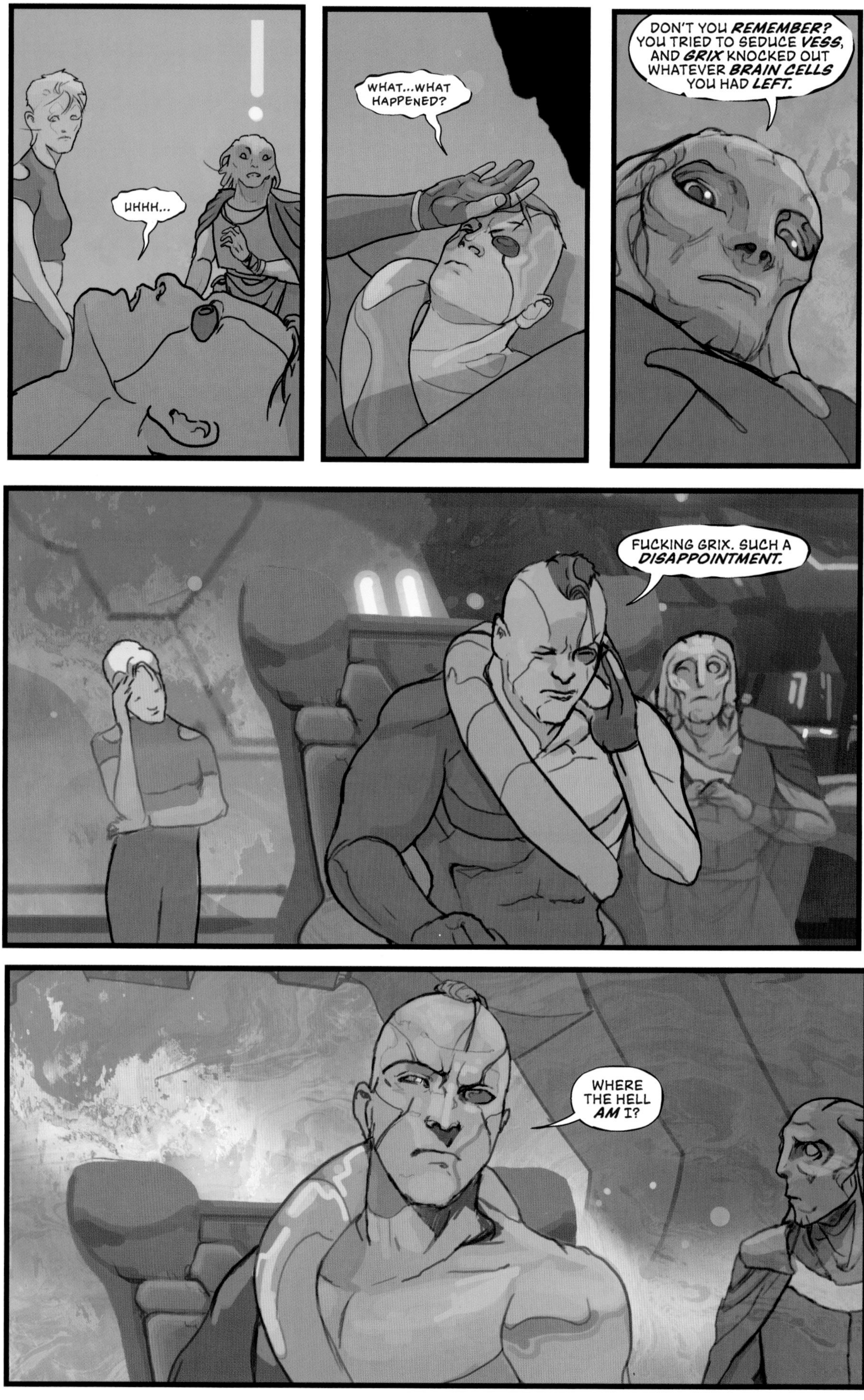
UHHH...
WHAT...WHAT HAPPENED?
DON'T YOU REMEMBER? YOU TRIED TO SEDUCE VESS, AND GRIX KNOCKED OUT WHATEVER BRAIN CELLS YOU HAD LEFT.
FUCKING GRIX. SUCH A DISAPPOINTMENT.
WHERE THE HELL AM I?

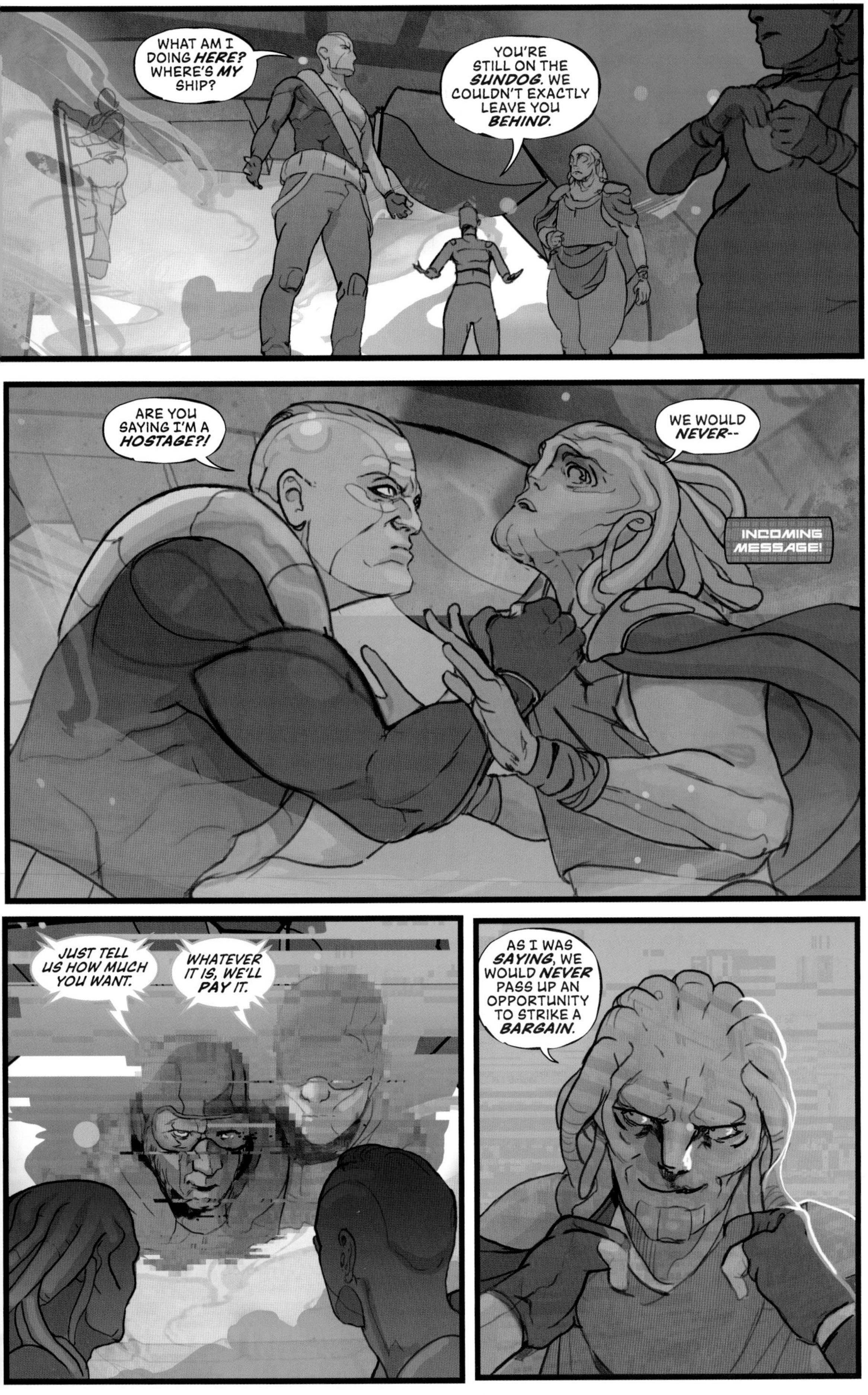
WHAT AM I DOING *HERE?* WHERE'S *MY* SHIP?
YOU'RE STILL ON THE *SUNDOG.* WE COULDN'T EXACTLY LEAVE YOU *BEHIND.*
ARE YOU SAYING I'M A *HOSTAGE?!*
WE WOULD *NEVER--*
INCOMING MESSAGE!
JUST TELL US HOW MUCH YOU WANT.
WHATEVER IT IS, WE'LL *PAY* IT.
AS I WAS *SAYING,* WE WOULD *NEVER* PASS UP AN OPPORTUNITY TO STRIKE A *BARGAIN.*

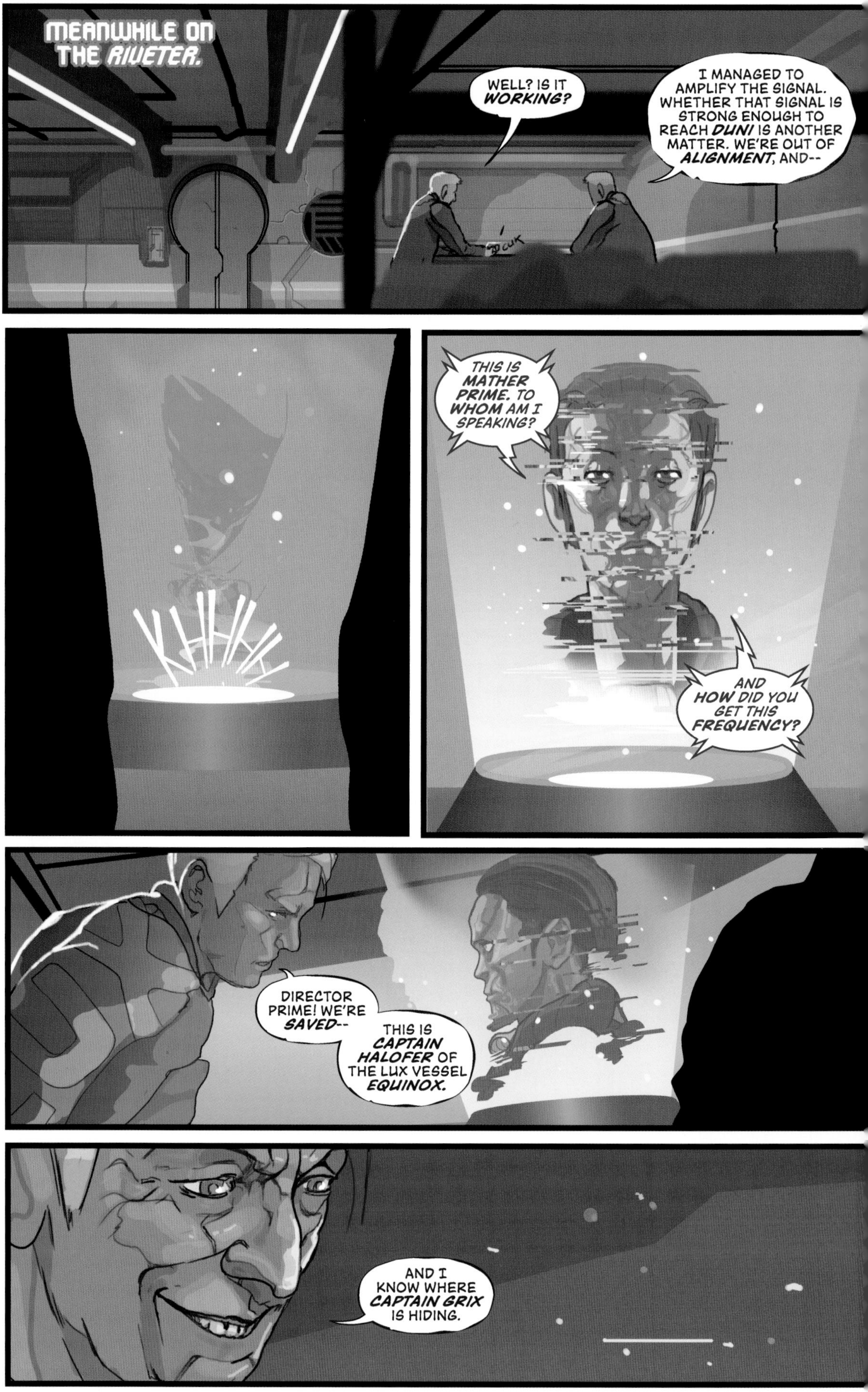
MEANWHILE ON THE *RIVETER.*
WELL? IS IT *WORKING?*
I MANAGED TO AMPLIFY THE SIGNAL. WHETHER THAT SIGNAL IS STRONG ENOUGH TO REACH *DUNI* IS ANOTHER MATTER. WE'RE OUT OF *ALIGNMENT*, AND--
KHHHK
THIS IS *MATHER PRIME*. TO *WHOM* AM I *SPEAKING?*
AND *HOW* DID YOU GET THIS *FREQUENCY?*
DIRECTOR PRIME! WE'RE *SAVED*--
THIS IS *CAPTAIN HALOFER* OF THE LUX VESSEL *EQUINOX.*
AND I KNOW WHERE *CAPTAIN GRIX* IS HIDING.

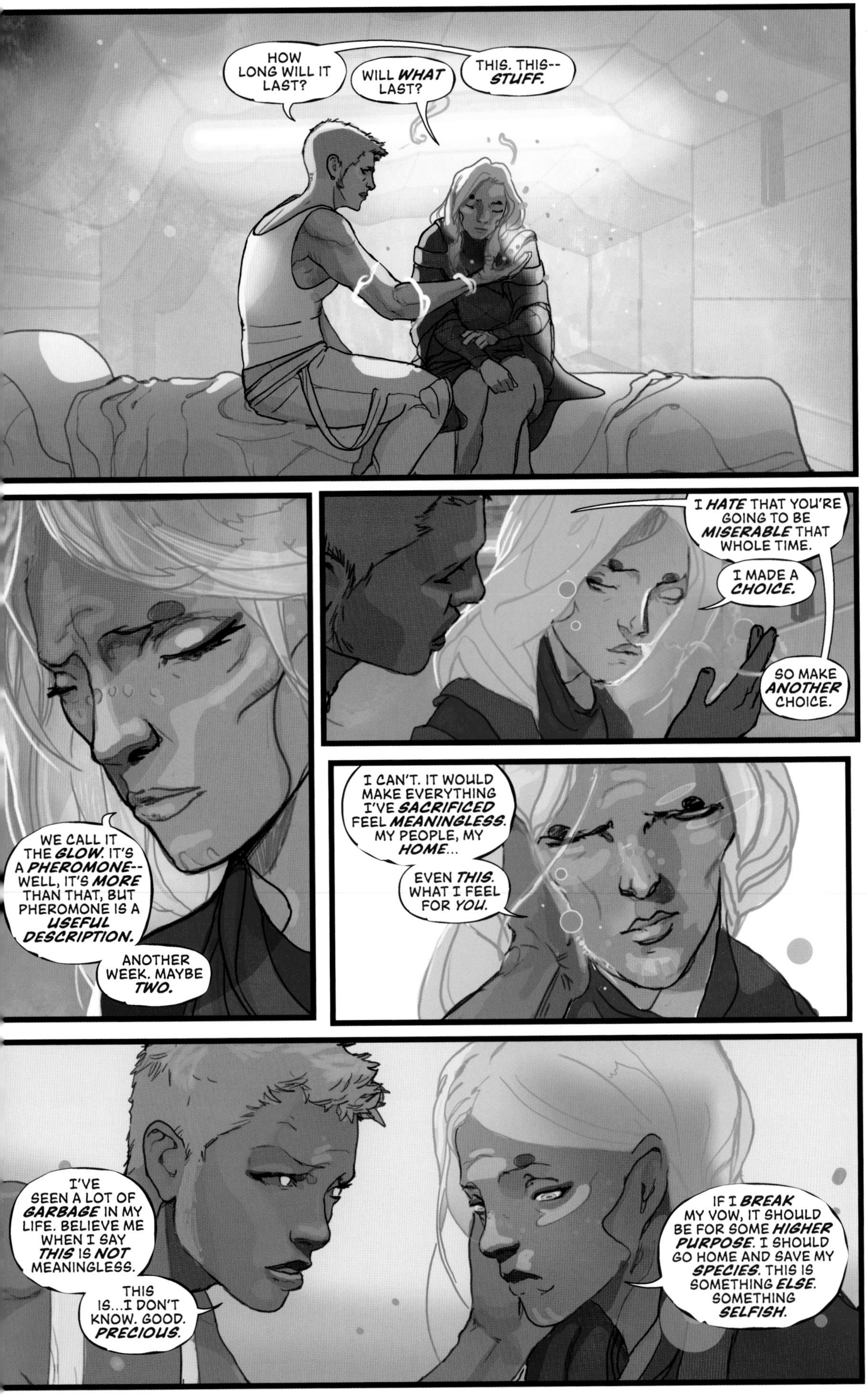
HOW LONG WILL IT LAST?
WILL WHAT LAST?
THIS. THIS-- STUFF.
WE CALL IT THE GLOW. IT'S A PHEROMONE-- WELL, IT'S MORE THAN THAT, BUT PHEROMONE IS A USEFUL DESCRIPTION.
ANOTHER WEEK. MAYBE TWO.
I HATE THAT YOU'RE GOING TO BE MISERABLE THAT WHOLE TIME.
I MADE A CHOICE.
SO MAKE ANOTHER CHOICE.
I CAN'T. IT WOULD MAKE EVERYTHING I'VE SACRIFICED FEEL MEANINGLESS. MY PEOPLE, MY HOME...
EVEN THIS. WHAT I FEEL FOR YOU.
I'VE SEEN A LOT OF GARBAGE IN MY LIFE. BELIEVE ME WHEN I SAY THIS IS NOT MEANINGLESS.
THIS IS...I DON'T KNOW. GOOD. PRECIOUS.
IF I BREAK MY VOW, IT SHOULD BE FOR SOME HIGHER PURPOSE. I SHOULD GO HOME AND SAVE MY SPECIES. THIS IS SOMETHING ELSE. SOMETHING SELFISH.

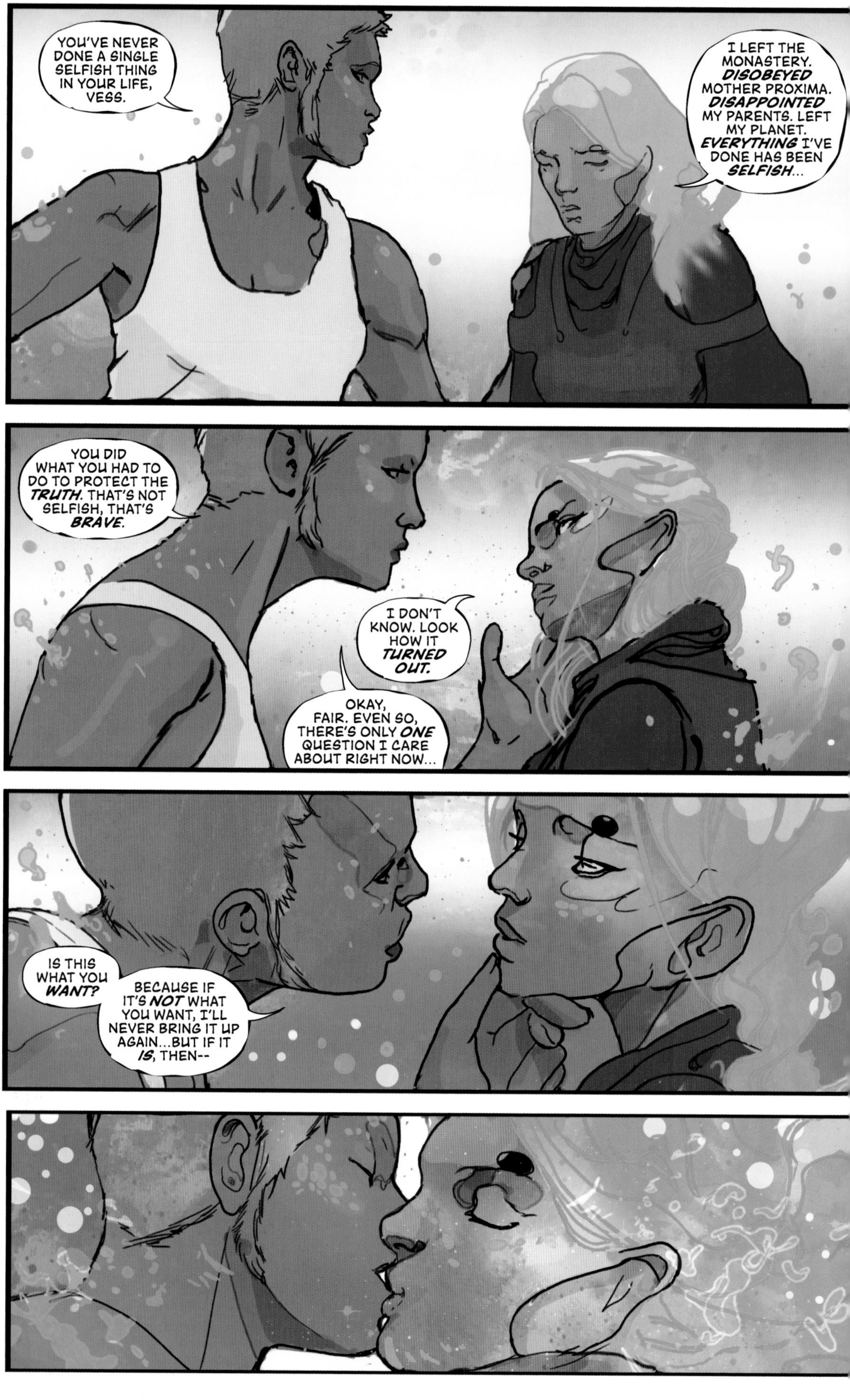
YOU'VE NEVER DONE A SINGLE SELFISH THING IN YOUR LIFE, VESS.
I LEFT THE MONASTERY. DISOBEYED MOTHER PROXIMA. DISAPPOINTED MY PARENTS. LEFT MY PLANET. EVERYTHING I'VE DONE HAS BEEN SELFISH...
YOU DID WHAT YOU HAD TO DO TO PROTECT THE TRUTH. THAT'S NOT SELFISH, THAT'S BRAVE.
I DON'T KNOW. LOOK HOW IT TURNED OUT.
OKAY, FAIR. EVEN SO, THERE'S ONLY ONE QUESTION I CARE ABOUT RIGHT NOW...
IS THIS WHAT YOU WANT?
BECAUSE IF IT'S NOT WHAT YOU WANT, I'LL NEVER BRING IT UP AGAIN...BUT IF IT IS, THEN--

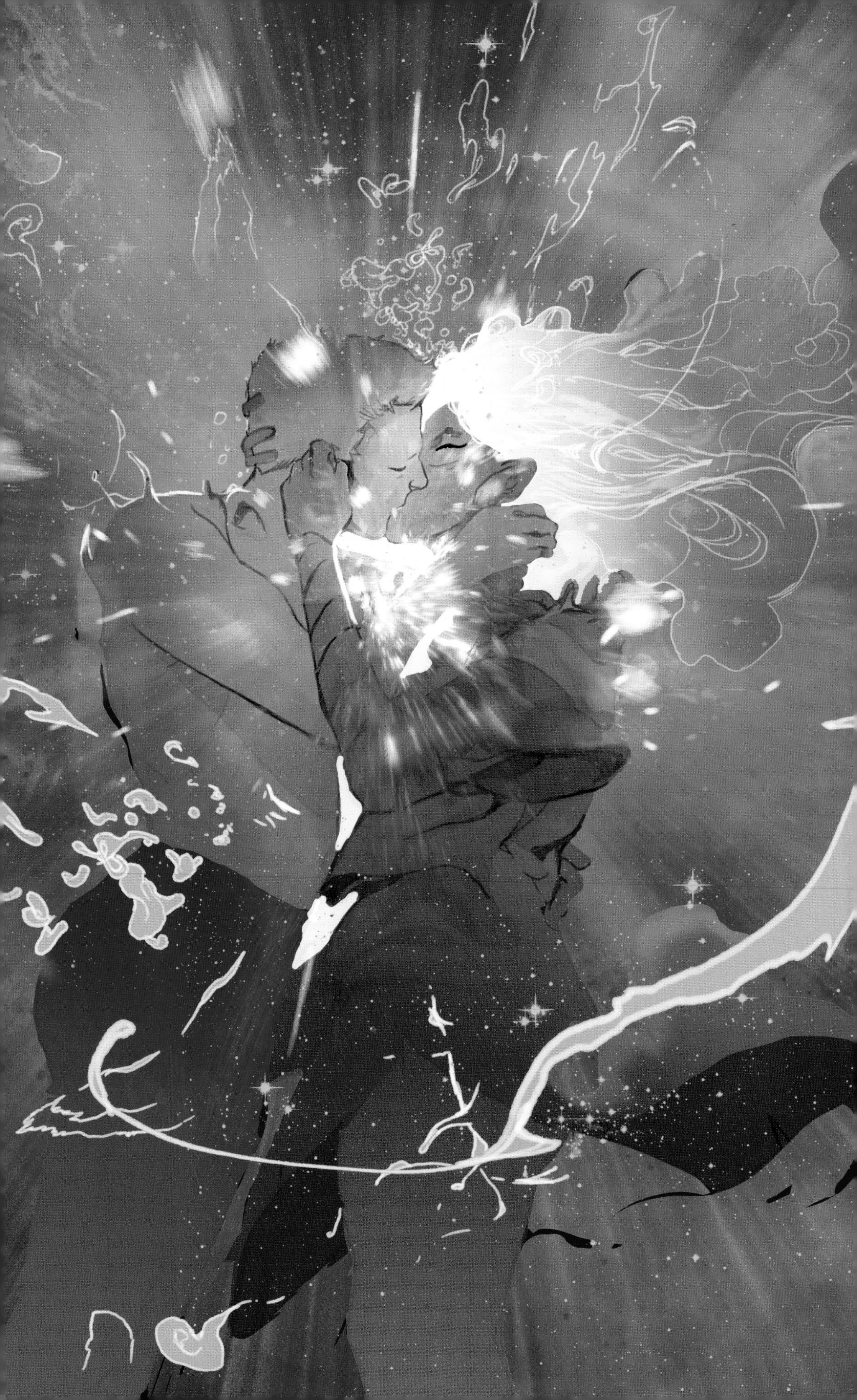

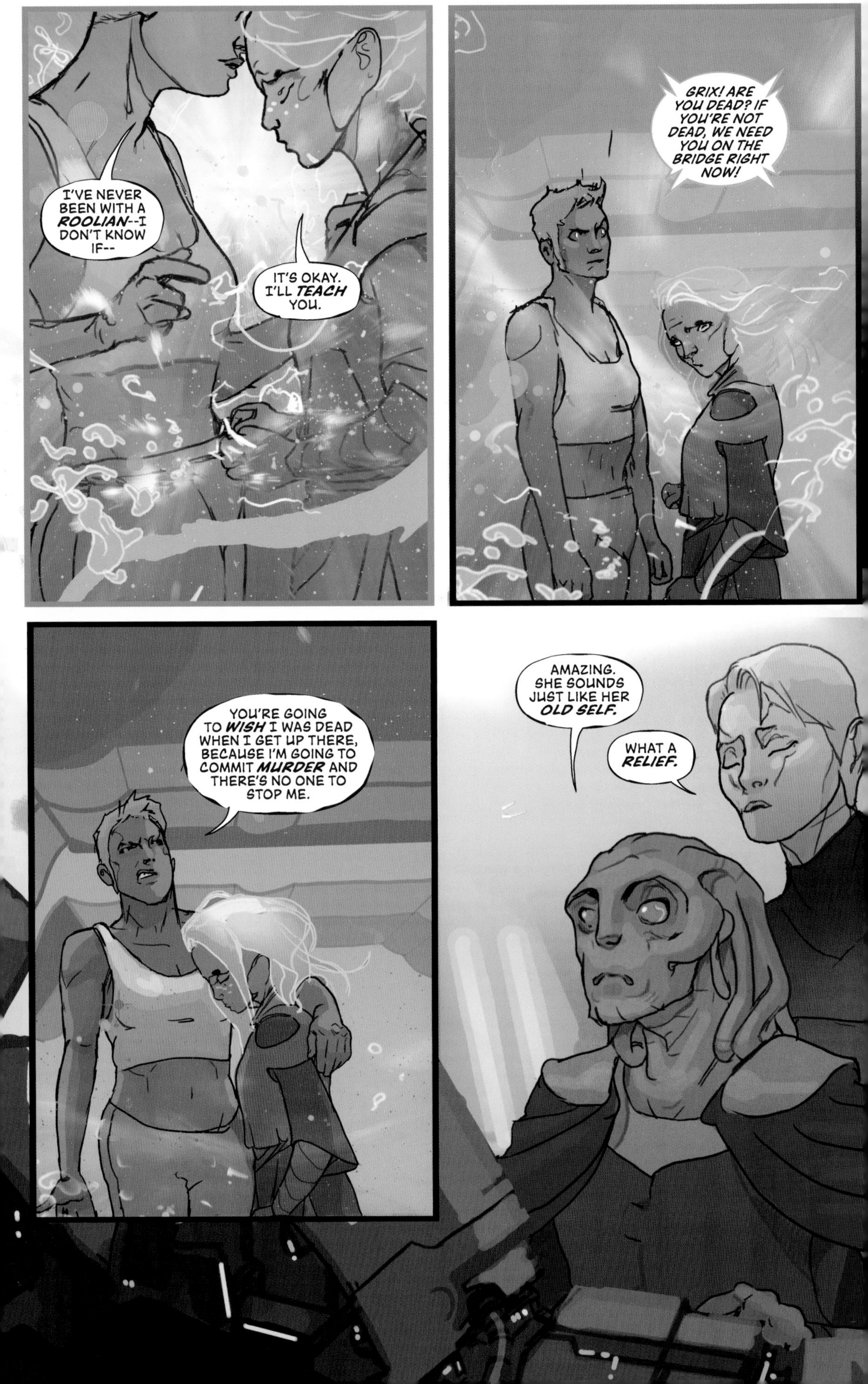
I'VE NEVER BEEN WITH A ROOLIAN--I DON'T KNOW IF--
IT'S OKAY. I'LL TEACH YOU.
GRIX! ARE YOU DEAD? IF YOU'RE NOT DEAD, WE NEED YOU ON THE BRIDGE RIGHT NOW!
YOU'RE GOING TO WISH I WAS DEAD WHEN I GET UP THERE, BECAUSE I'M GOING TO COMMIT MURDER AND THERE'S NO ONE TO STOP ME.
AMAZING. SHE SOUNDS JUST LIKE HER OLD SELF.
WHAT A RELIEF.

IDIOTS...
I'M SORRY, I'M NEVER SO FORWARD--I DON'T KNOW WHAT HAPPENED--
DON'T SAY THAT. DON'T APOLOGIZE. THAT MEANS THIS WAS A MISTAKE, AND I DON'T WANT IT TO BE A MISTAKE.
WHAT DO YOU WANT IT TO BE?
A BEGINNING. A--
HNGH
GRIX!
THIS IS RIDICULOUS. YOU NEED TO REST.
I'M FINE.
THIS WILL ALL FALL APART WITHOUT SOMEONE ON THE BRIDGE GIVING ORDERS.
SHHHK!

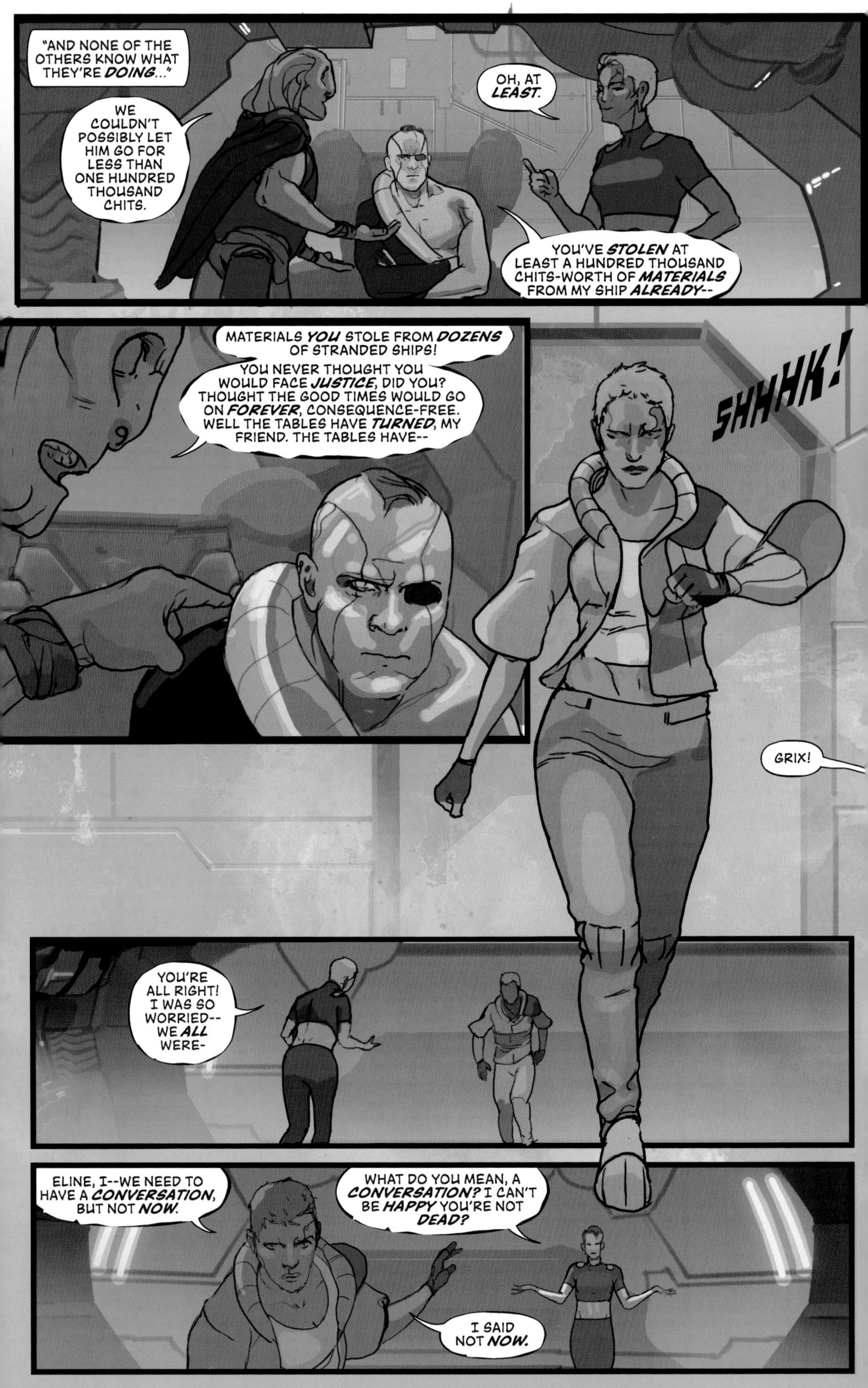
"AND NONE OF THE OTHERS KNOW WHAT THEY'RE DOING..."
WE COULDN'T POSSIBLY LET HIM GO FOR LESS THAN ONE HUNDRED THOUSAND CHITS.
OH, AT LEAST.
YOU'VE STOLEN AT LEAST A HUNDRED THOUSAND CHITS-WORTH OF MATERIALS FROM MY SHIP ALREADY--
MATERIALS YOU STOLE FROM DOZENS OF STRANDED SHIPS!
YOU NEVER THOUGHT YOU WOULD FACE JUSTICE, DID YOU? THOUGHT THE GOOD TIMES WOULD GO ON FOREVER, CONSEQUENCE-FREE. WELL THE TABLES HAVE TURNED, MY FRIEND. THE TABLES HAVE--
SHHHK!
GRIX!
YOU'RE ALL RIGHT! I WAS SO WORRIED-- WE ALL WERE-
ELINE, I--WE NEED TO HAVE A CONVERSATION, BUT NOT NOW.
WHAT DO YOU MEAN, A CONVERSATION? I CAN'T BE HAPPY YOU'RE NOT DEAD?
I SAID NOT NOW.

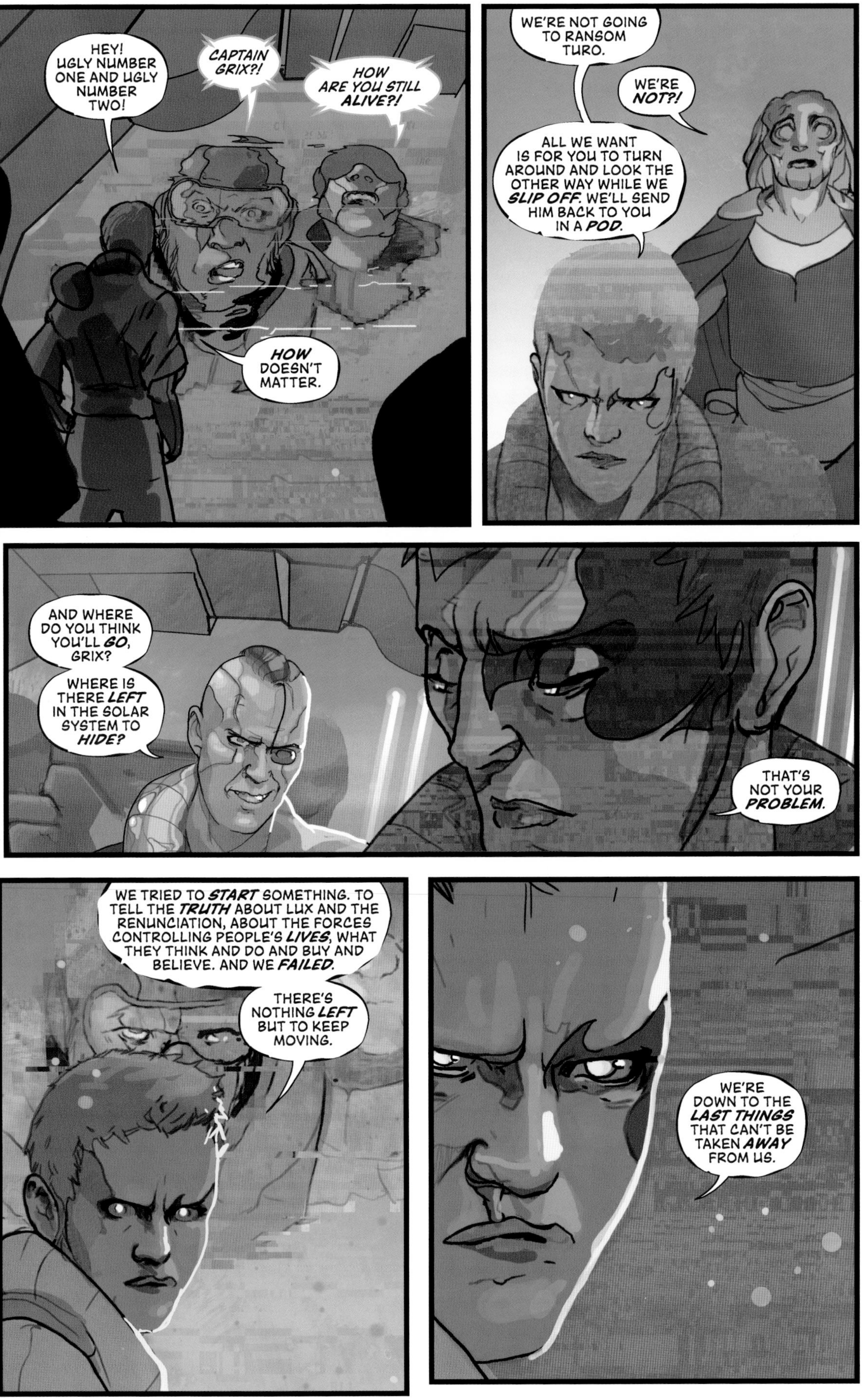
HEY! UGLY NUMBER ONE AND UGLY NUMBER TWO!
CAPTAIN GRIX?!
HOW ARE YOU STILL ALIVE?!
HOW DOESN'T MATTER.
WE'RE NOT GOING TO RANSOM TURO.
WE'RE NOT?!
ALL WE WANT IS FOR YOU TO TURN AROUND AND LOOK THE OTHER WAY WHILE WE SLIP OFF. WE'LL SEND HIM BACK TO YOU IN A POD.
AND WHERE DO YOU THINK YOU'LL GO, GRIX?
WHERE IS THERE LEFT IN THE SOLAR SYSTEM TO HIDE?
THAT'S NOT YOUR PROBLEM.
WE TRIED TO START SOMETHING. TO TELL THE TRUTH ABOUT LUX AND THE RENUNCIATION, ABOUT THE FORCES CONTROLLING PEOPLE'S LIVES, WHAT THEY THINK AND DO AND BUY AND BELIEVE. AND WE FAILED.
THERE'S NOTHING LEFT BUT TO KEEP MOVING.
WE'RE DOWN TO THE LAST THINGS THAT CAN'T BE TAKEN AWAY FROM US.

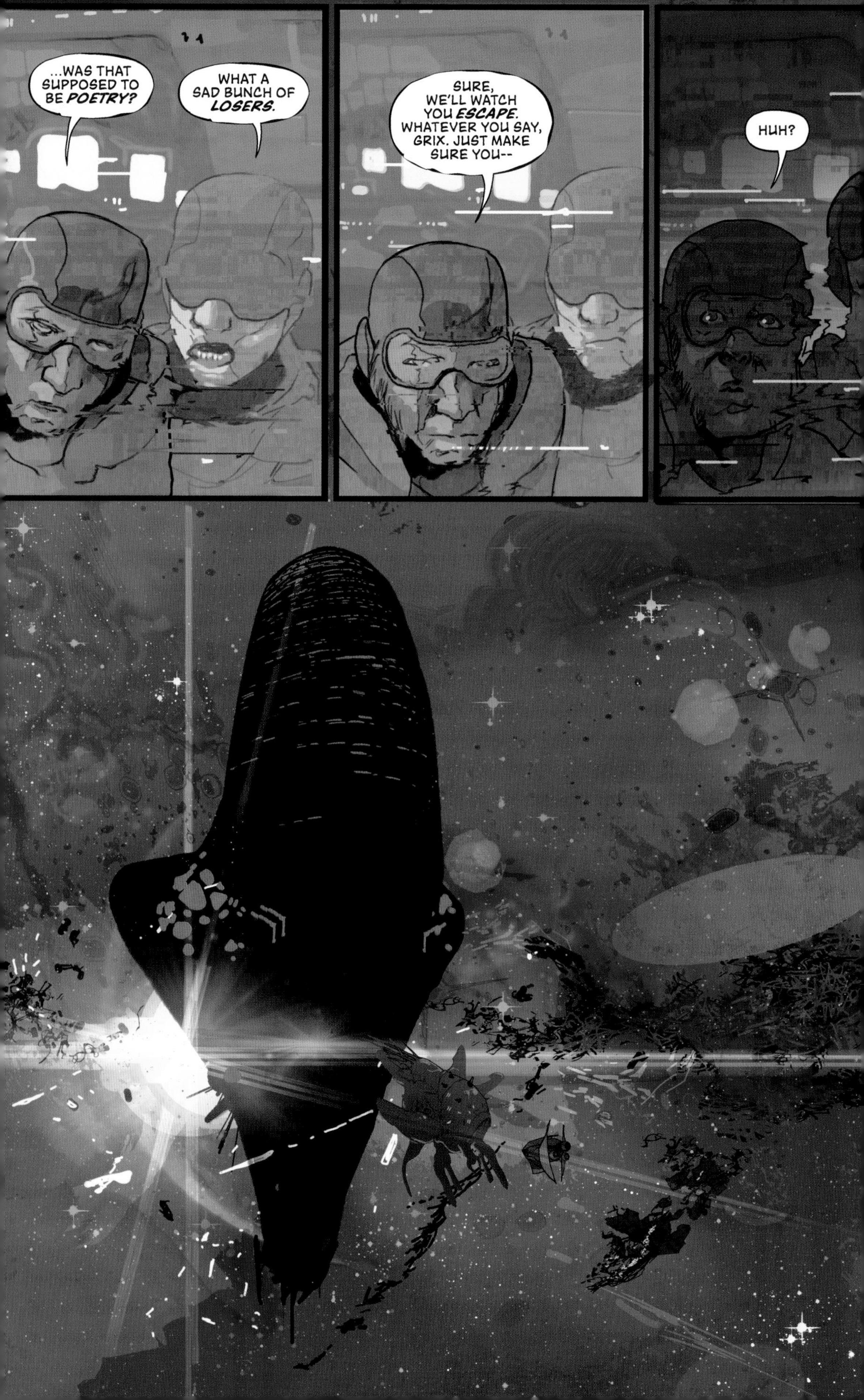
...WAS THAT SUPPOSED TO BE POETRY?
WHAT A SAD BUNCH OF LOSERS.
SURE, WE'LL WATCH YOU ESCAPE. WHATEVER YOU SAY, GRIX. JUST MAKE SURE YOU--
HUH?

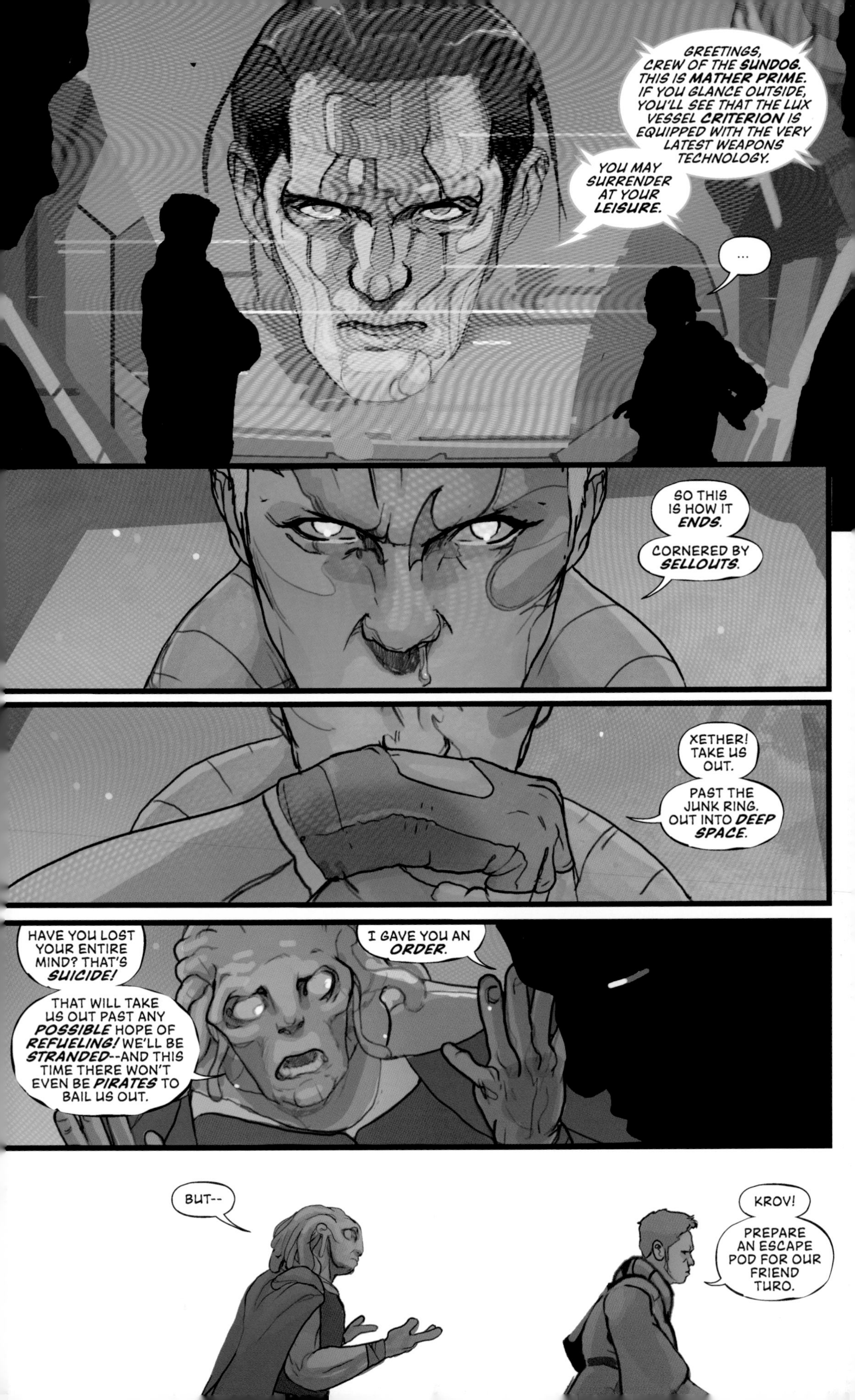
GREETINGS, CREW OF THE SUNDOG. THIS IS MATHER PRIME. IF YOU GLANCE OUTSIDE, YOU'LL SEE THAT THE LUX VESSEL CRITERION IS EQUIPPED WITH THE VERY LATEST WEAPONS TECHNOLOGY.
YOU MAY SURRENDER AT YOUR LEISURE.
...
SO THIS IS HOW IT ENDS.
CORNERED BY SELLOUTS.
XETHER! TAKE US OUT.
PAST THE JUNK RING. OUT INTO DEEP SPACE.
HAVE YOU LOST YOUR ENTIRE MIND? THAT'S SUICIDE!
THAT WILL TAKE US OUT PAST ANY POSSIBLE HOPE OF REFUELING! WE'LL BE STRANDED--AND THIS TIME THERE WON'T EVEN BE PIRATES TO BAIL US OUT.
I GAVE YOU AN ORDER.
BUT--
KROV!
PREPARE AN ESCAPE POD FOR OUR FRIEND TURO.

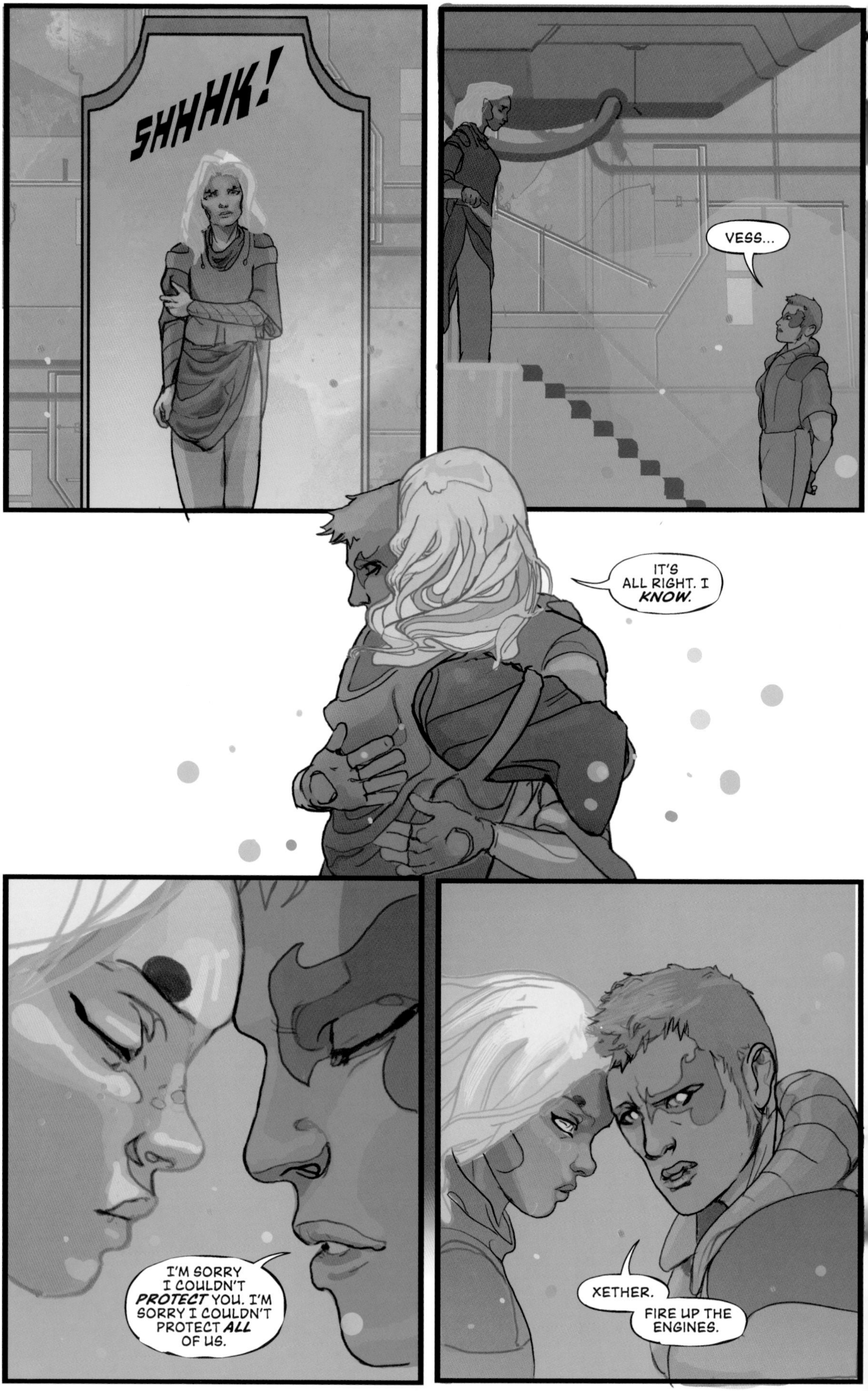
SHHHK!
VESS...
IT'S ALL RIGHT. I KNOW.
I'M SORRY I COULDN'T PROTECT YOU. I'M SORRY I COULDN'T PROTECT ALL OF US.
XETHER.
FIRE UP THE ENGINES.

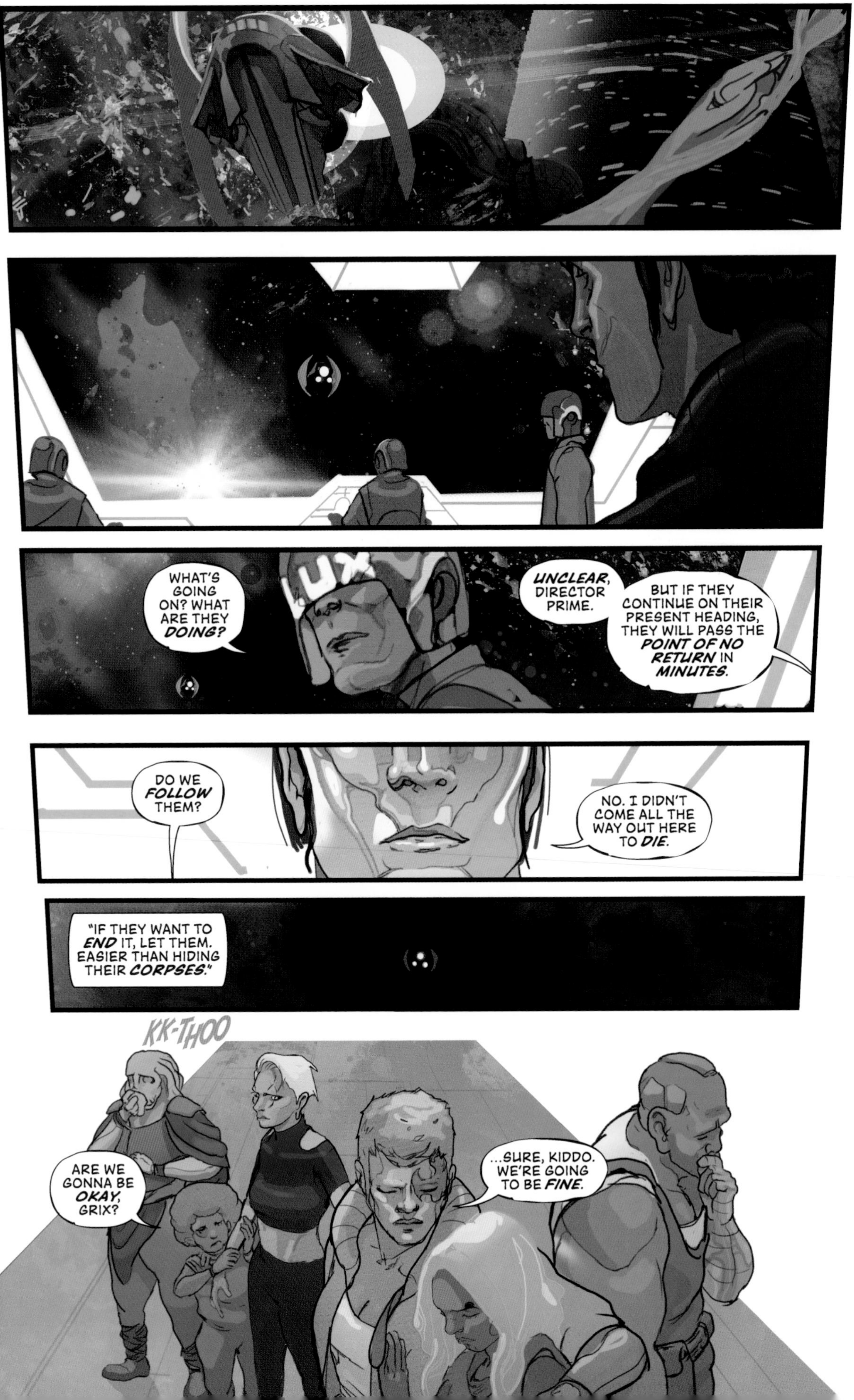
WHAT'S GOING ON? WHAT ARE THEY DOING?
UNCLEAR, DIRECTOR PRIME.
BUT IF THEY CONTINUE ON THEIR PRESENT HEADING, THEY WILL PASS THE POINT OF NO RETURN IN MINUTES.
DO WE FOLLOW THEM?
NO. I DIDN'T COME ALL THE WAY OUT HERE TO DIE.
"IF THEY WANT TO END IT, LET THEM. EASIER THAN HIDING THEIR CORPSES."
KK-THOO
ARE WE GONNA BE OKAY, GRIX?
...SURE, KIDDO. WE'RE GOING TO BE FINE.

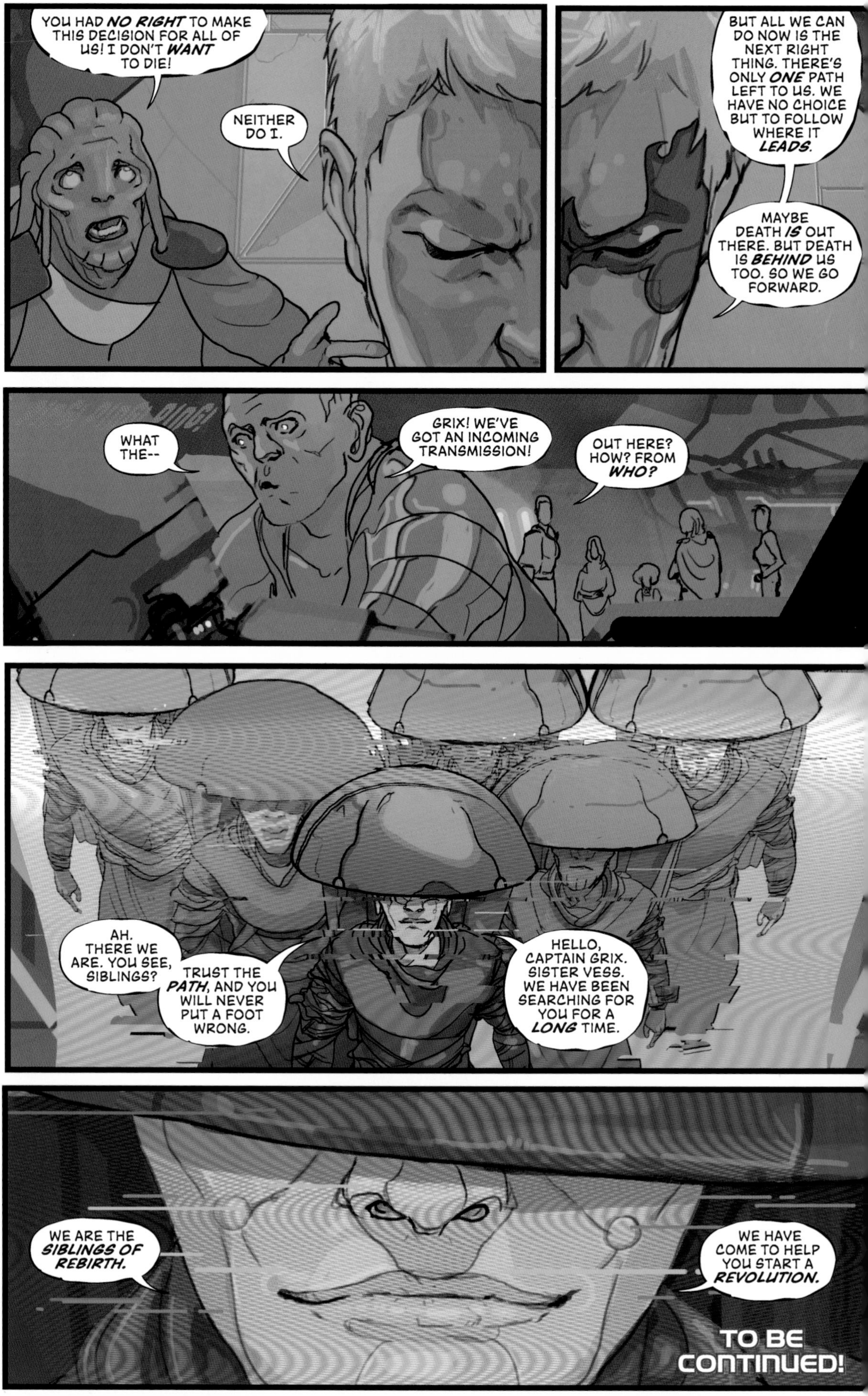
YOU HAD NO RIGHT TO MAKE THIS DECISION FOR ALL OF US! I DON'T WANT TO DIE!
NEITHER DO I.
BUT ALL WE CAN DO NOW IS THE NEXT RIGHT THING. THERE'S ONLY ONE PATH LEFT TO US. WE HAVE NO CHOICE BUT TO FOLLOW WHERE IT LEADS.
MAYBE DEATH IS OUT THERE. BUT DEATH IS BEHIND US TOO. SO WE GO FORWARD.
WHAT THE--
GRIX! WE'VE GOT AN INCOMING TRANSMISSION!
OUT HERE? HOW? FROM WHO?
AH. THERE WE ARE. YOU SEE, SIBLINGS?
TRUST THE PATH, AND YOU WILL NEVER PUT A FOOT WRONG.
HELLO, CAPTAIN GRIX. SISTER VESS. WE HAVE BEEN SEARCHING FOR YOU FOR A LONG TIME.
WE ARE THE SIBLINGS OF REBIRTH.
WE HAVE COME TO HELP YOU START A REVOLUTION.
TO BE CONTINUED!

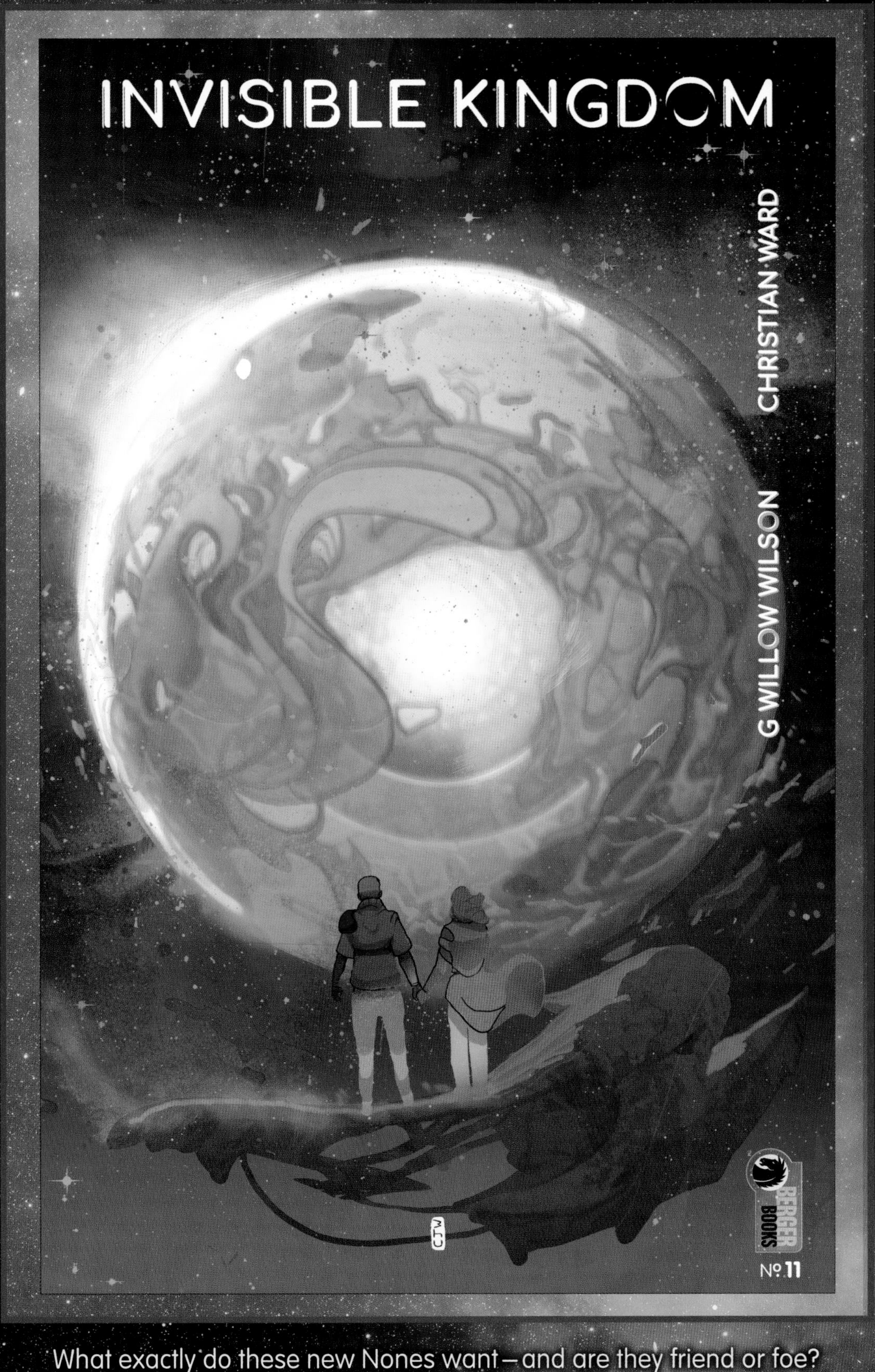
INVISIBLE KINGDOM
G WILLOW WILSON
CHRISTIAN WARD
BERGER BOOKS
Nº 11

BERGER BOOKS™

The Must-Have Graphic Novel Library

RUBY FALLS

Deluxe Softcover, 112 Pages

$19.99 ◊ ISBN 978-1-50671-495-0

Big secrets in a small town.

Lana Blake obsessively chases down the cold case of a infamously progressive "disappeared" woman in this neo-noir thriller.

A new kind of Noir...
Ruby Falls™
MISSING
HAVE YOU SEEN THIS GIRL?
DON'T BE A BETTY
ANN NOCENTI ✶ FLAVIA BIONDI
LEE LOUGHRIDGE

SHE COULD FLY
Vol. One: Obsessive Propulsion

Deluxe Softcover, 144 Pages

$19.99 ◊ ISBN 978-1-50670-949-9

A fantastic, unknown flying woman suddenly explodes mid-air. No one knows how she flew, or why. Luna Brewster, a disturbed 15-year-old, becomes obsessed with finding out. Will the truth free her...or shatter her life?

"Full of unexpected pleasures... masterful, joyful, poignant... A must-read."
–G. Willow Wilson
SHE COULD FLY
CHRISTOPHER CANTWELL
Co-Creator of HALT AND CATCH FIRE
AMC's Acclaimed TV Series
AND
MARTÍN MORAZZO
WITH
MIROSLAV MRVA

EVERYTHING
Vol. One: Grand Opening

Deluxe Softcover, 128 Pages

$19.99 ◊ ISBN 978-1-50671-492-9

EVERYTHING is a gleaming new mega-department store which arrives to extraordinary thrill—and rapidly escalates to inexplicable mania in the small town of Holland, Michigan.

Who—or what—exactly is in charge here . . . and what insidious plans are in store?

"This book bubbles with energy and inventiveness."
—JEFF LEMIRE
EVERY THING
SALE!
Christopher Cantwell
I.N.J. Culbard
Shirley

SHE COULD FLY
Vol. Two: The Lost Pilot

Deluxe Softcover, 128 Pages

$19.99 ◊ ISBN 978-1-50671-276-5

After discovering clues about the Flying Woman's missing family, Luna's obsession reignites. Will this twisting and dark path ultimately lead Luna to some peace of mind or her ultimate downfall?

SHE COULD FLY
THE LOST PILOT
"Devastating and wonderful."
— BLEEDING COOL
CHRISTOPHER CANTWELL
MARTÍN MORAZZO
MIROSLAV MRVA

ANTHONY BOURDAIN'S HUNGRY GHOSTS

Hardcover, 128 Pages

$17.99 ◊ ISBN 978-1-50670-669-6

Inspired by the Japanese game 100 Candles, a circle of chefs gather to outscare each other with modern tales of fear and food from around the world—and pray that they survive the night.

Includes original recipes by Bourdain.

Tales of Fear and Food from Around the World
ANTHONY BOURDAIN'S
HUNGRY GHOSTS
PLUS 5 ALL-NEW ORIGINAL RECIPES
with Joel Rose & Comics' Top Horror Artists

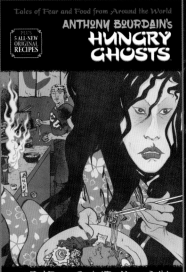

INVISIBLE KINGDOM
Vol. One: Walking the Path

Deluxe Softcover, 136 Pages
$19.99 ◊ ISBN 978-1-50671-227-7

In a distant galaxy, a young religious acolyte and an antagonistic freighter pilot join forces when they uncover an unconceivable conspiracy between the world's dominant religion and the mega-corporation that controls society.

G WILLOW WILSON CHRISTIAN WARD
INVISIBLE KINGDOM
"Sharp, funny and utterly breathtaking..." – Kelly Sue DeConnick
volume one
WALKING THE PATH

OLIVIA TWIST:
Honor Among Thieves

Deluxe Softcover, 136 Pages
$19.99 ◊ ISBN 978-1-50670-948-2

In dystopian future London, teenage orphan Olivia Twist joins a girl gang of thieves to save a new friend.

But Olivia has more power than she knows... and it comes at a great cost.

"Terrifically relevant and of-our-moment." – Jonathan Lethem
OLIVIA TWIST
HONOR AMONG THIEVES
DARIN STRAUSS
NATIONAL BOOK CRITICS CIRCLE AWARD WINNER
ADAM DALVA
EMMA VIECELI
LEE LOUGHRIDGE

J.M. DEMATTEIS CORIN HOWELL JAMES DEVLIN
the girl in the bay
"J.M. DeMatteis has evoked actual magic here" – Brian Keene

THE GIRL IN THE BAY

Deluxe Softcover, 112 Pages
$17.99 ◊ ISBN 978-1-50671-228-4

A supernatural coming-of-age mystery begins in 1969, when Kathy Sartori is murdered– only to reawaken in 2019, where another version of herself has lived a full life. And her "killer" is about to strike again.

Nnedi Okorafor
HUGO & NEBULA AWARD-WINNER
LAGUARDIA
Tana Ford & James Devlin
EQUALITY AND JUSTICE
NO HATE NO FEAR
ALIENS ARE CITIZENS
BABY ON BOARD
ALIENS ARE PEOPLE TOO

LAGUARDIA

Deluxe Softcover, 136 Pages
$19.99 ◊ ISBN 978-1-50671-075-4

In an alien-integrated world, a very pregnant doctor named Future Nwafor Chukwuebuka smuggles an illegal, sentient plant through LaGuardia International and Interstellar Airport, and their arrival to New York marks the abrupt start of a an amazing new life – for everyone!

"Engrossing...proudly exemplifies the graphic novel."–The New York Times
MAT JOHNSON WARREN PLEECE
INCOGNEGRO
A GRAPHIC MYSTERY

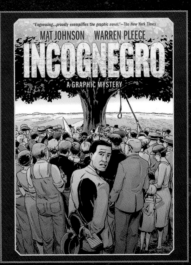

INCOGNEGRO:
A GRAPHIC MYSTERY

Hardcover, 144 Pages
$19.99 ◊ ISBN 978-1-50670-564-4

Reporter Zane Pinchback goes "incognegro", traveling from Harlem to the deep south to investigate the arrest of his brother.

A fast-paced mystery and riveting exploration of race and identity.

Also look for

INCOGNEGRO:
RENAISSANCE

Hardcover, 128 Pages
$19.99 ◊ ISBN 978-1-50670-563-7

Set in the Roarin' 20s, our race-bending protagonist penetrates a world where he feels stranger than ever before.

The story
starts here:

"Highly
recommended."
Saladin Ahmed
(Ms. Marvel, Black Bolt)

"Two master creators
doing a barrel roll just
outside our atmosphere.
You want this book."
Gail Simone
(Birds of Prey, Batgirl)

"It's my kind of
space opera."
Nnedi Okorafor
(LaGuardia)

...and only from

BERGER
BOOKS
on sale now

G WILLOW WILSON   **CHRISTIAN WARD**

"Sharp, funny and
utterly breathtaking..."
Kelly Sue DeConnick
(Pretty Deadly, Captain Marvel)

INVISIBLE KINGDOM™

volume one:
WALKING
THE PATH

Invisible Kingdom Volume Two: Edge of Everything, May 2020.

Published by Dark Horse Comics LLC., 10956 SE Main Street, Milwaukie, Oregon 97222. Text and illustrations of Invisible Kingdom™ © 2020 G. Willow Wilson and Christian Ward. The Berger Books Logo, Dark Horse Comics ® and the Dark Horse logo are trademarks of Dark Horse Comics LLC, registered in various categories and countries. Berger Books ® is a registered trademark of Karen Berger. All rights reserved. No portion of this publication may be reproduced or transmitted, in any form or by any means, without the express written permission of Dark Horse Comics LLC. Names, characters, places, and incidents featured in this publication either are the product of the author's imagination or are used fictitiously. Any resemblance to actual persons (living or dead), events, institutions, or locales, without satiric intent, is coincidental.

Published by
Dark Horse Books

A division of
Dark Horse Comics LLC.
10956 SE Main Street
Milwaukie, OR 97222

DarkHorse.com
ComicShopLocator.com

This volume collects Issues
#6-10 of Invisible Kingdom.

First Edition: May 2020
ISBN 978-1-50671-494-3

Printed in China

Names: Wilson, G. Willow, 1982- author. | Ward, Christian (Christian J.), artist. | Cipriano, Sal, letterer. Title: Edge of everything / script, G. Willow Wilson ; art, Christian Ward ; letters, Sal Cipriano. Description: First edition. | Milwaukie, OR : Dark Horse/Berger Books, 2020. | Series: Invisible Kingdom Volume II | "This volume collects Issues #6-10 of Invisible Kingdom" | Identifiers: LCCN 2020002767 | ISBN 9781506714943 (trade paperback) | ISBN 9781506714899 (ebook) | Subjects: LCSH: Comic books, strips, etc. | Classification: LCC PN6728. I574 W47 2020 | DDC 741.5/973--dc23 LC record available at https://lccn.loc.gov/2020002767